T0265251

The Economics of the UK Health and Social Care Labour Market

The Economics of the UK Health and Social Care Labour Market

How Labour Economics Can Inform Policy toward the Frontline Care Workforce

ROBERT ELLIOTT

OXFORD
UNIVERSITY PRESS

OXFORD
UNIVERSITY PRESS

Great Clarendon Street, Oxford, OX2 6DP,
United Kingdom

Oxford University Press is a department of the University of Oxford.
It furthers the University's objective of excellence in research, scholarship,
and education by publishing worldwide. Oxford is a registered trade mark of
Oxford University Press in the UK and in certain other countries

Published in the United States of America by Oxford University Press
198 Madison Avenue, New York, NY 10016, United States of America

British Library Cataloguing in Publication Data

Data available

Library of Congress Control Number: 2023947572

ISBN 9780198883142

DOI: 10.1093/oso/9780198883142.001.0001

Printed and bound in the UK by
Clays Ltd, Elcograf S.p.A.

To Sue, Andrew, Nicky, Iona, and Munro

Preface

Much of this book was written during lockdown in the UK. Along with most of the population, I observed the instruction to 'stay at home' throughout much of 2020 and the first half of 2021. A major exception to this instruction was the workers who deliver health and social care. The continued presence of these frontline care workers in our hospitals, surgeries, and care homes was critical to the well-being of far too many of the UK population. During this period they were prominent in all our thoughts, and they should remain so.

The services that frontline care workers deliver are among the most important contributions any professionals make to our lives. We encounter them at most of the major junctures in our lives, and the care they provide at each stage is fundamental to the quality of our lives. Frontline health and social care workers touch our lives like no other professionals. Our health and wellbeing depend on their skill and dedication, and never was there a time in the living memory of current generations when we were so acutely aware of their importance or more deeply indebted to them than during lockdown.

Frontline workers make up a very large part of the UK workforce and there can be very few amongst us who do not count some of these workers amongst our friends and acquaintances. Yet as I tracked the progress of the rollout of the vaccine, on some rather excellent charts and diagrams presented on the website of my local paper *The Press and Journal*, it became clear that, as I was discovering from my research, no one knew how many frontline workers there really were: after a time the website reported that 100 per cent of frontline workers in Scotland had been vaccinated, but the number underpinning that percentage kept changing!

Most people have little idea how many people in the UK deliver frontline health and social care, nor what the gender and ethnic composition of this workforce is. They have little understanding of why people might have chosen this work, what investment in training they have made, or how well, or poorly, they are paid. Still fewer will know how we as a society decide what they should be paid, why there is a labour shortage in all the largest occupations in this workforce, and why in some areas of the country the shortage is acute. Foreign trained workers make up a large part of the workforce, but most people do not know why. If we are to have the workforce we need, we require a much better understanding of these issues and of the factors that should guide government policy toward this workforce. Labour economics provides us with the conceptual framework we need if we are to achieve this understanding.

Labour economics is the study of the markets in which people work. Those without a background in economics, and even some with that background, may react rather negatively to discussion of markets in the context of health and social care. However the concept of a market, when the term is employed by labour economists, is simply that of a space, either physical or conceptual, in which there is resolution of the ambitions of those who wish to work in a particular job (sellers) and those organizations who wish to employ people to deliver a particular type of output (buyers).

In the labour market, institutions and social arrangements play an important role and influence the resulting exchange. One such exchange is that of working time, labour, for money and other benefits, and the market in which this exchange takes place is the labour market. This market plays a central role in all our lives, and in this book we focus on the part of it in which the people who deliver frontline health and social care operate.

This book will detail and explain five economic theories which are key to understanding the workings of the labour markets for frontline health and social care workers. They are the theories of net advantages, human capital, the production function, the labour demand schedule, and equilibrium in the labour market.

All markets have two sides—sellers and buyers, a supply side and a demand side—and the labour market is no exception. The conceptual framework for understanding the supply side of this market originates in the writings of Adam Smith, who advanced the two theories which remain fundamental to this understanding. The first is the theory of net advantages, which explains how people balance the different characteristics of jobs when deciding which to take, and the second is the theory of human capital, which explains why people decide to undertake training. On the demand side of the labour market, the two key theories are those of the production function, which details the relationship between the inputs to and the outputs from production,[1] and the demand for labour schedule, which shows, as a result of the contribution of labour to production, how much labour an organization will want to employ. The fifth theory is that of labour market equilibrium, of balance in the labour market, which enables us to identify the forces producing balance between the supply and demand sides of the market and stimulating change if there is imbalance.

Labour economics, like all economics, is a blend of the theoretical and empirical. A blend of models which are constructed through deductive reasoning and then subject to empirical testing through exposure to data. Sound policy requires the collection and analysis of data and its interpretation within a coherent

---

[1] This theory owes its development to the work of several economists, though the contribution of von Thunen is regarded by many as the seminal contribution. For discussion of the development of this theory see Gordon and Vaughan (2011).

analytical framework. The data that Adam Smith had at his disposal was rudimentary, yet through observation and deductive reasoning he developed a coherent theory of the labour market which is relevant today. That it remains of fundamental importance to understanding how modern labour markets work is testimony to his intellectual power.

To analyse and understand labour markets and to design labour market policy, we need high-quality data and a conceptual framework with which to interpret the data. Data alone tell us little; we need a framework which enables us to construct models which integrate the disparate strands of evidence into a logical and coherent whole. This is what economics offers, in the words of Keynes, 'economics is the science of thinking in terms of models joined to the art of choosing models which are relevant to the contemporary world'. Models structure our thinking; they require us to identify the main drivers of the behaviours we seek to explain, and to draw them together into a coherent, unifying framework. Labour economics offers the models required to understand and interpret behaviour in labour markets; it exemplifies that amalgam of logic and intuition, together with a wide knowledge of the facts which was declared by Keynes to be 'required for economic interpretation in its highest form' (Moggeridge D, 1973)[2]. This book identifies the economic models relevant to the frontline care labour market.

For too long, policy toward the frontline care workforce has been piecemeal and ill-informed, and the data available to inform policy have been poor. The labour markets which have emerged after the Covid-19 pandemic appear to be much changed, and they will present further challenges to policymakers. The pandemic has affected the level and the pattern of demand for health and social care, it has made people much more aware of the importance of the work that frontline workers do, and of the risks to their health that these workers face. The increased profile and status of frontline work may attract more people to this work, while increased understanding of the risks that frontline workers run may deter others from seeking these jobs. One major consequence of the pandemic is an increase in working from home. Frontline health and social care workers are not afforded this opportunity, and this will make recruitment to health and social care jobs more difficult.

What remains unchanged is the need to offer terms and conditions of service that attract the able and energetic and retain the experienced to jobs in frontline health and social care. In turn, this means understanding what attracts people to seek work in health and social care and what retains and motivates them once they have joined the workforce. It means ensuring that pay and reward appropriately compensate for the work that frontline workers do and the conditions under which they work. Pay must also reflect conditions in the many different areas of

---

[2] Both of the above quotations are to be found in this volume at pages 296–297.

the country in which frontline workers are employed. Only by offering competitive and attractive rewards can we eliminate labour shortages.

Many frontline care workers are highly trained, and we need to shape policy toward training to ensure that we deploy the limited resources government has available to spend on training effectively and efficiently. In turn this requires an understanding of the many ways in which we produce health and social care and how different occupations contribute to their production, for only then can we produce appropriate and integrated recruitment and training strategies. Moreover, until we can quantify the improvements in health and well-being that will result from investing in increased numbers of frontline staff, we cannot know whether we are investing wisely.

The focus of this book is on the frontline workforce—it is on the people who deliver health and social care.[3] Though we shall often talk about 'the' labour market for frontline health and adult social care workers, we must remember that this market comprises several different but highly interconnected occupational labour markets. The frontline workforce comprises all those occupations whose day-to-day activities deliver health and social care to the UK population. They are the workers who contribute to the spectrum of care we receive 'from the cradle to the grave'. They are the occupations we encounter in hospitals, community health care, residential, and domiciliary care settings. The Covid-19 crisis has reminded us all that adult social care workers are an integral part of our care system, a system within which the boundaries of care are now being redrawn. The largest three frontline occupations are doctors, nurses, and adult social care workers, but there are also many other workers involved: paramedics, optometrists, podiatrists, osteopaths, to name just a few of the occupations that are called Allied Health Professions.

Beyond the frontline workforce, the health and social care industry workforce is larger still. In their daily work, frontline workers are supported by a legion of administrative, managerial, technical, and IT workers. To be clear, this book is not about these support workers. Their work is vital to the delivery of health and social care services, but the labour markets in which their skills are bought and sold are not confined to health and social care. They operate in much broader labour markets, labour markets which extend to other industries. The focus here is upon the labour markets for frontline workers.

One reason for this focus is that these markets have seldom, if ever, been in balance: the labour markets for doctors, nurses, and adult social care workers have typically been characterized by acute shortages in at least some areas of the UK.

---

[3] The scholarly definition of a health care worker is different to the more popular definition. A Google search under 'health care worker' will take the enquirer to either the Wikipedia entry for Health Professional or the recruitment agency site, Totaljobs, where social care jobs are included under health care jobs. See: https://en.wikipedia.org/wiki/Health_professional and https://www.totaljobs.com/salary-checker/average-healthcare-worker-salary

This book identifies the analytical tools essential to understanding why shortages persist and where we should look for solutions to eliminate them. A second reason is that while, the labour markets for support workers have been the subject of analysis elsewhere, the specific factors that affect frontline labour markets have been less recognized and studied. The labour market for frontline care workers has a number of important features which are specific to this market, and these have been little recognized. An understanding of the particular features of frontline care labour markets is essential to designing sound policy. The purpose of this book is to bring together in a single accessible source the principal concepts from the economics of the labour market which enable us to understand and interpret developments in the UK labour market for frontline health and adult social care workers.

The vast majority of frontline care workers are employees, but there are also a considerable number who are self-employed. GP principals constitute the largest of these occupational groups, which also include most dentists and many Allied Health Professions. The self-employed have invested money and time in both human and physical capital, while employees have invested in 'only' human capital. The risks and rewards associated with investment in physical capital extend beyond those associated with investment in human capital, and analysis of them would take us into fields of economics which are beyond the scope of this book. For this reason, this book will have less to say about the self-employed, though they are an important part of the frontline workforce.

The publicly available data do not allow the frontline care workforce to be distinguished with precision. In some cases, the occupational groups that can be identified include some workers who are not in frontline jobs but are supporting or managing frontline care workers; where this occurs it will be flagged. The discussion of social care in this book is restricted to adult social care, to those caring for adults in either a residential care home or in a domiciliary setting. This part of the social care workforce is the most intimately connected to health care: some of the occupations we find in community and hospital health care we also find in adult social care. As this implies, the boundaries between primary, secondary, and adult social care labour markets overlap—some procedures undertaken in a community health care setting are also undertaken in residential care homes or in domiciliary care settings and vice versa.

There has been too little analysis of the labour markets in which frontline care workers operate, while analysis of those in which adult social care workers operate is in its infancy.[4] The reasons for this are several. The data available to labour economists until relatively recently was insufficiently detailed to allow detailed

---

[4] Notable exceptions are the Low Pay Commission and two research units, the *Personal Social Services Research Unit* (PSSRU) and the Health Foundation.

analysis of occupational labour markets, and so the focus of labour economics was on the labour market as a whole. Additionally, the health care labour market is among the most regulated of any labour market in the UK, and knowledge of the rules and institutions which shape this labour market is required for analysis. As a result, analysis was left to health economists who had better knowledge of these institutions. However, few health economists studied labour markets, their attention was focused on health technology analysis because policymakers in health and social care judged this more important, and research funding was concentrated on the clinical and cost-effectiveness of the procedures and technologies of health care.[5] The perversity of this neglect becomes evident when we reflect that it is the workforce which carries out these procedures and employs these technologies, and that a large part of all health and social care spending goes on workforce.[6]

The labour markets in health and social care and those in the rest of the economy were severely disrupted by the Covid-19 pandemic. The pandemic had a profound effect on the employment and pay of millions in the UK. The data for 2020 and 2021 reveal that these years are very different from those in the immediately preceding period and likely very different from the period that follows. For this reason we use data for the period prior to the onset of the pandemic, data up to and including 2019.[7] While it is as yet unclear how the pandemic has affected the labour market in health and social care, affect it, it certainly has, and so in Chapter 8 we discuss the ways in which this appears to be happening. What is clear is that, if we are to interpret and understand developments in this labour market, we shall need the analytical framework discussed and explained here.

This book is intended to be read widely, in particular by those working in frontline health and adult social care in the UK. It is intended to be read by those who are interested in understanding how these labour markets work and why they are characterized by persistent shortages. It is also intended to be read by those charged with setting the pay of these workers, by those in leadership and management roles in health and adult social care, and by those constructing workforce policy and strategy toward the development of this workforce. It should also be

---

[5] Analysis has been left to a small band of health and labour economists, whose names will crop up throughout this book.

[6] Scrutiny of the annual reports of hospital trusts reveals that spending on staff and associated labour costs typically accounts for around 65 per cent of hospital operating expenses. Staff and associated labour costs account for a higher percentage of operating costs in care homes and community care. Of course not all spending on workforce is on frontline staff. As best can be determined, about 80 per cent of all NHS spending on workforce is on frontline workforce, and if the same is true of the typical hospital, then just over half of the annual operating expenditure of a typical hospital goes on the frontline workforce.

[7] Only data which is publicly and readily accessible, either online or in publications available from any university or public library, have been used. Manipulation of extracted data has been kept to a minimum and is clearly explained.

essential reading for those studying and training to become part of this workforce. It is intended that this book will help inform and shape policy toward the frontline workforce, and it is intended to provoke discussion of what that policy, and in particular pay policy, should be. It will raise many questions, answer some, and leave others for further research, research which is urgently required. It is perverse that we spend so little resource researching those parts of the health and social services on which we spend the most.

Acknowledgements

The idea for this book originated in a commission I undertook for the World Health Organization. Michelle McIsaac and Ibadat Dhillon at WHO who oversaw this commission offered many perceptive and constructive comments and suggestions during the course of my research and it was my discussions with them that provided the motivation to write this book. I am deeply indebted to them both.

The book would not have been completed without the encouragement, advice, and help of many colleagues. Principal among them is Martin Chalkley, with whom I have discussed several of the theories covered in this book and who is responsible for helping me develop the ideas in Chapter 3. I also owe considerable thanks to Diane Skatun and Tony Scott, with whom I have worked closely over the years to research health care labour markets. Both offered expert advice and support as I transitioned from mainstream labour economics to researching health care labour markets. I am deeply grateful to all three for their friendship, expertise and wise counsel over the years.

Anita Charlesworth at The Health Foundation; Andrew Lloyd-Kendall at the British Medical Association; John Henderson, who was a senior economist at the Department of Health and Social Care; Mandy Ryan, Graham Scotland, and Dwayne Boyers in HERU; and Colin Tilley, Head of Programme, NHS Education for Scotland also offered helpful and constructive comments on parts of the book. Three of my clinical colleagues in the Medical School in Aberdeen also read and commented on chapters. They offered a complementary perspective and wise and invaluable advice; my heartfelt thanks to Paul Bachoo, Siladitya Bhattacharya, and in particular Steve Baguley, who also advised me of the developments noted in Chapter 1 footnote 14. All the above gave of their time generously and proffered their comments and suggestions with a politeness and grace that was not always merited by the material they were sent.

Tim Butcher at the Low Pay Commission provided invaluable help extracting data from the Annual Population Survey and NOMIS the service provided by the Office for National Statistics (ONS), while Louisa Daffin, Neil Higginbottom, and Roger Smith at the ONS helped with interpretation of data from the Annual Survey of Hours and Earnings (ASHE). Mark Pearson at the OECD smoothed the path to use of their excellent data while Heidi Wong and Kevin Smith in the IT department of the University of Aberdeen guided me with patience and goodwill through the numerous IT challenges and software changes at the University of Aberdeen that threatened my sanity. David Burns at HERU provided invaluable assistance with literature searches.

During my academic career I have had the good fortune and privilege of researching and writing with many outstanding labour and health economists. They have been based in the UK, Australia, France, Italy, and the United States and have revealed the benefits of working in a truly open and collaborative international research community. The stimulating discussions I have held with them have contributed to my thinking on the topics covered in this book. I owe them all a huge debt of gratitude for their patience and forbearing, and for all they taught me. Too numerous to mention individually, their names appear as my co-authors on publications.

During my time as Director and subsequently as Emeritus Professor I have had the privilege of working with many fine health economists in the Health Economics Research Unit at the University of Aberdeen. They, together with the outstanding support staff in HERU, have created the very best environment in which to undertake research. There has been no better place in the UK in which to undertake research. My thanks to the present director, Mandy Ryan, and to all my colleagues in HERU for their support and encouragement over the years. My particular thanks go to Shona Christie for her support over the years, and to Lesley Innes for her help preparing this manuscript for submission to OUP.

At OUP I have benefited from the support of my editors Kayley Gilbert and Adam Swallow, the efficiency of the production team headed by Sandhiya Babu and the excellent copy editing of Philip Dines. It should be made clear that none of the above is responsible for the errors and omissions in this book.

Finally, my thanks go to Susan, my wonderful wife, constant companion, and improving influence throughout our time together. She has quietly and patiently encouraged my efforts to complete this book, and throughout our time together has borne my evident shortcomings with stoical forbearance.

Contents

1

The Frontline Care Workforce

The focus of this book is on the frontline health and adult social care workforce, on the people who deliver health and adult social care to the UK population. They are workers we encounter at every stage of our lives and in a wide range of different settings. We encounter them at birth, in our infancy, youth, middle and old age, and in hospitals, surgeries, clinics, and care homes and even, in some circumstances, in our own homes. They interact with us when they deliver this care for they must provide the care in person. Health and social care are services which must, with very few exceptions such as telemedicine, be delivered in person.

Frontline care workers form part of the broader health and social care industry workforce.[1] This industry workforce comprises both frontline workers and those workers who support them. Prominent among these support workers are managers, administrators, IT and HR specialists, technicians, and statisticians as well as many other professions and trades. They too provide a vital service, because the work they do enables frontline workers to do their jobs, and in carrying it out they help shape the form and content of the care which frontline workers deliver. During lockdown many of these support workers worked from home, like others in these occupations in different industries. Their presence at the workplace was not a prerequisite for discharging their duties. In contrast, frontline care workers had to attend their place of work to deliver care.

The work support workers do is vital to delivering health care, but this book is not about them. The skills they have acquired have application in many industries beyond health and social care. The labour markets in which they operate thus have much wider scope than the labour markets for frontline workers, and a broader range of factors affect the supply and demand for their labour. The focus of this book is on the labour markets in which frontline care workers operate and on the specific factors which affect the supply and demand for labour in these markets.

We will identify frontline care jobs by occupational title. Occupational titles distinguish the type of work that is done and the training and skills that are required

---

[1] WHO defines the health care workforce as 'all people *engaged in actions* (own italics) whose primary intent is to enhance health' (WHO, 2008). This identifies the health and social care *industry* workforce which extends beyond those who deliver health and social care and includes those who support the deliverers. The focus of this book is on the people whose primary role is the *delivery* of health and social care.

The Economics of the UK Health and Social Care Labour Market. Robert Elliott, Oxford University Press.
© Robert Elliott (2024). DOI: 10.1093/oso/9780198883142.003.0001

to do that work. The occupational title is one of the two ways in which a labour market is distinguished, the other is by its geographical coverage. Occupational labour markets are often linked together, through the interconnectedness of the work that is done and the resulting complementarity or substitutability of the skills that are required to do the work. The occupational labour markets in which the frontline health and social care workforce operate cover a wide range of training and skills and range from the highly local to the global. The aggregate of all these occupational labour markets, 'the' health and social care labour market, is accordingly large and complex.

In this first chapter we set out to address the following questions about this workforce. How many frontline health and social care workers are there in the UK? What are the main frontline occupations? What proportion of the UK working population work in health and social care and how does this compare to other countries? How have these numbers grown over the years and in particular since the establishment of the NHS? Are there differences between the four countries that make-up the UK and what is the gender and ethnic composition of the different occupations that make up the frontline workforce?

We will discover that the frontline care workforce is the largest workforce in the UK. Frontline care jobs account for nearly one in every ten jobs in the UK and are found in every county and region of the UK. The frontline care workforce is ethnically diverse and most of these workers are highly trained. A large part of the workforce trained abroad but has now settled in the UK. Women account for almost 80 per cent of the workforce, and frontline care jobs are a major source of employment for women; today one in every five jobs done by women in the UK is in frontline care.

We will further discover that this workforce has increased rapidly in size since the establishment of the NHS which is widely recognized to be the UKs largest employer and one of the largest in the world. We will see that the health and social care workforce has grown more rapidly than has employment in general with the result that it has come to account for an increasing share of UK jobs.

The frontline workforce has grown more rapidly than employment in general both because we have been spending an increasing share of our national income on health and social care and most importantly, because the delivery of health and social care is labour intensive. If we want more and better health and social care we will have to employ more frontline workers. Care is delivered by people and there is therefore much less scope for substituting labour by capital than there is in other service industries. The services of the GP, the hospital consultant, the qualified nurse, and the care worker have to be delivered in person and if we want more of these services we will need more of these workers.

1.1 The Size and Occupational Composition of the Frontline Care Workforce

The frontline health and social care workforce comprises all the people who deliver health and adult social care as part of their normal work. There are in principle two ways of distinguishing this total: either using data from employers who record the type of jobs their employees do, or from surveys of the working population in which respondents report the types of jobs they do. Because there is no employer data which covers the whole of the health and social care workforce[2] we use data gathered from surveys of the working population. Appendix 1.1 describes the main statistical sources available for counting this workforce.

The most robust and comprehensive survey suitable for our purpose is the Annual Population Survey conducted by the Office for National Statistics.[3] The APS asks a representative sample of the UK population to describe the jobs they do and the skills and training they have acquired. Their responses are then used by coders to identify the occupation which best describes their work. The coders use the Standard Occupational Classification (SOC) system to classify jobs. From the resulting list of occupations we can distinguish all those occupations where the primary purpose is to deliver health or adult social care.[4]

Table 1.1 lists the frontline occupations and details the number of workers in each occupation in calendar year 2019. Table 1.1 reports the SOC title and code number of all the occupations identified in the Survey in which all, or the vast majority, were delivering health or social care. Frontline care workers are pre-dominantly employees, though three important groups—GP principals (partners in GP practices) and many dentists and Allied Health Professions (AHPs)[5]—are self-employed.

---

[2] Workforce statistics compiled by NHS Digital report the total number of NHS Hospital and Community Health Service (HCHS) workers employed by NHS Trusts and Care Commissioning Groups in England. The data are extracted from the NHS HR and Payroll system and are available as head-count and full-time equivalents for all months from 30 September 2009 onwards. However, these data exclude people working in primary care and social care. Similar NHS data are also available for the other three UK nations, but they too omit important groups of frontline workers.

[3] The Annual Population Survey (APS) combines the boosted samples of the Labour Force Survey (LFS) and provides rolling four-quarter labour market data for the four UK nations. The APS is the ONS Approved Statistic for employment estimates. The survey provides details of the employment circumstances of the UK population, identifying the number of people working, either as employees or as self-employed in the UK.

[4] Covid-19 has of course reminded us that the jobs health care workers do can sometimes change very quickly and when this happens occupational classification systems may fail to keep pace. The pandemic saw the reassignment of many doctors and nurses previously in managerial or research roles in universities and the NHS to frontline duties in the NHS. We are using data from 2019 the year prior to the pandemic so this will not affect the results we report here.

[5] Allied Health Professions (AHPs) are a distinct group of health professionals who apply their expertise to prevent disease transmission, diagnose, treat, and rehabilitate people of all ages and all specialties. They deliver direct patient care in the form of rehabilitation, treatment and health improvement interventions to restore and maintain optimal physical, sensory, psychological, cognitive and social functions of patients.

The total number of frontline workers in the UK in 2019 was 2,995,700. Just five occupations, GPs and hospital doctors listed as Medical Practitioners (SOC 2211), Nurses, Midwives, and Nursing auxiliaries (SOCs 2231, 2232, and 6141 respectively), and Care Workers and Home Carers (SOC 6145) accounted for 70 per cent of the frontline workforce. Nurses, Midwives, and Nursing auxiliaries

Table 1.1 The Make-up of the Frontline Care Workforce in the UK in 2019

Standard Occupational Code and Title	Number Employed (Thousands)
221 Health Professionals	570.8
2211 Medical Practitioners	296.4
2212 Psychologists	35.6
2213 Pharmacists	69.8
2214 Ophthalmic Opticians	17.8
2215 Dental Practitioners	41.0
2217 Medical Radiographers	33.9
2218 Podiatrists	12.1
2219 Health Professionals (Not Elsewhere Classified)	64.2
222 Therapy Professionals	203.3
2221 Physiotherapists	73.0
2222 Occupational Therapists	47.4
2223 Speech and Language Therapists	20.1
2229 Therapy Professionals n.e.c.	62.8
223 Nursing and Midwifery Professionals	713.0
2231 Nurses [Qualified]	668.5
2232 Midwives	44.5
321 Health Associate Professionals	166.0
3213 Paramedics	28.4
3216 Dispensing Opticians	8.8
3217 Pharmaceutical Technicians	33.0
3218 Medical and Dental Technicians	42.0
3219 Health Associate Professionals n.e.c.	53.8
614 Caring Personal Services	1,324.2
6141 Nursing Auxiliaries and Assistants	337.4
6142 Ambulance Staff (Excluding Paramedics)	23.3
6143 Dental Nurses	51.9
6144 House Parents and Residential Wardens	49.2
6145 Care Workers and Home Carers	772.2
6146 Senior Care Workers	76.9
6147 Care Escorts	13.3
9271 Hospital Porters	18.4
Total Frontline Care Workforce	2,995.7

Source: ONS Annual Population Survey, NOMIS, January–December 2019. All in employment by four-digit occupation. SOC 2010

alone numbered over one million. Table 1.1 also records that there were large numbers of frontline workers in a range of other occupations, collectively titled Allied Health Professions (SOCs 222 and 321, 2212–2214, and 2218). Three of the SOCs listed in Table 1.1 are residual categories, Health Professionals (SOC 2219), Therapy Professionals (SOC 2229), and Health Associate Professionals (SOC 3219) which include further frontline occupations that are too small to be listed separately.

In 2019 there were a total of 32,508,300 employees and self-employed workers in the UK. The 2,995,700 frontline care workers therefore accounted for 9.2 per cent of total employment in the UK in 2019 or, put another way, almost one in every ten workers in the UK in 2019 was a frontline care worker.

1.2 Frontline and Support Workers: The Health and Social Care Industry

Frontline workers play an important role in generating jobs in the rest of the economy. The jobs of those who support, assist, and direct the activities of frontline workers evidently depend directly on the presence of the workers delivering care. The jobs of the managers, administrators, IT specialists, laboratory workers, maintenance workers, cleaners, and security guards who work in GP surgeries, care homes, hospitals, NHS Trusts, and in NHS Boards and Commissioning agencies all depend on the presence of frontline workers. If there were no frontline care workers there would be no call for the managers, administrators, and IT specialists who support them.

These support workers together with frontline workers constitute the health and social care *industry* workforce. We can distinguish the size of this industry workforce using the APS because it also asks respondents to identify the main activity of their employer or business and the APS coders use their replies to identify the industry in which they work.[6] We can then identify among these industries all those in the business of providing health and social care and, by counting the number who work in these industries, distinguish the size of the health and social care industry workforce. Table 1.2 reports these data together with the total number employed in that year. The data reveal that in 2019 the size of the health and social care industry workforce was 4.3 million and that they accounted for 13.3 per cent of the total UK workforce. In 2019, one in every 7.5 people working in the UK worked in the health and social care industry.

The incidence differed between the four nations of the UK as is also shown in Table 1.2. The data reveal that while 13.1 per cent of total employment, or one in every 7.5 jobs, in England and Northern Ireland was in the health and social care

---

[6] Industries are classified using the Standard Industrial Classification (SIC).

Table 1.2 Share of Total Employment Accounted for by Health and Social Care Industry, 2019

	England	Northern Ireland	Scotland	Wales	UK
Total Health and Social Care Industry Workforce	3,594,800	113,900	399,200	221,500	4,329,400
Total Workforce (Employees and Self-Employed)	27,523,500	866,800	2,660,100	1,457,800	32,508,300
Health & Social Care Industry Share of Total Employment	13.1	13.1	15.0	15.2	13.3

Source: ONS Annual Population Survey, NOMIS, January–December 2019 and Section Q in Standard Industrial Classification titled Human Health and Social Work [Care] Activities. ONS

industry in 2019, the share was higher in Scotland and Wales, where it was 15.0 and 15.2 per cent respectively. In both these last two countries the health and adult social care industry accounted for around one in every 6.5 jobs.

Of course these are not the only jobs generated by frontline care activity. The jobs of workers in a range of other industries which provide products and services to the health and social care industry also depend upon the presence of frontline workers. The jobs of workers in the pharmaceutical industry, medical devices, and health research industries, and in parts of the higher education, transport, consultancy, and IT industries all originate in the requirement for frontline care.[7] Moreover some of these workers, such as IT specialists and management consultants, will be employed on NHS premises doing work that was previously done by NHS workers, but which has now been outsourced.

These industries are all part of a wider set of economic activities that are dependent on the activity of frontline care workers, though they are not classified as part of the health and social care industry. The publicly available data do not enable us to distinguish in detail just how many people are employed in all these other industries dependent upon frontline care, but a reasonable estimate is that the grand total of jobs in the UK dependent on and including frontline care workers is over five million, amounting to almost one in every six jobs in the UK in 2019. Frontline care is a major generator of jobs throughout the UK economy.

---

[7] These industries are also some of the drivers of growth in the UK economy and as a result their share of economic activity is likely to increase still further.

1.3 Differences between the Nations of the UK

The importance of frontline jobs to the economies of the four nations in the UK differs. The share of total employment accounted for by jobs in frontline health and social care is greater in Northern Ireland, Scotland, and Wales than in England. Table 1.3 reports the total number employed in frontline jobs together with the total numbers in employment in each of the four countries in 2019. It reveals that frontline workers accounted for 8.9 per cent of total employment in England, 10 per cent in Northern Ireland and 11 per cent in both Scotland and Wales. Thus around one in every nine workers in Scotland and Wales, one in ten in Northern Ireland, and one in eleven workers in England were employed delivering frontline care in 2019.

Table 1.4 then details the occupational composition of the frontline care workforce in each nation. The occupations listed are, like Table 1.1, those in which all, or the vast majority of workers were delivering frontline health or social care. The data reveal that the composition of the health and social care workforce differs between the nations of the UK to quite a degree and though care workers, qualified nurses, nursing auxiliaries, and doctors remain the four largest occupational groups, they account for rather different shares of the frontline workforce in each country.

Care workers are the largest occupational group in every country, but Wales employs relatively more than the other three. In Wales they account for nearly 29 per cent of the frontline workforce compared to just over 23 per cent in Northern Ireland and just under 26 per cent in both England and Scotland. Doctors, GPs, and hospital doctors account for a larger share of the frontline workforce in Scotland than in any of the other three countries. They account for nearly 11 per cent of the frontline workforce in Scotland, less than 10 per cent in England, and less than 9 per cent in Northern Ireland and Wales.

Table 1.3 Frontline Care Workforce Share of Total Employment, 2019

	England	Northern Ireland	Scotland	Wales	UK
Frontline Care Workforce	2,456,000	87,100	292,600	160,000	2,995,700
Total Workforce (Employees and Self-Employed)	27,523,500	866,800	2,660,100	1,457,800	32,508,300
Frontline Care Workforce Share of Total Workforce*	8.9	10.0	11.0	11.0	9.2

Source: As for Tables 1.1 and 1.2

Table 1.4 The Occupational Composition of the Frontline Health and Social Care Workforce in England, Northern Ireland, Scotland, and Wales in 2019

Standard Occupational Code and Title	England		Northern Ireland		Scotland		Wales	
	Number	% of Total	Number	% of Total	Number	% of Total	Number	% of Total
221 *Health Professionals*	471,600	19.20	18,800	21.58	53,700	18.35	26,700	16.69
2211 Medical Practitioners	244,000	9.93	7,500	8.61	31,500	10.77	13,400	8.38
2212 Psychologists	31,400	1.28	200	0.23	2,500	0.85	1,500	0.94
2213 Pharmacists	56,300	2.29	4,500	5.17	4,900	1.67	4,100	2.56
2214 Ophthalmic Opticians	13,300	0.54	700	0.80	2,700	0.92	1,100	0.69
2215 Dental Practitioners	36,100	1.47	1,800	2.07	2,600	0.89	500	0.31
2217 Medical Radiographers	28,500	1.16	900	1.03	2,700	0.92	1,800	1.13
2218 Podiatrists	9,900	0.40	200	0.23	1,100	0.38	900	0.56
2219 Health Professionals n.e.c.	52,100	2.12	3,000	3.44	5,700	1.95	3,400	2.13
222 *Therapy Professionals*	172,200	7.01	6,500	7.46	15,900	5.43	8,700	5.44
2221 Physiotherapists	59,800	2.43	2,800	3.21	7,400	2.53	3,000	1.88
2222 Occupational Therapists	38,900	1.58	1,800	2.07	4,600	1.57	2,100	1.31
2223 Speech and Language Therapists	17,400	0.71	700	0.80	1,200	0.41	800	0.50
2229 Therapy Professionals n.e.c.	56,100	2.28	1,200	1.38	2,700	0.92	2,800	1.75
223 *Nursing and Midwifery Professionals*	578,900	23.57	21,800	25.03	76,000	25.97	36,300	22.69
2231 Nurses	540,400	22.00	21,400	24.57	72,800	24.88	33,900	21.19
2232 Midwives	38,500	1.57	400	0.46	3,200	1.09	2,400	1.50
321 *Health Associate Professionals*	142,200	5.79	3,600	4.13	12,100	4.14	8,100	5.06
3213 Paramedics	24,000	0.98	200	0.23	3,100	1.06	1,100	0.69

Occupation	Count	%	Count	%	Count	%	Count	%
3216 Dispensing Opticians	7,600	0.31	200	0.23	500	0.17	500	0.31
3217 Pharmaceutical Technicians	28,300	1.15	900	1.03	2,200	0.75	1,600	1.00
3218 Medical and Dental Technicians	36,700	1.49	200	0.23	2,900	0.99	2,200	1.38
3219 Health Associate Professionals n.e.c.	45,600	1.86	2,100	2.41	3,400	1.16	2,700	1.69
614 *Caring Personal Services*	1,075,500	43.79	35,700	40.99	133,900	45.76	79,100	49.44
6141 Nursing auxiliaries and Assistants	272,500	11.10	8,100	9.30	35,300	12.06	21,500	13.44
6142 Ambulance Staff (Excluding Paramedics)	19,500	0.79	500	0.57	2,000	0.68	1,300	0.81
6143 Dental Nurses	39,400	1.60	3,200	3.67	7,000	2.39	2,300	1.44
6144 House Parents and Residential Wardens	39,000	1.59	1,600	1.84	5,300	1.81	3,300	2.06
6145 Care Workers And Home Carers	631,100	25.70	20,200	23.19	75,300	25.73	45,600	28.50
6146 Senior Care Workers	64,700	2.63	1,100	1.26	6,900	2.36	4,200	2.63
6147 Care Escorts	9,300	0.38	1,000	1.15	2,100	0.72	900	0.56
9271 Hospital Porters	15,600	0.64	700	0.80	1,000	0.34	1,100	0.69
Total Frontline Care Workforce	2,456,000		87,100		292,600		160,000	

Source: ONS Annual Population Survey, NOMIS, January–December 2019, All in employment by four-digit occupation. SOC 2010

Scotland also employs relatively more qualified nurses and midwives, they account for 26 per cent of the frontline workforce in Scotland compared to 25 per cent in Northern Ireland, 23.5 per cent in England, and less than 23 per cent in Wales. Which means that doctors together with qualified nurses and midwives account for 37 per cent of the frontline workforce in Scotland compared to 34 per cent in England and Northern Ireland and just 31 per cent in Wales. When auxiliary nurses are included, the share of doctors and nurses in the frontline workforce increases to 49 per cent in Scotland compared to 45 per cent in England and Wales, and 43 per cent in Northern Ireland. Wales's share is brought into line with England because it employs relatively more auxiliary nurses than any of the other three countries, while Scotland's share of doctors and nurses in the total frontline workforce remains much higher than any of the other three because it also employs a relatively large number of auxiliary nurses.

Pharmacists account for a much larger share of the frontline workforce in Northern Ireland; over 5 per cent, double the share in any of the other three countries. There are relatively more psychologists in England and Dental Practitioners and Dental Nurses in Northern Ireland. Northern Ireland also has relatively more Physiotherapists but fewer podiatrists. There appear to be considerable differences in the composition of the frontline workforce between the four nations.

Should we expect workforce composition to be the same in each country? We might, because the NHS delivers by far the largest part of health care services in each country and it uses the same procedures (clinical interventions), technologies, and adheres to the same protocols throughout the UK. However, there will be differences in the health care needs of the populations of the four countries and in the priority that the four administrations assign to meeting these needs. Meeting these different needs will require a different mix of skills. There will also be differences between the four countries in the way that they organize the delivery of care—the division between primary, secondary, and social care. These differences will result in differences in the pattern of labour demand in the four countries, which we shall discuss further in Section 3.4.

That there can be sometimes quite striking differences between the four nations in frontline workforce composition is illustrated by the larger share of the frontline workforce accounted for by Dentists and Dental Nurses (SOCs 2215 and 6143) in Northern Ireland. What might account for this? It might be because Northern Ireland assigns higher priority to dental health, and this in turn might be because there is a greater need for dental care (poorer dental health) in Northern Ireland. If this is the explanation, then it lies on what economists call the 'demand-side' of the labour market. However, the difference between Northern Ireland and the rest of the UK might be due to differences on the 'supply side' of the market. For example, perhaps there is a much greater supply of dentists and dental nurses in Northern Ireland, and it is therefore cheaper to employ them here than it is in the rest of the UK. Or perhaps dentists and dental nurses prefer to work in Northern Ireland

Table 1.5 The Number of Qualified Nurses and Midwives and Doctors in the Countries of the UK in 2019

	England	Northern Ireland	Scotland	Wales
Nurses and Midwives	578,900	21,800	76,000	36,300
Doctors	244,000	7,500	31,500	13,400
Ratio of Nurses to Doctors	2.4	2.9	2.4	2.7
Nurse/Doctor Ratio Relative to England	*1.0*	*1.21*	*1.0*	*1.13*

Source: Table 1.3

and, as a result, vacancy rates are much lower in these occupations in Northern Ireland than in other parts of the UK. Though it seems unlikely this last could alone explain the large differences we observe, this brief discussion serves to reminds us that we need to take account of factors on both the supply and the demand sides of the labour market when we seek to explain the occupational composition of the frontline workforce and that the level of employment results from the interaction of factors on both sides of the market.

One aspect of workforce composition which is frequently the focus of analysis and discussion is the number of qualified nurses and midwives relative to the number of doctors. In the past this ratio might have been described as the number of nurses available to support doctors, and a century ago that might have been an appropriate description of what most nurses did. However, today nurses have their own roles, some are members of clinical teams, but many others work independently of doctors across the complete range of health care settings. How this ratio differs between the four nations of the UK is reported in Table 1.5. The Table shows that in 2019 there were 2.9 nurses for every doctor in Northern Ireland, 2.7 nurses to every doctor in Wales, and 2.4 to every doctor in both England and Scotland. The final row of Table 1.5 shows how the ratio differs from that in England.

The table raises some interesting questions, but we will postpone discussion of them until Section 1.8 where we look at the differences in this ratio between the UK and other European countries. First we look at the long-run growth in the frontline workforce and at how the ratio of nurses to doctors has declined over the century to 2011.

1.4 The Long-Run Growth in the Frontline Care Workforce

Health and social care have a long history. People have been delivering some form of health and social care since they populated the Earth, though the accurate recording of the numbers involved is relatively recent. The decennial Census of Population provides data on the jobs people do and allows us to track how the size of the health and social care workforce has increased through time. We use this data to look at the growth in the workforce over the century to 2011, and to distinguish, as far as the data allow, growth in the period prior to and after the creation of the NHS.

From the Census we can distinguish the number of people working in the two most established occupations delivering health care, doctors and nurses, for over a century. The 1911 Census recorded the numbers working as Physicians and Surgeons and the number working as Midwives (then called Registered Practitioner Midwives) and Nurses (Sick Nurses and Invalid Attendants).[8] The 1951 Census also provided this detail, recording the number working as physicians and surgeons and as midwives and trained nurses, but it also recoded the number working as assistant and student nurses, as medical auxiliary professions, as pharmacists and physiotherapists, as hospital and ward orderlies, and as dental practitioners. With the introduction of the Standard Occupational Classification system in 1990 still more detail became available. The 2011 Census used the 2010 version of the SOC and identified frontline occupations using the occupation titles reported in Table 1.1. Over the century from 1911 the decennial Censuses have used an increasing number of titles to describe the occupations of people working in frontline health and social care, providing evidence of the increasing range of skills required to deliver frontline care.

A count of the numbers working in the health and social care occupations recorded in the Censuses of 1911, 1951, and 2011 provides an estimate of the number of frontline care workers in each of these years. By expressing this total as a percentage of the total number of people recorded as working in the Census of the same year, we can obtain an estimate of the share of total employment accounted for by frontline health and social care workers in each of these years. Nurses and doctors are identified in each Census so we can also document how the numbers working in these two occupations have grown over the century to 2011.[9] Over the century as a whole, the number of qualified nurses and midwives increased nearly seven-fold from 83,662 to 558,834 while the number of doctors increased over eight-fold, from 23,469 to 195,329.

The 1951 and 2011 Censuses also asked respondents to identify the main activity of their employer or business and used the Standard Industrial Classification

---

[8] In 1911, there will also have been a small number of other workers delivering health and social care who, though not classified as such at that time, would today be identified as community nurses and care workers. In 1911, they provided health and social care within a domestic setting and would have been classified as domestic servants. In 1911, domestic service was by far the largest source of employment for women, accounting for over a quarter of all women's employment at that time.

[9] At the time of writing, the publicly available data for the 1911 and 1951 Censuses only distinguished health and social care occupations at the level of detail required for this analysis in England and Wales.

Table 1.6 Share of Working Population Accounted for by the Frontline Workforce and the Broader Health and Social Care Industry in England and Wales, 1911–2011

	1911	1951	2011
Frontline Health and Social Care Workforce Share of Total Working Population	1.1	2.1	8.0
Health and Social Care Industry Share of Total Working Population	N/K	2.8	12.5

Source: Census of Population accessed through 'A Vision of Britain Through Time' and Central Statistical Office, Census of Population, England, and Wales, 2011, Table CT0347

(SIC)[10] to categorize their responses. We can therefore identify the number working in the Health and Social Care Industry in those years and so distinguish both the frontline and the industry workforces in these two years. The results are shown in Table 1.6.

Table 1.6 records the dramatic increase in the share of the total working population in England and Wales that was accounted for by the frontline health and social care workforce over the century to 2011. In 1911 just 1.1 per cent of the working population in England and Wales worked in frontline care, but by 2011 this had risen to 8 per cent. In 1911 one in every ninety workers worked in frontline care, but by 2011 this had increased to one in every 12.5. The increase in the broader health and social care industry workforce was even more dramatic. Over the sixty years between 1951 and 2011, the share of the working population in England and Wales working in this industry increased from 2.8 per cent in 1951 to 12.5 per cent in 2011. In 1951 those working in the health and social care industry accounted for one in every thirty-six of the working population, but by 2011 they accounted for one in every eight. The data reveal the dramatic increase in the importance of health and social care as a source of employment and income.

The growth in the frontline workforce occurred in two quite distinct phases. During the first forty years, between 1911 and 1951, the frontline care workforce grew at a rate which was only slightly faster than the rate of growth of the workforce in general: over this period the frontline workforce increased from 1.1 to 2.1 per cent of the total workforce. The period encompassed two world wars, which placed huge demands on the health care system, and yet despite this the health care workforce grew at only a slightly faster rate than the workforce as a whole.

The second period witnessed much more dramatic growth. The NHS was founded in 1948 and so the Census of 1951 was the first conducted after its founding, and the period 1951 to 2011 therefore captures the growth of the NHS.

---

[10] The Standard Industrial Classification system was introduced in the UK in 1948. Industrial activities were allocated to the appropriate Minimum List Heading.

Between 1951 and 2011 the share of the frontline care workforce in the total workforce nearly quadrupled from 2.1 to 8 per cent, while the share of the broader health and social care industry grew almost fivefold, from 2.8 per cent to 12.5 per cent of total workforce. Over this period the number of nurses almost quadrupled, and the number of doctors increased almost five-fold.

One striking feature of developments over the century is the increasing share of the frontline workforce accounted for by AHPs and auxiliary nurses. This becomes evident from a comparison of Tables 1.6 and 1.7 where the latter records the share of the total workforce accounted for by just doctors and nurses.

In 1911 the frontline care workforce comprised largely doctors and qualified nurses and midwives. Together they accounted for 0.9 per cent of the total working population in England and Wales (Table 1.7) at a time when the total frontline workforce accounted for just 1.1 per cent of the total working population (Table 1.6). Thus, other frontline care occupations accounted for just 0.2 per cent of the total working population in 1911. In 1951, doctors and qualified nurses and midwives still accounted for 0.9 per cent of the total working population (Table 1.7), but now the total frontline workforce accounted for 2.1 per cent of the working population (Table 1.6). Thus, the increase in the share of frontline care workers in the total working population (from 1.1 to 2.1 per cent) was entirely due to the increase in the number of AHPs and auxiliary nurses. These occupations which had accounted for just 0.2 per cent of the total working population in 1911 had increased in number to such an extent that they accounted for 1.2 per cent of the total working population in 1951. The same is evident over the period from 1951 to 2011. Over this period the share of the working population accounted for by doctors and qualified nurses increased from 0.9 per cent to 2.8 per cent while the frontline workforce as a whole increased from 2.1 per cent to 8 per cent of the total working population

The data also reveal something of the prominence of different occupations. With only 0.2 per cent of the working population working as doctors in 1911 and 1951, a doctor in those years was something of a 'rare' occupation; just one in every 500 people working in England and Wales worked as a doctor. However, the dramatic increase in their number between 1951 and 2011, meant that a doctor became a much more commonplace occupation. By 2011, one in every 140 of the working population in England and Wales was a doctor.

Nursing was always a more commonplace occupation; even in 1911, one in every 150 people working in England and Wales worked as a nurse, and this remained unchanged through to 1951. However, with the founding of the NHS there was a substantial increase in the number of nurses as recorded in the Censuses of 1951 and 2011. Over this period nursing numbers increased to such an extent that by 2011 nursing accounted for one in every fifty jobs in England and Wales.

Table 1.7 Increase in Nurse and Doctor Numbers in England and Wales, 1911–2011

	Qualified Nurses and Midwives			Doctors			Doctors and Nurses Number	Doctors and Nurses share of total working population	Ratio of Nurses to Doctors
	Number	% of Working Population	% Increase from Earlier Census	Number	% of Working Population	% Increase from Earlier Census			
1911	83,662	0.7%	–	23,469	0.2%	–	107,131	0.9%	3.6
1951	149,323	0.7%	78.5	42,839	0.2%	82.5	192,162	0.9%	3.5
2011	558,834	2.1%	274.2	195,329	0.7%	356.0	754,163	2.8%	2.9

Source: Census of Population accessed through 'A Vision of Britain Through Time' and Central Statistical Office, Census of Population, England, and Wales, 2011, Table CT0347

The 1951 and 2011 Censuses reveal that, since the founding of the NHS, the number of doctors and nurses employed in England and Wales has increased at a much faster rate than the working population, and this is also almost certainly the case in Scotland and Northern Ireland. Furthermore, because the number of doctors increased at a faster rate than that of nurses, doctors have come to assume a more prominent role in the delivery of health care. Over the century to 2011, the ratio of qualified nurses to doctors in England and Wales as reported in Table 1.7, fell from 3.6 to 1 to 2.9 to 1. All of this reduction occurred in the period after the founding of the NHS.

The Censuses show that in England and Wales health care has increasingly become a doctor-intensive service, as indeed it has in many other advanced industrial countries, as we shall see in Section 1.8 below. The development of a doctor-led service means that over the years since the founding of the NHS the production of health care has become more intensive in higher cost labour, and this has contributed to the UKs' rising expenditures on health care over this period. We can see this much more clearly if we look at employment growth in just the NHS.

1.5 Employment Growth in the NHS

The growth in the number of doctors and nurses following the establishment of the NHS is revealed by data for England and Wales published on the seventieth anniversary of the founding of the NHS (NHS Digital, May 2018). The data was taken from the NHS employment records and report the numbers of doctors and nurses working in NHS hospitals in England and Wales in 1949 and 2018.[11] The data for nurses is recorded on a headcount basis while doctors are recorded as full-time equivalents (FTEs), which means they are not directly comparable.

The data reveal that there were 11,735 full-time equivalent (CF) hospital doctors, including 3,488 consultants, working in the NHS in England and Wales in 1949 and that by 2018 the number of FTE hospital doctors had risen to 109,509, including 46,297 consultants.[12] Thus, between 1949 and 2018 the number of consultants increased 50 per cent faster than the medical workforce in general. Over this period the number of consultants increased more than twelve-fold, while the total number of doctors working in the NHS increased over eight-fold.

---

[11] NHS Digital report the number of medical staff on a full-time equivalent (FTE) basis. The number of staff counted on an FTE basis will be fewer than the number recorded by a headcount because some staff only work part-time. FTEs provide a better measure than headcount of the quantity of labour that is at the disposal of the NHS. On the other hand, headcount provides a better indicator of the prominence of medical and nursing staff among the workforce in general and a better guide to how these occupations feature among individual's career choices.

[12] The number include the small number of dental staff employed by the NHS.

The number of qualified nurses working in NHS hospitals in England and Wales also increased rapidly over this period. In 1949 there were 73,650 registered nurses and midwives working in NHS hospitals in these two countries, but by 2018 their number had risen to 346,941. Between 1949 and 2018 the number of nurses increased nearly five-fold.

The Census data reported in Table 1.7 recorded the number of nurses on the same basis as NHS Digital, on a headcount basis, and it is illuminating to compare the two. The Census reported a total of 149,323 nurses and midwives working in all settings in England and Wales in 1951. NHS Digital report that in 1949, two years earlier, a total of 73,650 registered nurses and midwives worked in hospitals in England and Wales. Thus, it would appear that in the very early days of the NHS, at the start of the 1950s, around half of all qualified nurses and midwifes worked in the community. Many worked as district nurses and midwives and were employed by county councils, the predecessors of the current local authorities.

Both the Census and NHS Digital report a substantial rise in the number of qualified nurses and midwives over the following decades. The Census (Table 1.7) reported that between 1951 and 2011 the number working in all settings almost quadrupled, while NHS data reported that between 1949 and 2018 the number working in hospitals increased nearly five-fold. Thus, it appears that since the founding of the NHS the nursing workforce has grown more rapidly in hospitals than in community and other settings. Nonetheless in 2018 there were still around 200,000 qualified nurses and midwives working in the community and other settings in England and Wales.

The NHS Digital data also make clear that the NHS has become a doctor-led, and more specifically, a consultant-led service. In 1949 there were 8.3 qualified nurses and midwives for every doctor and twenty-one for every consultant working in the NHS in England and Wales. By 2018 this had fallen to just 3.2 per doctor and 7.5 per consultant. Moreover, we noted above that the numbers of doctors, consultants, and nurses were recorded on a different basis: doctors and consultants as FTEs, and nurses by a headcount. Though many nurses work part time, their numbers are not adjusted to take account of this. Thus, the ratios above overstate nursing capacity—the fall in the number of nursing hours per doctor and consultant in NHS hospitals in England and Wales has been even more pronounced than the simple numbers suggest.

The same NHS Digital data also tell us something about the growth in the GP workforce in England and Wales, though the data are only available for a shorter period. The data reveal that in 1963 there were 22,159 GPs in England and Wales and that their numbers had risen to 41,693 by 2018. It also reveals a very striking change in the gender composition of this workforce. In 1963 90 per cent of all GPs were men, but by 2018 men accounted for just 48 per cent of the GP workforce. Over the period, the number of men working as GPs fell by 13 per cent while the number of women working as GPs increased almost nine-fold. In 1963, there had been nine male GPs for every woman GP, but by 2018 there were five women GPs for every four male GPs.

What the NHS data tell us is that since the inception of the NHS the production of health care in hospitals in England and Wales has become increasingly dependent on those types of labour that cost the most; those which command the highest salaries and require the greatest investment in training. This change in the composition of the NHS workforce provides part of the explanation for rising expenditures on health care in England and Wales, but it also has other consequences. Because doctors and in particular hospital consultants take many years to train and are generally highly specialized, the service is much less agile. It now takes more time to respond to changing health care needs because it is difficult to allocate highly specialized consultants to new roles and it takes a long time to train a person to assume a new consultant role. We might reasonably question whether this development has produced the workforce we need and constitutes the most efficient way to produce health care?

1.6 Frontline Workforce Composition in General Practice and Hospitals

In the UK, health care is delivered in both the community and hospitals. Primary and secondary care have different workforce requirements, and the occupational composition of the overall frontline workforce is therefore affected by the share of total care delivered by each sector, by what is termed the balance of care between the two sectors.

The difference between the composition of both the total workforce and, within that, the frontline workforce, in general practice and in hospitals in England is reported in Table 1.8.[13] In general practice, GPs account for 51.5 per cent of the frontline workforce, while in hospitals doctors account for only 14.6 per cent of the frontline workforce. In hospitals, nurses and AHPs play a more prominent role than they do in general practice. Nurses account for 38.9 per cent and AHPs 46.6 per cent of the frontline workforce in hospitals but only 26.4 per cent and 22.1 per cent respectively in general practice.

The direction of policy in the UK is to move care from hospitals to general practices and this will therefore change the overall composition of the frontline care

---

[13] The data is only available for England. Most striking is the difference between the two sectors in the share of support staff. Administrative support accounts for 51.5 per cent of the primary care workforce compared to only 19.5 per cent in the secondary sector.

Table 1.8 Composition of the General Practice and Hospital Workforces in England in September 2019 (Headcount)

	General Practice Workforce (% of Total) % of Frontline Workforce	Hospital Workforce (% of Total) % of Frontline Workforce
Nurses	(12.8) 26.4	(31.3) 38.9
AHPs	(10.7) 22.1	(37.5) 46.6
Administrative Support	(51.5)—	(19.5)—
Doctors	(25.0) 51.5	(11.8) 14.6

Sources: England: 'Healthcare Workforce Statistics' for England. Hospital extracted from NHS Hospital & Community Health Service (HCHS) monthly workforce statistics: HCHS staff for England, and General Practice comes from General Practice Workforce Statistics. See https://digital.nhs.uk/data-and-information/publications/statistical/nhs-workforce-statistics/october-2019

workforce.[14] The policy means switching care from a sector which employs a relatively large number of nurses and AHPs to one which employs relatively few and from one which employs relatively few doctors to one which employs relatively more. However, this change in the balance of care will also provoke a change in the composition of the general practice workforce because, as the sector takes on new responsibilities and delivers procedures previously done in hospitals, it will need to employ some of the same skills as hospitals, and so the composition of its workforce will develop in the direction of that in hospitals.

One other striking feature of Table 1.8 is the much greater administrative support that general practices require. One explanation for this is the small scale and associated diseconomies of many primary care organizations, but this too will change as general practices seek to overcome these diseconomies through amalgamation and growth. The composition of the workforces in both general practice and hospitals are in a state of transition.

1.7 The Gender and Ethnic Diversity of the Frontline Workforce

A striking feature of the frontline care workforce is its gender composition, and a second is its ethnic diversity. In this section we reveal that the delivery of frontline care in the UK depends heavily on women and workers from ethnic minority

[14] Though a senior consultant advises that a trend over the last decade has been for previously fatal or untreatable conditions to become chronic diseases and cites as examples, CML or chronic granulocytic leukaemia, myeloma, and macular degeneration. This development has increased the requirement for hospital specialists to manage the complex medications and side effects of these treatments. In consequence, specialists in hospitals rather than GPs will directly manage more chronic diseases. In the past GPs would lead the management of chronic disease, and hospital-based specialists would contribute as required.

backgrounds, which means that jobs in frontline care are a very important source of employment for these workers.

Women have always accounted for a majority of the frontline care workforce, and UK survey data[15] tell us that their share has increased over the last fifty years, which is perhaps surprising given the general expansion of job opportunities for women over this period. In 1970, women accounted for around 75 per cent of employees in frontline health and social care jobs, and this had risen to 78 per cent in 2019. Furthermore, because, as we saw in Section 1.4, employment in health and social care has expanded at a faster rate than UK employment in general, jobs in frontline care have come to account for an increasing share of the jobs done by women. In 1970, jobs in frontline care accounted for one in every eight of the jobs done by women, but by 2019 this had risen to one in every five. By 2019, 20 per cent, or one in every five women employed in the UK were working in frontline care.

Even though jobs in frontline care are a much less important source of employment for men than they are for women, the rapid growth in jobs in frontline care in the UK has meant that these jobs have also become a more important source of employment for men. In 1970, one in every fifty jobs done by men was in frontline health and social care, but by 2019 this had risen to one in twenty.

Jobs in health and social care are also an important source of employment for non-white workers. Research by NHS England compared the ethnic composition of the NHS workforce in England in 2019 to that of the working age population, 16–64 year-olds, recorded in the 2011 Census (NHS Workforce, 2020). It reported that workers of Asian or Asian British ethnicity accounted for 10 per cent of the NHS workforce in 2019 compared to 8.1 per cent of the working age population in 2011, while people of Black or Black British ethnicity accounted for 6.1 per cent of the NHS workforce in 2019 compared to 3.4 per cent of the working age population in 2011. These data are shown in columns (2) and (4) of Table 1.9 and show that in 2019 the workforce in NHS England was more ethnically diverse than the working age population of England in 2011.

However, the NHS workforce data used in the research included support as well as frontline workers and so do not reveal the ethnic composition of the frontline workforce. For this reason the research also looked at the ethnic composition of four large frontline occupations in NHS England, doctors, nurses, midwives, and ambulance workers and compared this to the population of working age in 2011. Column (3) of Table 1.9 reports the results and shows that in 2019, 13.6 per cent of the total working in these occupations were Asian or Asian British, 7 per cent were Black or Black British, and 73.1 per cent were white. In 2011, Asian or Asian

---

[15] The share of men and women in employment in different occupations in the UK can be distinguished in the New Earnings Survey and its successor the Annual Survey of Hours and Earnings. These datasets are the only ones which enable us to distinguish the gender composition of occupations each year from 1970 onwards. As noted earlier, these datasets exclude the self-employed.

British and Black or Black British accounted for 8.1 and 3.4 per cent respectively of the working age population, and so the report concluded that workers from these ethnic minorities played a disproportionately large role in the delivery of frontline care in the NHS.

In fact, this was only true of workers of Black or Black British ethnicity because the research used data that were not appropriate for such an analysis. It compared the composition of the four frontline occupations to the composition of the population of working age when the appropriate comparator was that part of this population which was working. This is because the ethnic diversity of the population aged 16–64 will differ from the ethnic diversity of those from among this population who are working. It will differ because access to jobs and the experience of unemployment will differ between ethnic groups if some ethnic groups suffer discrimination. It will differ if ethnic groups differ in their desire to work, and in the opportunities to undertake non-market work, to remain in education, and to retire from work.

For all these reasons, the ethnic diversity of the working population will differ from that of the working age population. By referencing the ethnic composition of the population aged 16–64 who are working, we capture the labour market realities facing different ethnic groups. Data on the working population can be obtained from the 2019 Annual Population Survey and are reported in column 5 of Table 1.9. They are for the same year as the data on the ethnic composition of the NHS workforce and thus more directly comparable.

Table 1.9 reveals this to be important. Those of Asian or Asian British ethnicity make up a greater share of the population aged 16-64 who are working, column (5), than the population of working age, column (4). Now we find they are less likely to be working in the four largest frontline occupations than they are to be working elsewhere: at 13.6 per cent and 14.1 per cent, respectively, they account for a slightly smaller share of employment in these four occupations than they do of the working population. However, this is not the case for those of Black or Black British ethnicity; they still account for a larger percentage of these four frontline occupations than they do of either those aged 16–64 who are working or the working age population. Frontline jobs are a more important source of employment for people of Black or Black British ethnicity than for the other ethnicities.

What sort of jobs do workers from these ethnic groups do? Are they distributed evenly across frontline jobs or are they concentrated in particular occupations? The answer is provided in Table 1.10, which reports the ethnic composition of the Hospital and Community workforce in NHS England in 2019. The table shows that, in that year, nearly 30 per cent of doctors were Asian or British Asian, and that, in total, non-white workers accounted for over 44 per cent of all doctors. The table also shows that workers of Black and Black British ethnicity were prominent among the nursing, midwifery, and ambulance workforces, while workers

Table 1.9 Ethnic Composition of the NHS Workforce in England: March 2019

	Number Employed in NHS (March 2019) (1)	Percentage of NHS Workforce (March 2019) (2)	Percentage of Four Large Frontline Occupations (March 2019) (3)	Percentage of Working Age (16–64) Population (Census Data 2011) (4)	Percentage of People Aged 16–64 Who Are Working (Annual Population Survey 2019) (5)
Asian	118,396	10.0	13.6	8.1	14.1
Black	72,321	6.1	7.0	3.4	3.3
Mixed	20,607	1.7	1.8	1.8	1.2
White	934,544	79.2	73.1	85.6	79.8
Other	27,169	2.3	4.5	1.1	1.7

Source: NHS Workforce (2020) and Annual Population Survey 2019

Table 1.10 Ethnic Composition of Frontline Occupations in NHS England: March 2019 (Percentage of Occupation)

	Asian	Black	Chinese	Mixed	Other	Total Non-White
Doctors	29.7	4.6	2.5	3.2	4.3	44.3
Nurses	9.7	8.3	0.4	1.4	3.8	23.6
Midwives	2.0	7.0	0.3	1.6	0.6	11.5
Ambulance Workers	1.2	8.3	0.1	1.2	0.2	11.0
All Frontline Occupations	13.6	7.0	0.8	1.8	3.7	26.9

Source: Hospital and Community Health Services (2019)
Note: This table uses the ethnic categories reported by HCHS

of Chinese ethnicity were more likely to be working as doctors than as nurses, midwives, or in the ambulance service.

There is no comprehensive data on the ethnic composition of the adult social care workforce though some details are available for those employed by local authorities in England (NHS Digital February 2020). These data show that 84.5 per cent of adult social services jobs within local authorities in 2019 were carried out by white workers, with 15.5 per cent of jobs carried out by workers from minority ethnic groups. Among these minorities the largest group, which accounted for 7.9 of the 15.5 per cent, was Black, African/Caribbean/Black British. Table 1.9 revealed that 3.3 per cent of the population aged 16–64 who were working identified as Black or Black British, and thus it would appear they play a more prominent role in the adult social care workforce than in the workforce in general and that working in local authority adult social care is an important source of employment for people of this ethnicity.

In summary, it is evident that there is a very marked gender imbalance in the frontline health and social care workforce in the UK and that in England the NHS and local authority social care workforces display greater ethnic diversity than the working age population in general. Why should this be? What factors on either the supply or the demand side of these labour markets might explain this? It seems unlikely that it is factors on the demand side of the market because, jobs are not specific to ethnicities and employers cannot express a preference for a person of a particular ethnicity or gender when seeking to fill a job vacancy. The explanation, therefore, must surely lie on the supply side.

The ready supply of large numbers of foreign trained workers willing to work in frontline care in the UK will be part of the explanation for the ethnic, and perhaps the gender, composition of the frontline workforce. Further women and people from ethnic minorities may be more attracted to the type of work that is done in health and social care and the conditions of employment and pay in frontline jobs may also be perceived as better than in other parts of the UK economy.

It may also be the case that health and social care workplaces are more conveniently located for women and ethnic minorities, NHS hospitals are located in large metropolitan areas and if minority ethnic groups are more likely to live in metropolitan areas, hospitals will be a major source of local jobs. No research has to date investigated the relative importance of each of these in explaining the gender and ethnic composition of the frontline workforce, yet this is evidently important.

What is clear from the data in this section is that frontline health and social care jobs are a very important source of employment and income for women and people who identify as from an ethnic minority background and that the delivery of frontline services relies heavily on the contribution of these workers.

1.8   The UK Compared to Other Countries

How does the health and social care workforce in the UK compare to that in other countries and in particular to those developed countries with whom we typically compare our health service? The best data available to make such comparisons is that produced by the Organisation for Economic Co-operation and Development (OECD) because it goes to considerable lengths to ensure the comparability of data reported for each country.[16] The OECD data allows comparisons with countries with which the UK usually compares itself: France, Germany, the Scandinavian countries, and the USA.

The OECD collects data on the share of total employment accounted for by employment in health and social care in all member countries. The data is taken from national income accounts where the data on employment comes from company records and is therefore likely to differ from that derived from population surveys, such as the APS, where the data result from the responses of individuals. Moreover, national income accounts data distinguish employment by industry and will therefore include people who are working in non-frontline occupations who support, assist, and direct the activities of frontline health and social care workers. It is thus similar in coverage, though the source is different, to the data we reported in Table 1.2.[17]

Figure 1.1 shows the shares of total employment accounted for by employment in the health and social care industry in 2000 and 2017 in selected OECD countries (OECD 2019a). The data record that in 2017, 12.3 per cent of the employed

---

[16] The OECD used to be called the 'rich nations' club when membership comprised exclusively high income countries but over the last two decades OECD membership has broadened, and it now counts among its members a number of middle income countries. As a result the 'average for OECD countries', the OECD 36, now represents a much less useful point of comparison for the UK than it once did.

[17] The data in Table 1.2 came from a population survey, while the data in Figure 1.1 are derived from company records. We would not therefore expect data from these two sources to produce exactly the same results, though they are clearly compatible. Table 1.2 reports the share as 13.3 per cent in 2019 while Figure 1.1 reports it as 12.3 in 2017.

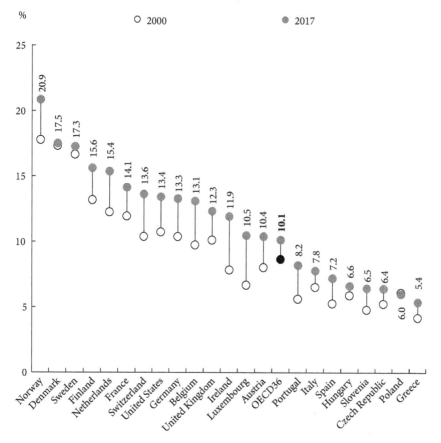

Figure 1.1 Employment in Health and Social Care as a Percentage of Total Employment in 2000 and 2017

Source: OECD 2019a Figure 8.1 StatLink 2 https://doi.org/10.1787/888934017215

population in the UK were working in the health and social care industry, up from 10.1 per cent in 2000. Figure 1.1 reveals that the share of the health and social care industry in total employment varies very substantially between countries in OECD membership. Among Scandinavian and large Continental European countries, Norway at the top of the range had over 20 per cent of its' workforce employed in health and social care in 2017, while Spain at the bottom had just 7.2 per cent. In Norway one in every five jobs was in the health and social care industry, while in Spain it was only one in fourteen.

Though the share in Norway is particularly high, it is noticeable that other Scandinavian and Nordic countries also have high shares of total employment in health and social care. In Denmark, Sweden, and Finland it ranges between 15.6 and 17.5 per cent. France, the USA, and Germany also have larger shares of employment in these industries than does the UK. Indeed, among the large European countries with whom we traditionally compare ourselves, only Italy and Spain at 7.8 and 7.2 per cent respectively are below the UK. Moreover, though the share of employment in health and social care in the UK advanced from 10.1 per cent in 2000 to 12.3 per cent in 2017, the share also advanced in these other countries, and the UK therefore remains below (in many cases well below) that of most other large European countries.

These data reveal the importance of jobs in this industry. One in every five jobs in Norway, one in every seven in France, and one in every 7.5 in Germany is in the health and social care industry. In contrast, fewer than one in thirteen in Italy and Spain and only one in nineteen in Greece are in this industry. These differences in the importance of this industry reflect differences in the share of national income spent on health and social care, which is reported in Figure 3.1, but as will be evident, high spending does not necessarily lead to a correspondingly large share of health and social care jobs in total employment.

The USA exemplifies this. In Chapter 3 we will report that the USA spends a much higher proportion of its national income on health and social care than any other OECD country and though at 13.4 per cent the share of total employment in health and social care industry in the USA in 2017 was well above the OECD average, this was a smaller percentage of total employment than seven other countries, all of whom devoted a smaller share of national income to health and social care spending. The USA employs relatively fewer health and social care workers despite its high spending. One explanation for this could be the higher administrative costs of running the USA health care system, a large part of which are not workforce costs (Frakt 2018). Another and more likely explanation is that, in the USA, labour costs in health care are much higher relative to labour costs in the rest of the economy than they are in any other country. In the USA, health care workers are relatively better paid than they are in other countries, so the USA uses relatively less labour input than other countries when it produces health care.

No data enable us to distinguish the occupational composition of the frontline health and social care workforce in different OECD countries. However, we can gain insight into an aspect of this by looking at OECD data on the number of doctors and nurses and the ratio of nurses to doctors in selected member states. The data enables us to distinguish countries' relative reliance on nurses and doctors to deliver health care as we did earlier, in Section 1.3, for the four nations of the UK. Figure 1.2 reports the ratio of nurses to doctors in selected OECD countries.

The Figure reveals substantial differences between countries in their reliance on these two occupations to deliver health care. In 2017, the USA employed 4.3 nurses per doctor, while among the countries of the European Community the ratio ranged from 4.4 in Finland to 1.0 in Greece. The Figure shows that, at 2.8 nurses per doctor in 2017, the UK had many fewer nurses relative to doctors than some Nordic countries (Finland, Iceland, and Norway) but more than some others (Sweden and Denmark). It also shows that the UK ratio was only slightly lower than that in France at 3.1, and Germany and the Netherlands at 3.0. Thus, the UK was not significantly different from many of the countries with which it typically compares.

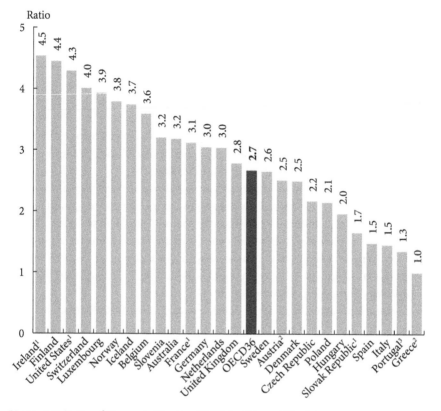

Figure 1.2 Ratio of Nurses to Doctors, 2017 (or Nearest Year)

Source: OECD 2019a Figure 8.11 StatLink 2 https://doi.org/10.1787/888934017405

Earlier, in Table 1.5, we reported the ratio of nurses to doctors in the four nations of the UK as 2.4 in England and Scotland, 2.7 in Wales, and 2.9 in Northern Ireland. These data were for 2019 and from a different source to those reported by the OECD,[18] but they record a picture compatible with that reported by the OECD. Thus the ratios in the nations of the UK are only slightly lower than those in most of the countries with which the UK usually compares.[19]

What are the reasons for the differences between countries in the occupational composition of the frontline workforce, of which the ratio of doctors to nurses is just one aspect? Once again there will be factors on both the demand and the supply sides of the labour market which account for these differences. On the demand

---

[18] In Section 1.4 we used Census data to reveal the decline in the ratio of nurses to doctors in England and Wales over the century from 1911 to 2011 (Table 1.7). In Section 1.3 we used APS data to report differences in the ratio in the four countries of the UK in 2019 (Table 1.5). Both of these datasets are surveys and they are therefore likely to produce slightly different results to the OECD data reported in this section which are derived from employer records.

[19] The OECD data and the data in Table 1.5 are across all sectors and the ratio of nurses to doctors will differ between the hospital and the community care sectors though we do not have data to distinguish this detail.

side will be factors such as the age and gender composition of the population and the extent of deprivation, all of which affect the pattern of demand for health care and therefore for particular health care skills. On the demand side there will be further differences in the way in which these health care needs are met in each country; differences in the procedures and interventions they employ and in the protocols which guide and regulate how they are to be done, which also affect the demand for different health care occupations. On the supply side will be differences in incentives to invest in the skills required to become a doctor or a nurse and, once qualified, to work as trained; the relative pay of doctors and nurses in each country will be a major driver of these decisions.

All the above will produce differences in workforce composition, although in advanced economies like these there are also forces pushing in the opposite direction, toward greater uniformity in workforce composition. High income countries increasingly employ similar protocols and procedures and therefore require the same skills to treat conditions such as cancer, heart disease, and diabetes. Moreover these conditions, together with obesity, account for a very large part of health care activity in most high income countries.

It is therefore surprising that the nurse to doctor ratios differ so much between high income countries. It is perhaps more surprising to find such substantial differences between the three Scandinavian countries, Denmark, Norway, and Sweden. These countries are relatively homogeneous with respect to population health needs, and all have high-performing health systems, yet, as Figure 1.2 reveals, they exhibit big differences in nurse to doctor ratios.

These differences in the ratio of nurses to doctors, in relative nursing capacity, raise important questions for policymakers. Does greater nursing capacity mean that nurses are undertaking tasks that are done by doctors in other countries, and does this help reduce health care expenditure? Or does greater nursing capacity enable doctors, and the health system, in these countries to deliver more output, to undertake more procedures and consultations? Or is the benefit of employing relatively more nurses realized in higher quality, better clinical outcomes? Again, there is no research that looks at the impact of differences between countries in frontline workforce composition on health care expenditure, health care output and health care outcomes.

Though the UKs reliance on nurses relative to doctors to deliver health care is not very different from some other European countries, the number of nurses and (in particular) doctors it employs is. OECD data show that in 2017 the UK employed fewer doctors and nurses per head of population than France, Germany, and the Scandinavian countries and fewer doctors, though more nurses, per head of population than either Italy or Spain. These data are reported in Table 1.11.

Column (2) of Table 1.11 shows that, with 2.8 doctors per 1000 population in 2017, or one doctor for every 357 citizens, the UK had fewer doctors per head of population than any of the countries reported in Table 1.11. Only France, with 3.2

Table 1.11 Nurse and Doctor Densities in 2017 in Scandinavia and Large European Countries

	Practising Nurses per 1,000 population	Practising Doctors per 1,000 population	Practising nurses and doctors per 1,000 population	Ratio of Practising Nurses to Practising Doctors
	(1)	(2)	(3)	(4)
UK	7.8	2.8	10.6	2.8
Denmark	10.0	4.0	14.0	2.5
Norway	17.7	4.7	22.4	3.8
Sweden	10.9	4.1	15.0	2.5
France	10.5	3.2	13.7	3.1
Germany	12.9	4.3	17.2	3.0
Italy	5.8	4.0	9.8	1.5
Spain	5.7	3.9	9.6	1.5

Source: OECD (2019a), Figures 8.3 and 8.10

doctors per 1,000 population, came close to the UK, though it still had fourteen per cent greater medical capacity per head of population than the UK. The highest provision was in Norway, which had 4.7 doctors per 1000 population, or one doctor for every 213 citizens: Norway had 70 per cent greater medical capacity per head of population than the UK.

Norway also had many more nurses per head of population than the UK. The table shows that, at 17.7 nurses per 1000 population, Norway had more than double the number of practising nurses per head of population than the UK had at 7.8. Norway and Germany stand out as two countries which employ relatively large numbers of nurses. Norway had one nurse for every fifty-six of the population and Germany one for every seventy-eight, compared to the UK, where there was only one nurse for every 128 of the population.

Figure 1.2, which reported the ratio of nurses to doctors, revealed that the UK employed fewer nurses per doctor than either France or Germany, and thus, that compared to these countries, in the UK, health care delivery relied more heavily on doctors. Yet as Table 1.11 makes clear, in 2017 the UK employed fewer doctors per head of population than either France or Germany. Thus, though the UK was more poorly provided with doctors, it was still more dependent on them than France and Germany.

This section has raised important questions about the drivers of frontline workforce composition and about the consequences of such differences. More research is required to understand what is driving the differences we have reported above and to distinguish what benefit can be derived from changing these ratios.

1.9 Summary and Conclusions

In this chapter we have reported the numbers and occupations of those working in frontline health and social care in the UK. We have reported how these numbers have grown over the years, and in particular since the establishment of the NHS. We have reported the differences between the nations that make up the UK and the gender and ethnic composition of the frontline care workforce, and we have compared the numbers employed in the UK to those in other countries. The key points to take away from this chapter are as follows.

Since the founding of the NHS the number of jobs in frontline care has increased at a much faster rate than the number of jobs in the UK economy as a whole. Frontline work in health and social care has become an increasingly important source of employment in the UK. In 2019 there were almost three million workers in frontline health and social care in the UK; frontline care accounted for one in every eleven jobs in the UK. These jobs were more important in Northern Ireland, Scotland, and Wales than in England. In Northern Ireland and Scotland they accounted for one in every nine jobs, in Wales one in every ten, and in England one in eleven.

Four occupations dominated the frontline workforce in the UK in 2019. They were care workers, qualified nurses and midwives, auxiliary nurses, and doctors; together they accounted for almost three-quarters of the total. The NHS is the dominant employer of frontline workers. In 2018 the NHS in England and Wales employed almost 110,000 hospital doctors, 42,000 GPs, and 350,000 nurses. Nearly half of these hospital doctors—46,000—were consultants. Over the years between 1949 and 2018, the number of consultants working in the NHS in England increased more than twelve-fold, the number of doctors more than eight-fold, and the number of nurses five-fold.

Frontline care generates large numbers of jobs in the rest of the UK economy. There are a large number of workers in jobs supporting frontline care. These support workers together with frontline workers make-up the health and social care industry workforce, which numbered over 4.3 million and accounted for over 13 per cent of total UK employment in 2019. Again, these industry jobs were more important in Northern Ireland, Scotland, and Wales than they were in England. Yet more people work in industries which supply goods and services to the health and social care industry, they are workers in the pharmaceutical, medical devices, consultancy, and research industries. When they are included in the count of jobs, over five million jobs, or getting on for one in every six jobs in the UK in 2019 resulted from the provision of health and social care.

Frontline jobs are a much greater source of employment for women than men and, despite the expansion of employment opportunities for women over the past half century frontline work has become a more important source of employment for women over this period. By 2019 women accounted for a larger part of the frontline workforce than they did fifty years earlier and by 2019 one in five women, compared to one in twenty men, working in the UK worked in frontline care. In 2018, a majority of GPs were women, while in 1963, the vast majority, nine out of every ten GPs, had been men. It is clear that jobs in frontline care are central to the working lives of a great many women and households in the UK. We need research to better understand why frontline jobs have particular appeal to women; of the importance of pay, working conditions, the type of work and location of work in the appeal of these jobs to women.

Jobs in frontline care were shown to be of particular importance to the working lives of many Asian and Asian British and Black and Black British workers. Workers of Black and Black British ethnicity were prominent among the nursing, midwifery, and ambulance workforces, and they also formed an important part of the Local Authority adult social care workforce. Workers of Asian or British Asian ethnicity were a very important part of the medical workforce, where they accounted for over 30 per cent of all consultant and senior doctor posts and nearly a third of all junior doctor posts in NHS England. In contrast, less than five per cent of doctors in NHS England were Black or Black British. Data to allow similar analysis for Scotland and Northern Ireland were not publicly available, and in general, data on the ethnic composition of the NHS workforce was patchy and unsatisfactory. The ethnic composition of the frontline workforce may in large part be explained by the recruitment of foreign trained workers, but this does not tell us all we need to know. We need research to detail and explain the representation of people of Black British and Asian British ethnicity in the frontline workforce.

The data showed that, over the life of the NHS, the UK health care system had become a doctor-led, and more specifically, a consultant-led service: the number of doctors and consultants increased much faster than the number of nurses and other health care occupations. Among the four nations of the UK the increasing reliance on doctors was most pronounced in England and Scotland. For every doctor that was employed there was 21 per cent more nursing capacity in Northern Ireland and 13 per cent more capacity in Wales than in either England or Scotland.

Policy in the UK is to shift care from hospitals to primary care organizations, where doctors play a much more prominent role in the delivery of care. Doctors accounted for over 50 per cent of the frontline workforce in primary care in England in 2019 but only around 15 per cent of the hospital workforce. Unless there is a substantial change in the composition of the primary care workforce, this shift in the provision of care will increase the reliance of the UK health system on doctors.

International comparisons revealed that the UK employed fewer nurses and doctors per head of population than those European countries with which the UK generally compares its health system: France, Germany, and the Scandinavian countries. The data showed that the UK had constructed a health system which was more heavily reliant on doctors than France and Germany, though it employed relatively fewer doctors than either of them. What the data did not tell us was whether the UK was also more heavily reliant on consultants than other countries. Perhaps the UK employed relatively fewer doctors because it employed relatively more of the most expensive 'type' of doctor, consultants? Or perhaps it employed relatively fewer doctors because doctors in the UK are relatively better paid than in other countries?

The analysis of the occupational composition of the frontline workforce raised many questions. Why does the composition of the frontline workforce differ so substantially between high income European countries and what is the effect of these differences on health care expenditures, outputs and outcome? Does the UK employ fewer doctors per head of population than France and Germany because doctors are relatively better paid in the UK or is it because we employ relatively more of the highest paid among doctors, consultants? Is a consultant-led hospital workforce, as appears policy in the UK, the most cost-effective workforce configuration? The consultant workforce is a high cost, relatively inflexible workforce. It is a highly specialized workforce, and greater specialization usually means reduced flexibility. It also takes a long time to train consultants and thus to change the specialist composition of this workforce.

We have noted in this chapter that France, Germany, and Norway have higher nurse to doctor ratios than the UK. What are these countries doing differently to the UK and what do these differences mean for the quality and cost-effectiveness of care? There appear to be ways of producing health care that are more intensive in nursing care than the UK. Are these countries producing a different type of health care or the same type in a different way? The UK should certainly explore whether a more nurse-intensive health service might be a more cost-effective way of delivering health care. It has been shown that health care in Northern Ireland and Wales is more nurse-intensive than in either England or Scotland. We can learn from the experience of other counties and more locally we can gain insight by researching the differences between the four nations of the UK.

2

Labour Supply to Frontline Care

In the previous chapter we looked at some of the main characteristics of the health and social care workforce, we detailed the number of jobs that result from the provision of health and social care and the type of jobs that this provision generates. The chapter revealed the very sizeable role that the industry plays in the UK economy. Now we look a little deeper into this labour market and consider why people choose to work in frontline health and social care and to spend time and money investing in the skills they need to do frontline jobs. These are issues on the supply side of the labour market.

When economists analyse labour supply they distinguish two time periods, the long and the short run. Most jobs in frontline care are skilled jobs which require a period of formal training before they can be started. The period during which people are able to choose what training to undertake is called the long run. Once that choice has been made and the training completed we enter the period called the short run. In the short run the trained person decides how to use the skills they have acquired; if they are going to work, where they will work, and how many hours they will work. The long run is therefore a period during which a much wider range of choices are available than in the short run. The distinction between the long and the short run is important to understanding labour supply to health and social care jobs.

The most important long-run labour supply decision most people will make is what sort of training to undertake. Economists view training as a form of investment because investment creates assets and training creates the asset called human capital. People invest in assets because they expect them to generate returns and the asset, human capital, generates returns once people start work using the skills they have acquired through their training. As with any other form of investment, human capital investment is costly, and so people will only invest if they judge that the expected returns will exceed the costs of the investment. Many jobs in health care require substantial human capital investment, and so the balance between returns and costs has a very important influence on the numbers who undertake training in health care.

In health care, human capital investment decisions are strongly influenced by the interventions of the governments in the four UK nations, because they affect both the costs of training and the returns from training. Through subsidies to training, the governments reduce the costs that people incur to acquire health care skills, and through control of what health care workers are paid, they affect

The Economics of the UK Health and Social Care Labour Market. Robert Elliott, Oxford University Press.
© Robert Elliott (2024). DOI: 10.1093/oso/9780198883142.003.0002

the returns from their training. The decisions of the four administrations therefore strongly influence the numbers training in health and social care in the UK.

Investment in human capital differs from investment in physical capital in one very important respect: the ownership of the asset created by the investment. The asset created by investment in training is owned by the person who undertook the training, regardless of who paid for the training. One consequence of this difference is that the incentives for government to invest in human capital through subsidies to training are generally weaker than those for individuals to invest in training. In this chapter we shall explain why this is the case and we will explore its implications.

But first we discuss the reasons people work, and specifically why they choose to supply labour to frontline jobs. We will consider the role and importance of pay in the labour supply decisions of people working in frontline care. Much of the focus of analysis of labour markets is on pay, though labour economists recognize that there are other aspects of work which explain why people choose particular jobs. We will seek to identify what these are and their importance in frontline jobs. It has been argued that frontline work attracts people who are altruistic, people who are motivated less by financial rewards than by their desire to help and care for others. We shall examine these arguments and address the question that naturally follows for an economist, which is: how might this affect what frontline workers are paid?

In this chapter we will explore these issues in detail. We will look at the impact of pay on people's labour supply decisions and assess whether pay is less important to workers in frontline jobs. We will investigate the economics of human capital investment and explain why investment in human capital is different from investment in other types of capital. We will consider the incentives for individuals and government to invest in the human capital required to work in frontline health and adult social care in the UK and detail the scale of the government subsidies to this investment. We will detail the number of people investing in health and social care human capital in the UK, report how this has changed in recent years, and reveal how these numbers compare to those in other major European countries.

2.1 The Importance of Pay

Extensive research by economists has established that pay is of primary importance to people's labour market decisions; what people are paid affects the type of work they choose, where they work, how intensively they work, and how long they work. Pay matters because what people are paid determines the goods and services they can afford and the type of life they are able to lead. It affects whether they are able to enjoy a rich and varied lifestyle or merely subsist. What people are paid has a profound impact on their happiness and satisfaction with life.

When economists discuss pay, they anchor its value by translating it into the quantities of goods and services it can buy. Economists talk about pay in *real terms*. This means that if the price of goods and services rise then nominal pay, pay in money terms, must also rise if the same amount of goods and services as before are to be bought. If the same amount of goods and services can be bought then pay, in real terms, has not changed. We expect pay in real terms to be what matters to people, because we understand that it is the goods and services they can buy with the money they earn which matters to them. For this reason, when we talk about the influence of pay on labour supply we generally mean pay defined in real terms.

Pay constitutes the major part of the returns from work. Pay compensates people for the time they spend at work and the prospect of higher pay is one of the main reasons people invest in human capital. Pay is important to doctors, nurses, social care workers, and indeed to all frontline workers, and in this respect they are no different from other workers. Pay affects their long-run supply decisions, such as choice of training, of medical or nursing specialty, and of geographical area in which to work. It also affects their short-run labour supply decisions such as when to work and how many hours to work. A recent comprehensive review of the extensive research in this field attests to the importance of pay in the labour supply decisions of nurses and doctors (Lee et al. 2020).

2.2 The Impact of Pay on Labour Supply in the Short Run

Pay affects the labour market decisions of people in both the long and the short run. In labour market analysis, the short run is defined as the period of time during which the number of people with the requisite training is fixed.[1] In the short run, labour supply to an occupation can increase either because the number of trained people who wish to work increases or those already working are willing to work longer hours. The measure 'hours of work' captures both of these, and we will use it to define labour supply in what follows.

In the short run, an increase in pay makes work more attractive, and therefore we might expect this to result in an increase in the number of hours people are willing to work. However, though an increase in pay makes work more attractive, it also makes those already working better off, and as a result two countervailing

---

[1] Because of the time it takes to train, the short run can be quite lengthy for some health and social care occupations. On average it takes at least five years training before a doctor can start work, though they will still be in training, and three years before a nurse has completed training, and so for these occupations the short run is of the order of at least five and three years respectively. In the case of the adult social care workers the distinction between the short and long run only becomes relevant when considering senior, supervisory or training, posts. This is because qualifications and the mandatory training required can be acquired while working.

effects are at work. Economists label these two effects the substitution and the income effects.

The first of these, the *substitution effect*, works as follows. If real pay rises, work becomes more rewarding, and when people respond to this and work more they reduce the time they spend not working, time they had previously devoted to leisure and non-paid work. This response is called the substitution effect because people are substituting hours of paid work for hours previously devoted to leisure and non-paid work. Another way of looking at this is to recognize that leisure and non-paid work both have an implicit price. The 'price' is the opportunity cost, the pay that is forgone, when time is devoted to leisure and non-paid work. The price of both leisure and non-paid work is the pay that is not being earned when time is spent on them. Viewed in this way, we can see that when pay rises both leisure and non-paid work become more expensive and in consequence we might be expected to buy less. When we 'buy' less leisure and non-paid work when pay rises, we work more; we substitute paid work for leisure and non-paid work. The substitution effect therefore tells us that when pay increases people will want to work more.[2]

However, there is also an influence working in the opposite direction which is called the *income effect*; the increase in pay has had an effect on our income. It is simplest to think of this by considering someone already working. The increased rate of pay is applied to every hour this person was already working, and so even without working longer hours they are already better off. The pay rise has meant that each hour they are working now pays more. Now they must decide what to do with the additional income. One option is to 'spend' some of this increased income buying more leisure or devoting more time to non-paid work. Even though the price of both has risen, the pay rise means they are better off and so they can afford to buy more leisure and non-paid work. The income effect of the pay rise means that they may well choose to work less.

Evidently, we have two influences that can work in opposite directions. The substitution effect encourages the person to work more, while the income effect may result in them wishing to work less. Which effect dominates will determine whether the person ends up working more or less following the pay rise. If the substitution effect is stronger than the income effect, the net result is that the person will wish to spend more time working. If on the other hand the income effect is stronger than the substitution effect the person will wish to work less.[3]

---

[2] This is of course assuming that nothing other than pay has changed.

[3] Both influences may be evident during a person's working life, and which dominates could depend on the stage they are in. In the early years, when pay is usually at a relatively low level, the substitution effect is likely to dominate, and the labour supply schedule, like the one drawn in Figure 2.1, will be forward sloping. In later years when pay is higher, the income effect might dominate, and the schedule may become backward sloping. Thus, the slope of the schedule might change during a person's working life. How this then nets out at the level of an occupation will depend on the age composition of the occupation. If the majority are in the early stages of their career the schedule is likely to be forward

The above reasoning can be helpfully captured in diagrammatic form, in the form of a labour supply schedule. This conceptual device helps us to think carefully and rigorously about what might happen to labour supply as pay and indeed other things which affect people's decisions to work, change. It will also help us distinguish how the labour supply response might differ between doctors, nurses, social care workers, and other occupations. An example of a labour supply schedule is drawn in Figure 2.1. The Figure serves to focus our attention on the key factors which influence labour supply, because when drawing it we need to decide on both the slope of the schedule and its position in the diagrammatic space, and both are, as we shall later discover, very important for the occupations we are interested in.

In Figure 2.1 we depict a labour supply schedule for qualified nurses who are, for purposes of this discussion, supplying labour to the NHS. The schedule depicts the number of hours that qualified nurses are willing to work for the NHS at different rates of pay for NHS nurses. It is an example of a short-run labour supply schedule because underpinning the Figure is the assumption that the number of people with the training required to work as a qualified nurse is fixed, and therefore the only way that labour supply to the NHS can increase is if those already trained as nurses are willing to supply more hours to the NHS.

The hours those trained as nurses are willing to supply to the NHS will increase if any or all of the following happen in response to a rise in NHS pay. First, if those already working as NHS nurses are willing to work longer hours; second, if those who have trained as nurses but were working elsewhere are now willing to work as NHS nurses; and finally, if those who trained as nurses but subsequently decided not to work at all are willing to return to nursing in the NHS. The total number of hours that results is measured along the horizontal axis of Figure 2.1. Along the vertical axis of the Figure we measure different rates of pay for NHS nurses.

The labour supply schedule is constructed by plotting the points in this diagrammatic space which represent combinations of hours of work nurses are willing to supply to the NHS and those rates of pay for NHS nurses which encouraged this supply. The slope of the schedule is given by the relative magnitude of the substitution and income effects. If the substitution effect dominates the income effect, the labour schedule will have a positive slope, like that drawn in Figure 2.1. If the income effect dominates the substitution effect, the schedule will be backward sloping. In practice, which of the two countervailing influences dominates is an empirical matter and cannot be deduced a priori.

Drawing the labour supply schedule makes clear that we must consider two things, the slope of the schedule and the position of the schedule. The slope of the schedule in this Figure depicts the responsiveness of qualified nurses labour

sloping, if those in the late stages of their careers are in the majority, the schedule may well be backward sloping.

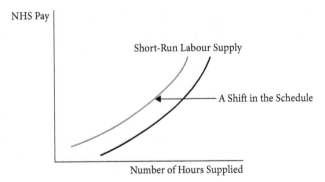

Figure 2.1 The Short-Run Labour Supply Schedule to the
NHS for Qualified Nurses

supply—the number of hours those who have nursing qualifications are willing to work—to changes in the rate of pay for nurses working in the NHS. If a small increase in pay results in a large increase in the hours they are willing to work for the NHS, labour supply is evidently very responsive to wage increases, and we would illustrate this by drawing a schedule with a shallow slope. Conversely, if a large increase in pay produces only a small increase in the number of hours they are willing to work in the NHS, then labour supply is relatively unresponsive to wage change and the schedule would be drawn with a steep slope.[4]

The slope of the labour supply schedule provides a visual representation of the responsiveness of the quantity of labour supplied to changes in pay. Responsiveness can be calculated by taking proportional changes in the two variables, the hours that those qualified to work as nurses are willing to work and pay, and contrasting the two. The measure of responsiveness is called the *elasticity of supply*. It is calculated by expressing the percentage change in labour supply over the percentage change in pay. The resulting number gives us our measure of elasticity. If it is greater than 1 (>1) then supply is very responsive to changes in pay, and described as elastic; if it is <1 then supply is unresponsive, and described as inelastic. Elasticity will be greater in the long run than in the short run, as must be clear from the discussion of the difference between the two time periods, and we shall return to discuss this further in Section 2.7. Elasticity is an important concept because it provides a measure of how much labour supply will respond to any increase in pay that might be offered. An employer who is seeking to increase the number of hours people work by offering an increase in pay should know this number.

---

[4] Under the assumption that the intervals between the numbers along the vertical and horizontal axis have not been distorted. Curves can be made to look steeper or shallower by compressing or increasing (respectively) the intervals between the units of measurement along the horizontal axis.

The position of the schedule in Figure 2.1 is also of great interest because the position of the schedule is determined by all the other things that affect nurses willingness to work in the NHS. These include pay in those jobs which nurses might consider alternatives to working for the NHS, and perhaps the pay of other family members. The position of the schedule may also be affected by things such as child care commitments and domestic arrangements, which make claims on the time of some nurses and affect how much time they can devote to working for the NHS. Moreover, the position also reflects things which are more difficult to measure but which nonetheless influence how much time they are willing to work, things such as social conventions or religious beliefs that may prevent some people from working at certain times in their life. The position of the schedule will also reflect things such as people's perceptions of the stress associated with health and social care jobs, or the safety of the workplace, or indeed other aspects of the working environment which affect the attractiveness of jobs.

All of the above position the labour supply schedule in the two-dimensional diagrammatic space, and when they change they shift the supply schedule, to either the right or left. The way these factors might influence labour supply can be illustrated by an example. Suppose we are mapping the labour supply schedule of people wishing to work in frontline care in adult residential care homes, and we have gathered data reporting what different care homes pay and the total number of hours that are being worked at these different rates of pay. When we plot each of these points and draw the line that best describes the pattern of these coordinates, we draw the labour supply schedule.

Now suppose that there is an increase in the rates of pay in other jobs that adult residential care workers can do, this will shift the labour supply schedule to adult care homes to the left. At any given level of pay in adult care homes, fewer people will wish to work in care homes because it is now more attractive to work elsewhere. Or suppose that government offered vouchers for free nursery care for the children of people who had a National Vocational Qualification (NVQ) in adult social care. For those with nursery-aged children, this would reduce the costs of nursery care and increase opportunities to take paid work by releasing time that had previously been devoted to looking after children of nursery age. The effect of this policy would be to shift the labour supply schedule to adult social care out to the right. At any given level of pay in adult care homes, the hours that people were willing to work in adult care homes would increase because more time is available for such work.

One of the most important factors influencing the position of the supply schedule for frontline workers is the availability of other jobs, jobs outside frontline care, that these workers are willing to consider and what these other jobs pay. What each of the frontline occupations considers to be an alternative source of employment to frontline care is of course subjective, it is in the end 'whatever they are willing to do'. But the range of other jobs that nurses and adult social care workers are willing to consider is likely greater than for doctors.[5] This means that the pay offered by these other jobs is a more important influence on the position of the short-run labour supply schedule to frontline care in the case of nurses and adult social care workers than doctors. If the pay in jobs outside frontline care rises while frontline pay remains the same, there will a greater leftward shift in the nursing and adult social care workers labour supply schedules than the doctors supply schedule. What other jobs pay is a much less important determinant of short-run labour supply to frontline care in the case of doctors than it is for these other two occupations.

The supply schedule in Figure 2.1 was depicted in terms of hours of work, but it could have been drawn in terms of the total number of people who wish to work at different levels of pay. In which case, the horizontal axis would have been defined in terms of the number of people qualified to work as a nurse. The advantage of a schedule defined in terms of hours of work is that it provides a more accurate measure of the total quantity of labour supplied because when supply is measured in terms of the number of people, by headcount, it takes no account of the fact that some of these people may be working or wish to work part time, and so it does not measure labour supply accurately. Of course when the schedule is drawn in terms of hours of work, we are not able to distinguish between an increase due to more hours supplied by the same number of people, or an increased number of people each supplying the same number of hours as before, or indeed some combination of the two. It will depend upon the analytical purpose for which we have drawn the Figure as to which is more useful, people or hours.

It is easy to understand that estimates of the elasticity of labour supply and the factors that shift the labour supply schedule are of great interest to both economists seeking to understand the health and social care labour market and policymakers trying to develop policies to attract people to work in health and social care. Economists have therefore attempted to estimate the elasticity of labour supply for health care occupations, though this has proved no simple matter. For example gathering data on the labour supply responses of health care workers to changes in NHS pay has proved difficult because NHS data at the required level of detail has often been unavailable. It has also proved difficult to collect data on, and therefore to control for, changes in the other factors which position the labour supply schedule. Moreover because the pay of health care workers who are employed in the NHS changes discontinuously, typically annually, many years of data are required before researchers can capture a sufficiently large number of changes in pay to allow them to estimate supply elasticities. When researchers are using

---

[5] Research has shown that qualified nurses can be found working in a wide range of jobs outside frontline care (Elliott et al. 2002). Though there is no comparable research for doctors, doctors may be less willing to consider other jobs because they are more reluctant than nurse to write off the, more substantial, investment in human capital they have made.

data stretching over many years they then have to allow for the possibility that important features of the labour market, and perhaps the behaviour of workers in response to these, may have changed over the period and the elasticity they estimated for the period as a whole may be unrepresentative of the way workers are responding by the end of the period.

An alternative approach has been to gather pay data from a large number of hospitals in a single year and use this to estimate the responsiveness of labour supply to differences in pay between these hospitals. However, here too there are problems because the system of national pay rates for health care workers in the NHS means there is very little variation in rates of pay between hospitals in the UK. There are as a result relatively few studies into labour supply elasticities for occupations in health and social care in the UK, but there are some.

Those estimates we have were obtained from surveys which asked frontline workers what they were paid and how many hours they worked, and most are for nurses and come from research conducted in the 1990s. This research concluded that in the UK, nursing labour supply was relatively inelastic (See Antonazzo et al. 2003 and Shields 2004). One study reported that a 10 per cent increase in nurses' pay would increase nursing labour supply by 3 per cent (Rice 2005) and another that it would reduce the annual leaving rate by 0.7 per cent (Frijters, Shields, and Price 2007). More recent estimates of nursing labour supply elasticities in Australia, where the nursing labour market has many similarities to that in the UK, suggests that these estimates now likely understate the elasticity of nursing labour supply to the NHS and hence new estimates are urgently required.

Australian research has confirmed that factors which shift the labour supply schedule are now of considerable importance. The pay of jobs outside nursing and child care commitments play an important role in the short-run labour supply of nurses. Researchers found that an increase in nurses' pay attracted back to nursing many who had been working in other jobs and many others who had stopped working altogether. The increase in nurses' pay made nursing more attractive and child care more affordable. In Australia, like the UK, a majority of nurses are women and many still assume the main responsibility for child care. Like the UK a large number of nurses choose to work in other jobs when nursing pay is uncompetitive. The research found that child care commitments affected whether nurses worked and how many hours they worked. It found that the labour supply of nurses who had young children was less responsive to pay change than the labour supply of those without young children (Hanel et al. 2014). From this research it can be concluded that what nurses are paid and government support for child care, which affects the cost of child care, are important influences on nursing labour supply, and though this research was for Australia it is likely that similar results would be found in the UK.

Research has distinguished still other factors which affect nurses labour supply. It has revealed that the predictability and timing of working hours is important to nurses in the UK (Eberth et al. 2015). Shift working is a feature of many nurses' jobs, and researchers found that nurses were not averse to this type of work but that it was the predictability of working hours which was important (Di Tommaso et.al. 2009; Scott et al. 2015).

Research of relevance to doctors labour supply in the UK is much more limited. It appears that having young children does not affect doctors labour supply and that labour supply elasticities do not vary much according to age, as would likely happen if supply was affected by the presence of young children. Reviewing the available empirical studies a recent survey concluded that in the short run doctors do not alter their labour supply much in response to changes in pay (Lee et al. 2019).

One reason why the elasticity of labour supply is greater for nurses than for doctors is because in the UK there are a much larger number of people holding nursing qualifications but not working as nurses (Elliott et al. 2003; Hanel et al. 2014) than people holding doctors qualifications but not working as doctors. One reason is doctors have many fewer job opportunities outside the NHS than do nurses, another is that there are likely to be fewer doctors who quit work altogether to assume child care responsibilities because the (higher) pay of doctors affords them more choice over how to manage child care responsibilities than is available to nurses.

Finally, we should note that there has been no research into the labour supply of adult social care workers, and so we know nothing about the elasticity of labour supply for this occupation. These workers are not covered by nationwide rates of pay and it therefore should be possible, and it is of some importance, to estimate labour supply elasticities for this occupation, though obtaining the required data would likely prove very challenging. We might expect that their labour supply will prove highly responsive to changes in their rates of pay. Adult social care workers have many employment opportunities outside adult care, while the gender composition of the workforce also suggests that many will have child care responsibilities. It seems highly likely that, as was reasoned above for nurses, a large number of adult care workers could be enticed back to work in adult care by increasing their pay. We will return to discuss this later in the book.

2.3 Does Altruism Attract People to Frontline Care?

Up to this point the discussion has been about the impact of pay on the labour supply of frontline workers. However, it has long been argued that frontline care workers are less concerned about what they are paid than other workers because they were attracted to this work by their desire to care for others. They have what can be described as an intrinsic motivation to care for the sick and elderly. This motivation has sometimes been described as vocation, on other occasions as a form of altruism. In this section we discuss whether there is evidence for this, whether frontline workers are different from other workers, and what this could mean for their pay.

It has already been contended that people who work in frontline care are in one respect just like people who work in other jobs, they work because work pays. It is also the case that people who work in other jobs are attracted to them by both pay and the characteristics of these jobs. Furthermore, frontline jobs are not the only jobs which have been called a vocation. What distinguishes frontline jobs is that they involve caring for others, and it this characteristic of the work which has led people to suggest that those who do this work must have some form of intrinsic motivation. Caring for the sick and elderly involves intimate, personal contact with people and it calls for special qualities. This type of work will certainly not appeal to everyone, some people will find this work too emotionally challenging, others may be deterred by the degree of intimacy between carer and cared for; it is possible that the people who have chosen to work in frontline care are in some way different from the rest of us.

Descriptions of what frontline work entails on job advertisement websites make clear that an important requirement of work in frontline care is 'the ability to put the emotional needs of your patients first by practising sensitivity, patience, and empathy [because it] can drastically improve patient outcomes. Displaying this level of compassion can ease your patients' anxieties and decrease their time in hospital'.[6] Sensitivity, patience, and empathy appear to be essential requirements of frontline work. Frontline jobs also require compassion because they involve working with people who are experiencing some of the most difficult and distressing times in their lives. Not everyone has the qualities required to undertake this type of work, nor does it appeal to everyone.

The idea that frontline work requires special qualities has been explored most fully in the case of nursing. Research has confirmed that empathy and compassion are vital for performing the jobs of nurses (Hoeve et al. 2014), it has revealed that some nurses regard nursing as a calling and that others claim that it provides them with a purpose in life (Wrzesniewski 2012). Several researchers have shown that the desire to care for others is a prominent motivation for choosing to become a nurse (McLaughlin et al. 2010; Wu et al. 2015) and others have found that this also applies to doctors in the UK (McHarg et.al. 2007).

Frontline work could be seen as a vocation. The term vocation means that people are driven to choose a particular type of work because they feel they have an aptitude, or in the extreme a 'natural talent', for it. However, frontline work is not the only vocation in the UK. There are other jobs and therefore other labour markets in which labour supply is likely to be affected in the same way. Teaching is

[6] See, for example, https://www.worktheworld.co.uk/blog/nursing-as-a-vocation#:~:text=Vocation%20Noun.,as%20worthy%20and%20requiring%20dedication

frequently described as a vocation and indeed the origins of the term lie with the job of the priest.[7] While a sense of vocation may indeed describe the motivation of many people attracted to frontline care, it does not distinguish frontline workers.

Altruism is a stronger form of intrinsic motivation, and it has been argued that, if frontline work is more than 'simply' a vocation, this is a better term to describe what motivates people to undertake this work. Altruism is the disinterested and selfless concern for the welfare of others, a commitment to put the interests of others first even at a cost to oneself, and frontline work offers a unique opportunity for expressing this form of intrinsic motivation. In its purest form it would mean that helping others was the only motivation of those who work in frontline care. The Hippocratic Oath and the Nightingale Pledge which in the UK doctors and nurses, respectively, agree could be seen as evidence for this. These oaths imply, though do not make explicit, that any tension between monetary reward and patient care must be resolved in favour of the latter.

The motivation of frontline workers matters for our discussion of labour supply because if they do care less about what they are paid than other workers they are likely to be less responsiveness to financial incentives than other workers. Extreme altruism would mean there was no relationship between how much work a frontline worker was willing to do and what they were paid. However, the research evidence tells us otherwise for at least significant parts of the frontline workforce. The research evidence on the elasticity of labour supply of nurses, discussed in the previous section, and of GPs' responses to payment by results, which we shall discuss in Section 6.3, reveals that altruism is neither the sole nor the dominant reason many people want to work in these frontline jobs.[8]

This does not mean that intrinsic motivation has no impact on the labour supply of some workers to frontline jobs; intrinsic motivation may have been what attracted many people to this work in the first place. However, motivation may change through time; the initial motivation to undertake this type of work may weaken when confronted with the realities of what frontline jobs pay and what that pay means for frontline workers standards of living. It is entirely possible that the motivation of workers, who were initially attracted to work on the frontline by some form of altruism, changes, and that through time pay assumes a more prominent role in explaining why they continue to work. It is possible that, confronted

[7] The word 'vocation' derives from the Latin vocare, to call, and its application to the labour market was first applied to that for priests 'called' to the ministry by God.
[8] In a further attempt to describe this intrinsic motivation, the term prosocial behaviour has been used. The term means the desire to make a difference to other people lives (Nesje 2015) and it has on occasion been used interchangeably with altruism (Batson 2002). However, the two are distinct because prosocial behaviour says nothing about the underlying motivation of the person, while altruism does. The desire to make a difference to other people's lives may reflect altruism, or it may result from the personal reward, the satisfaction, that is gained from making a difference to other peoples' lives. People may also engage in jobs which make a difference to other peoples' lives because these are jobs considered fulfilling and personally rewarding (Grant and Berg 2012), and that is not altruism.

by the challenges of the work, workforce shortages, and the need to deliver care in a resource-constrained environment, with the result that they are not be able to deliver the ideal care they originally envisaged, intrinsic motivation fades.

However, we lack evidence to support this contention—we have no research recording the motivation of a group of frontline workers through time, revealing how individual workers' motivation may have changed over the years they have worked on the frontline. The evidence about frontline workers' motivation we reported earlier is what researchers call cross-section evidence, evidence gathered in a particular point in time, a month, or year. There is no substantive research which has tracked how the motivation of a cohort of frontline workers might have changed over their working lives. This is what we need.

Theoretical economists have identified how cross-section data should be collected and analysed using the conceptual framework of the 'utility' function. A utility function captures the characteristics of the job which generate utility for workers. A utility function described for a health care worker would include both pay and, and because intrinsic motivation is expressed in concern for patients' health, some measure of the benefit that patients derive from treatment. In this framework the health care worker is then depicted as trading off pay and intrinsic motivation, proxied by the benefit to patients, and the importance they assign to the benefit that patients derive from their care then determines their responsiveness to changes in what they are paid. (Chalkley and Malcomson 1998; Ellis and McGuire 1990; Siciliani 2009). To date, this research has largely taken the form of model-building, though empirical evidence from laboratory experiments has begun to distinguish the weight that doctors attach to patient benefit (Godager and Wiesen 2013 and Hennig-Schmidt et al. 2011).

One final point to make is that our focus here has been on the characteristic of frontline jobs which might attract people motivated by altruism. This characteristic is of course just one of the characteristics of frontline jobs which will affect what they pay. Frontline jobs have other characteristics which will appeal to workers. They have characteristics which offer stimulation, challenge, prestige, and reputation—all of which have been shown to be attractive to doctors (Scott, 2001)—but in this respect frontline jobs are not alone. Our focus is on the distinguishing characteristics of frontline jobs which affect what they pay, and there are a number of these which we will discuss in Section 6.2. The point to make here is that frontline jobs have several distinguishing characteristics which affect what they pay and the characteristic of frontline work which attracts those motivated by altruism is just one of them.

This brief discussion has revealed something of the complexity of this issue and that there is as yet no agreement on how to describe the motivation of some frontline workers. Even though we have not pinned down what, if anything, sets some frontline workers apart from workers in other jobs, the fact that there is thought to be something different about at least some of the people who choose these jobs is evidenced by the extent and persistence of this discussion.[9] There is agreement that frontline jobs demand particular qualities, but there is no consensus as to what this means for what they pay. Nor do we understand how this motivation may have changed over the working lives of frontline workers.

The issues at stake can again be illustrated with the help of Figure 2.2. If some form of intrinsic motivation attracts people to frontline jobs then it increases labour supply to these jobs. This means the supply of labour to frontline jobs is greater at any rate of pay than it would be if there was no one with this motivation; diagrammatically, it shifts the labour supply schedules of frontline health and social care occupations to the right. Moreover, if the intrinsic motivation of frontline workers means that their labour supply is less responsive to changes in their pay, it also steepens the slope of their labour supply schedules. Both of these effects are depicted in Figure 2.2.

Labour economists are interested in the motivation of frontline workers because they want to know how it affects their pay. If intrinsic motivation results in an outward shift and steeping of the labour supply schedule, it is very likely to have an effect on pay. Precisely what that effect is we can only discover once we have taken account of labour demand. We need to marry the labour supply schedules in the absence and presence of intrinsic motivation to a labour demand schedule to distinguish the impact of this motivation on pay. In Chapter 3 we will derive the labour demand schedule for frontline workers and in Chapter 4 describe how this schedule, together with labour supply schedules, can be used to identify how changes in labour supply will affect pay.

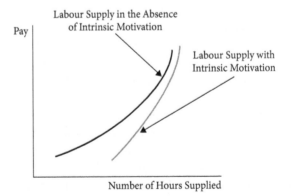

Figure 2.2 Labour Supply Schedule with Intrinsic Motivation

---

[9] A Google search of 'health care work as a vocation' or 'medicine as a vocation' will reveal an extensive and lively debate on this topic.

Most importantly, in Chapter 6 we shall discover that the impact of intrinsic motivation on pay will depend on how the pay of different health and social care workers is set. If it is set through competition, any increase in labour supply, while labour demand remains unchanged, will result in lower pay than would otherwise be the case. In a labour market where pay is set through competition, workers 'pay' for their intrinsic motivation because they receive a lower rate of pay than they could earn if they took a job which was in all other respects equivalent; equivalent in all respects save that the other job provided no opportunity for the expression of this intrinsic motivation.

In Chapter 6 we will see that the pay of neither health nor adult social care workers is set through competition. In health care, pay is set through an administrative process, while in social care, though the conditions appear appropriate for competitive pay-setting, competition does not set pay. Moreover, as we shall also see in Chapter 6 in recent years health and social care labour markets have been far from equilibrium and pay far from equilibrium levels. If pay were at the market-clearing level and labour supply were greater than would otherwise be the case, because the supply of some or many workers was motivated by altruism, then health and social care workers would pay for their altruism. However, we are not in that position and so how large the payment would be we cannot know.

2.4 Human Capital Investment and the Impact of Pay on Long-Run Labour Supply

The skills required to do frontline work are acquired through formal and informal training. Formal training is certified training and takes place in the classroom and sometimes at work, while informal training is learning-by-doing and takes place at work. The complete range of skills and competencies required to become a doctor, nurse, or social care worker are acquired through both formal and informal training in a very wide range of different settings, in universities and colleges and in hospitals, surgeries and care homes.

Among the frontline occupations, training is lengthiest for doctors; undergraduate education can take between four and six years, and this is followed by a mixture of classroom and on-the-job training, which takes a further three to eight years. In the UK it generally takes three years to complete a nursing degree. The training involves a mixture of classroom and work-based learning, clinical placements, with classroom training accounting for up to half of the time. The training for adult social care work consists of a number of short courses which can be undertaken at college, online at home, and on-the-job while working.

The type of training people choose is determined by their aptitude, the career they want to follow, and the costs and benefits of the training required to pursue that career. Their choice may be affected by the labour market status and ambitions of people close to them, people in their household, because the train-ing they choose may affect their choices. Economists view a person's decision to train as conceptually the same as an organizations decision to invest in a piece of machinery. In both cases the investment creates capital, an asset, which is expected to generate income in the future for the owner of the asset. Training creates the asset economists call human capital.[10]

The relationship between the initial costs of the investment and the income it is expected to generate is central to any investment decision. Both the person investing in human capital and the organization investing in physical capital spend money and time to create capital, and both have to judge whether their outlays will be covered by the income the capital is expected to generate. Both must under-take a cost–benefit analysis to establish whether the returns from their investment exceed the costs of their investment. When future income is expected to exceed the initial cost of the investment there is an incentive to invest.

The return to the organization which owns the physical capital is the flow of income that results from selling the product which the capital has produced. The returns to the owner of human capital are the monetary and non-monetary rewards they obtain when doing a job which requires the skills they have acquired. Pay is the most important of the returns to human capital, because it must, at a minimum, be sufficient to cover both the initial outlays on training and sub-sequently to ensure that the human capital remains in good working order, the person has enough to live on, and remains in good health. The expected level of pay is therefore of central importance to the human capital investment decision.

The cost–benefit analysis of the investment must also take account of the dif-ference in the timing of the outlays on the investment and the returns from the investment. The costs of investment will largely be incurred in the present, while the returns will accrue in the future. In general, it is thought that returns which accrue in the future are worth less than those earned now, and there-fore the investor needs to discount future returns. The application of a discount rate enables the investor to calculate the present value of the returns, which they can then compare to the costs. By comparing the present value of the returns to the (present value) of the costs they can calculate the *net present value* of the investment. The investment is worthwhile if the net present value is positive.

The relationship between initial outlays and returns on human capital is depicted in Figure 2.3. In this example, investment is in nurse training, which is hypothesized to take place between the ages of 18 and 21. The initial invest-ment costs incurred between 18 and 21 comprise both direct costs, expenditures on tuition fees, and learning materials, shown by the shaded area ABCD below

---

[10] The concept of human capital was developed by Gary Becker (1964), and the pioneering empirical work in this field was undertaken by Jacob Mincer (1974), yet the ideas underpinning this concept can be traced back to Adam Smith, who wrote of the 'costs of learning the business'. See Book 1, Chapter X, of *An Inquiry into the Nature and Causes of The Wealth of Nations*, published in 1776.

the horizontal axis, and opportunity costs, the pay that would have been received by working instead of training, shown by the shaded area RSAB above the line. These costs must be compared to the size of the discounted returns that would be expected from training. Pay after training, represented by line WV which measures 'discounted returns', is higher than the pay which would have been received if no training had been undertaken, represented by line SZ. The returns from training are therefore represented by the hatched area WVSZ which represents the discounted present value of the higher pay that it is expected to be earned in the jobs open to the trained person. If the area WVSZ in Figure 2.3 is greater than the area RSCD, the total of direct and opportunity costs, the net present value of the returns exceeds costs and the investment is worthwhile; the net present value of the investment is positive.

Of course, the investment choice is very unlikely to be between training and no training, rather it will be between training as, say, a doctor and training as a lawyer, an accountant, or even an economist. In which case Figure 2.3 would need to be modified to capture the difference in training costs and discounted returns between the two occupations. The most important of the returns from training for another occupation will be what the other occupation is expected to pay, and thus the expected pay of the doctor, nurse, or social care worker relative to that of the alternative occupation affects their investment decision.

The most important labour market decision most people make is the choice of career, and in choosing a career they also choose a type of training. People typically make their career choices when they are young and have neither a partner nor dependents, and it is therefore primarily the costs and benefits to them which influence their career choice and associated human capital investment decision. If, however, the choice is made when they have a partner and dependents, then the costs and benefits to these other members of the household enter the calculation. Moreover, other members of the household are also likely to contribute to the investment decision. The costs and benefits to other members of the household will be affected by whether they are working or planning to work.

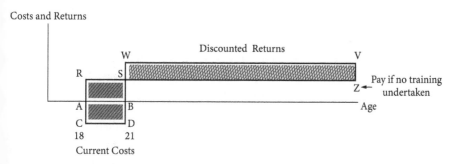

Figure 2.3 The Costs and Benefits of Human Capital Investment

One particular aspect of this merits comment. In recent decades the labour market participation of women has increased, with the result that many households in the UK now contain at least two people who are working. In these households, human capital investment decisions must be taken with regard to their impact on the work and career opportunities of other household members. If an investment restricts the opportunities available to other members of the household it increases the costs of the investment; if it increases the opportunities it reduces the cost. Household composition and the labour market status of other household members can therefore affect the cost–benefit calculation and the type of training chosen. Where the costs and benefits of the investment affect other household members, Figure 2.3 would again need to be modified to capture the costs and benefits to the household taken as a whole.

Of course, few if any individuals or households will engage in the finely calibrated calculations implied by the human capital model, indeed it is unlikely they can obtain all the information they would need to do so. The importance of the model is that it identifies the factors that individuals take into account when making career and training choices, and it conceptualizes the decision-making process. It identifies the most important things people pay regard to when making human capital investment decisions and, most importantly, makes clear that they weigh costs against benefits.

We should be in no doubt that if people are considering training to become a nurse and observe that the pay of nurses is little different from the pay of some other occupations which are no more demanding and require little or no training then this will deter at least some of them from undertaking nurse training. Or if they discover that the costs of investing in nurse training have risen while the pay of nurses has not, this too will deter some from training. Again, the person considering whether to train as a doctor will be deterred from doing so if they understand that the relative pay of doctors has been falling while investment costs have remained largely unchanged.

The implications of the theory of human capital are profound. It makes clear that the volume of investment in human capital is determined by the balance between the costs of the investment and the returns from the investment, by the net present value of the investment. It follows that an increase in net present value will lead to more investment in human capital while a fall in net present value will result in less investment. There are two ways of increasing net present value to encourage investment: either increase the returns to investment for a given level of costs or reduce the costs at a given level of returns.

More people will train if either returns, primarily pay, are increased at a given cost of training, or if training costs are reduced at a given level of pay. Conversely, if training costs increase and pay is unchanged, fewer people will train. The balance between training costs and pay is therefore a key influence on the size of the trained workforce. Recognizing this is key to policy aimed to affect the long-run supply of labour to frontline health care occupations.

2.5 Short- and Long-Run Labour Supply Schedules

From the foregoing discussion it will be evident that the responsiveness of frontline workers' labour supply to changes in what they are paid will differ in the long and short run. The short run is defined as a period in which the number of people with the required training is fixed, and therefore the only way that the labour supply to a frontline job, such as nursing in the NHS, can increase in the short run is if any, or indeed all, of the following occur, as detailed in Section 2.2. If those already working as NHS nurses are willing to work longer hours, those who have trained as nurses but were working elsewhere are now willing to work as NHS nurses and if those who trained as nurses but subsequently decided not to work at all are willing to return to nursing in the NHS. In the long run, the supply of nurses to the NHS can increase in any or all of these three ways and by an increase in the number of people undertaking and completing nurse training. From which it follows that the supply response to an increase in pay is greater in the long run than in the short run. This is the case for all frontline occupations which require investment in training.

The difference between labour supply schedules in the long and short run can again be illustrated using the diagrammatic method employed earlier in this chapter. In Figure 2.4 labour supply schedules in both the long and the short run are depicted. Labour supply is measured along the horizontal axis in terms of number of hours, because this captures all the ways in which supply can increase in both the long and the short run. The vertical axis again measures pay though in the long run it is expected pay, pay in the future, which drives the long-run investment decisions. What most people expect to be paid in the future will be strongly influenced by current pay, and therefore current pay has an important role in human capital investment decisions.

The Figure makes clear that any increase in pay will produce a greater supply response in the long run than in the short run: the more elastic supply response in the long run is depicted by the shallower slope of the long-run labour supply schedule. The difference between the long and the short run will differ between frontline occupations because of the time it takes to complete training. The difference is negligible in some cases such as adult social care workers where training can be done on the job, and as a result a rise in pay could produce an almost immediate increase in labour supply. But for other occupations, such as doctors, there will be a considerable difference between the long and short run, and it will take several years before the effects of a pay rise feed through into increased labour supply as a result of increased investment in human capital.

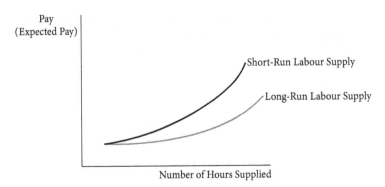

Figure 2.4 Short- and Long-Run Labour Supply Schedules to the NHS for Qualified Nurses

2.6 Government Investment in Frontline Skills

In the UK, the governments of the four nations invest in training health care workers. The level of investment in training the different health care occupations differs between the four nations, though in each of them the largest expenditure is on training doctors. Training for consultants and GPs comprises the years in medical school followed by a foundation programme with a health care provider. The costs to the trainee are tuition fees,[11] expenditure on accommodation and other living expenses, and the opportunity costs of the income that is foregone while training—had they not been training they might have been working and earning. The direct cost to government is the financial support they offer to some students, through bursaries and scholarships, reimbursement to universities for those training costs that are not covered by tuition fees, and reimbursement to health care providers for clinical placement costs and lost production costs-costs incurred when trainers are away from their posts- during foundation years. Universities are reimbursed through teaching grants,[12] and health care providers through placement fees (tariffs). Tuition fees cover only a small part of the undergraduate teaching costs in medical schools.

In 2017 it was estimated that in England the total direct cost to government of putting a UK or EU national through medical school was around £230,000 (Department of Health 2017) and the costs would have been similar in the other

[11] Scotland is an exception. Students who are recognized as resident in Scotland pay no fees provided they study in Scotland. Overseas students (except those from the EU who started in or before the 2020/21) and students from the rest of the UK (RUK) pay full fees. This should be understood as a qualification to statements about who pays fees in all that follows.

[12] Medical training is judged by The Office for Students to be a high-cost subject. The costs are judged to be more than double the fees paid by students and are defrayed by grants from government. See https://www.officeforstudents.org.uk/media/42d81daf-5c1d-49f6-961b-8b4ab1f27edc/ofs2018__21.pdf

nations of the UK. In the academic year 2017/18 there were 42,190 medical students in the UK. That year tuition fees in England totalled less than £40,000 and so the net cost to government in England of putting a UK or EU national through medical school was of the order of £190,000. In Scotland the net cost of putting most students through medical school would have been of the order of £230,000 per trainee, because tuition fees for students recognized as resident were paid by government.

Government investment in medical training continues beyond medical school. Following medical school, the newly qualified doctors undergo two years of foundation programme training, at which stage they are working and receiving pay.[13] The two years of foundation training constitute a general medical training programme, combining, predominantly, work experience with formal training. During these years the government also incurs the costs associated with the training and supervision of doctors who are learning on-the-job within a health care provider. Once they have completed foundation training, they choose between general practice, core training, and specialty training, which require similar levels of government support.[14] In 2019 there were just over 60,000 doctors in foundation and specialty group training in the UK (General Medical Council 2019).

In all it takes fourteen years to produce a consultant, and ten to produce a GP. It is estimated that in England in 2014 the total costs of training a consultant amounted to £727,000, while the total costs to train a GP was £485,000 (National Audit Office 2016). These costs do not include the opportunity cost of the income that is foregone while individuals are training, and of course today's training costs will be higher than those in 2014. Data suggest that in the UK the burden of the costs required to produce either a consultant or GP fall roughly two-thirds to government and one-third on the individual trainee (National Audit Office 2016).

It takes significantly fewer years training to become a nurse or AHP than it does to become a doctor. Typically, it takes three years to train as a nurse and four years to train to become an AHP, and thus both the direct and the opportunity costs of training are less. It has been estimated that in 2014 it cost £79,000 to train a general nurse (National Audit Office 2016). Prior to 2017, trainees paid no tuition fees and received either non-means-tested or means-tested bursaries and reduced-rate student loans to finance living costs, so most of these costs fell to government.

However, in recent years the level of government support for training nurses and midwives and some AHPs (occupational therapists, speech and language therapists, podiatrists, radiographers) has reduced substantially. This support was abolished in England in 2017, though not in Scotland. These changes in support

[13] In 2019 this comprised a basic salary ranging between £27,600 to £32,000 per annum plus pay for additional hours over forty per week, a 37 per cent enhancement for working nights, a weekend allowance for any work at the weekend, an availability allowance for on-call, plus some other pay premia.

[14] The modal age of those undertaking foundation training is 30–39 (GMC 2017).

for nurse training in England substantially changed the balance between the costs and benefits of investment in nursing human capital and resulted in a sharp reduction in the number of applicants to train as qualified nurses in England as reported in Box 2.1. This reduction in long-run labour supply to nursing was viewed with concern and partially reversed with the reintroduction of more modest support in England with effect from September 2020. From that time, nursing bursaries, worth at least £5000 and up to £8000 per year, were made available to those training as nurses and midwives.

The costs of training to become an adult social care worker are less than those required to become either a nurse or doctor. Not all jobs in care require formal training, though there are increasing pressures to improve the qualifications of those working in adult social care. Colleges offer training for NVQs in social care. Study is typically part-time and often online, and many train through apprenticeships. Courses allow carers to train while remaining at work. Both the costs of training and the duration of the training are less than those for health care workers. Typically, trainees bear the major part of the costs of investing in training in adult social care.

Box 2.1 Changing the Cost–Benefit Balance of Human Capital Investment

Prior to 2017, most nurses, midwifes, and AHPs training in the UK did not pay tuition fees. The waiving of fees was estimated to cost the exchequer £800 million per annum. In 2017, England decided to reduce this expenditure by restricting training places and requiring trainees to pay tuition fees. Loans were offered to cover tuition fees and maintenance costs. The Department of Health and Social Care stated that loans would give those in training about 25 per cent more financial support while they studied.

The change transferred some of the costs of human capital investment in nursing in England from government to the individual. Nursing is a generally transferable skill, and this change therefore introduced an element of economic logic into policy in this area. However, there was a risk attached to this change. Through this policy, the government had engineered a reduction in the returns from nurse training. The change increased the private costs of investing in nurse training, but there was no compensating increase in the rewards from that investment, for example through an increase in nurses' pay. The change therefore discouraged human capital investment in nursing. All else remaining the same, the number of applicants for training places would be expected to fall, which is what happened. In 2018, there was a 17.6 per cent fall in applications to study nursing.

Alongside expenditure on training, the governments in the UK incur additional costs because they have established institutions to attest to the trained persons competence to practice. In the UK this is done by the General Medical Council (GMC) and the Nursing and Midwifery Council (NMC). These Councils verify the completion of training and attainment of the required skills. The GMC awards licences to practise to those it judges have an acceptable primary medical qualification, and the skills and capabilities (including English language proficiency) required to practise medicine. The NMC does essentially the same for nurses and midwives. Licensure provides reassurance that a specified standard has been attained[15] and prohibits those who do not meet the minimum required standard from practising. This system is common to other professions, for example, teaching and parts of the legal profession.[16] These arrangements confer substantial powers on the licensing authority. The licensing authority determines the number permitted to practice and it therefore affects supply. It is therefore important that the licensing authority is independent and is not subject to influence by those who might benefit from manipulation of supply.

2.7 The Economics of Government Investment in Frontline Skills

There are powerful economic arguments which should caution government against investing in health and social care training. They result from the combination of an important distinguishing feature of human capital and the type of skills which investment in health care human capital creates.

The distinguishing feature of human capital is that the legal ownership of human capital resides with the person who was trained, the person embodying the human capital, and this ownership cannot be transferred. Human capital, unlike physical capital, cannot be bought and sold.[17] The ownership of human capital resides with the trained person regardless of who paid for the training. The significance of this is that it is the owner who will decide where, how, and when the

---

[15] It is interesting to note that during the early years of the French Revolution a different view was taken, which was that anyone should be able to practise medicine. In March 1791, all trade associations and guilds were abolished, and everyone had the right to follow the occupation of their choice (Crosland 2004). The motivation for this reform was to allow freedom of entry to all labour markets. It was argued that the public would be able to distinguish between the competent and incompetent practitioners and the latter would attract no business. The collapse and revival of medical education in France during the revolution is interestingly detailed in Vess (1967)

[16] Certification is another mechanism for signalling competence and is a feature of other professions, for example solicitors and accountants. However, while certification attests to competence it does not, unlike licensure, prevent those who fail to meet the standard from practising.

[17] Slavery was the most notorious example of buying and selling human capital, and though it is no longer legally permissible in the UK, there is evidence it continues, though not in either health or social care (See: https://www.antislavery.org/slavery-today/slavery-uk/).

human capital is to be brought to the labour market and these decisions affect the returns to human capital.

If the trained person decides to delay entry to the workforce or to work part time, the returns to training will be lower than if they started work immediately and worked full time. If the UK government paid for the training the returns they will receive will be lower if the trained person delays entry to work or works part time. Moreover, if the trained person decides to embark on a completely different career or to work overseas, the returns to government investment in training will be zero. Ownership affords control, and where the government has no ownership it has no control. This means that the returns to government investment in human capital are uncertain, and this uncertainty reduces the incentives for government to invest in the human capital.

This distinguishing feature of human capital is of particular significance in health care because the type of skills that are produced by the training front-line health and social care workers receive produces transferable skills. Skills are described as transferable when there is more than one organization that might want to employ the skills. The training that doctors, nurses, and social care workers undertake produces skills which can be employed by several organizations. As well as publicly funded health and social care providers, there are private health and social care providers in the UK, and health and social care providers abroad who have a demand for these skills. Where there are organizations outside the publicly funded health care service in the UK which have a demand for the skills that the training has produced, this reduces the incentives for governments in the UK to invest in producing these skills, they cannot be confident the trained worker will choose to work in the public sector.

Indeed, where government has invested in training it is at a disadvantage in bidding to employ the trained workers because it has incurred the costs of training and other organizations have not. As a result, these other organizations can afford to offer the trained workers higher pay.[18] It follows that the greater is the competition for any health care occupation from organizations in the UK private sector and abroad, the weaker are the incentives for the UK government to invest in training these occupations and the smaller should be government investment.

---

[18] Hiring workers whom another organization has trained is described as 'poaching' or 'free-riding'. The term poaching has been used to describe the behaviour of many high income countries which recruit trained health and social care workers from low and middle income countries. Recent initiatives have sought to counter this behaviour by persuading high income countries to sign 'no poaching' agreements—agreements not to hire trained workers from low income countries. However, there are clearly strong incentives for health and social care providers in high income countries to ignore such agreements, because if they can hire trained workers from abroad without incurring any financial penalty they can reduce their expenditure on training. The strong incentives to 'cheat' on 'no poaching' agreements mean these agreements have met with limited success.

The government in the UK has addressed this problem in the case of nurses and AHPs by transferring the costs of investment to the individual. Indeed, the argument for doing so is strengthened by the fact that workers derive greater benefits from human capital investment than employers. Workers derive greater benefit because the returns to human capital investment take both a monetary and a non-monetary form and the non-monetary benefits are likely to be valued more highly by workers than employers. An example of a non-monetary return from human capital investment would be the stimulation and enjoyment the highly trained person might derive from working with other highly trained people, an employer might judge this of little benefit to them. Moreover, the non-monetary benefits of training are intrinsically difficult to value because of their subjective nature, and thus even if an employer judged a non-monetary benefit was of some value to them, it is likely they would find it difficult to agree with the worker what that value was.

Economic theory tells us that government should reduce its' investment in health care human capital, yet if it simply transferred the costs of training onto health care workers and did nothing else we would expect the number of people investing in training to fall, as happened in nursing in 2017. Individuals would be unwilling to take on a larger share of investment costs unless there was a compensating increase in the returns from their investment. Pay constitutes the most important of the returns to human capital, and therefore pay would need to increase to compensate for the increased investment costs. In the case of doctors it would require a substantial pay rise to compensate them for the very substantial training costs they would assume. The evidence of recent years suggests that government is reluctant to award substantial pay increases to health care workers and so it seems unlikely they would fully compensate health care workers for any increased investment costs.

A further obstacle to transferring investment costs is the reluctance of banks and similar financial institutions to lend to finance human capital investment. If people were required to pay a larger part of the investment costs they would need to borrow to finance the investment. Financial institutions are reluctant to advance large sums for human capital investment for the same reasons that organizations are reluctant to invest in transferable skills: lending to finance human capital investment produces less certain returns than lending to finance physical capital investment.[19] Recall that this is because the people in whom the investment

---

[19] Banks or other financial institutions could reduce their exposure to risk by requiring collateral for human capital loans. However, this would disadvantage those who are unable to provide collateral and advantage wealthy families. People from wealthy families would then become disproportionately represented in those areas of the health and social care workforce which required the highest levels of human capital intensive, i.e., doctors. A concern would be that a less socio-economically diverse and representative workforce might be less able to deliver effective health and social care.

has been made own the human capital and their choices affect the rate of return on human capital investment.

One approach government could adopt would be to offer trainees loans, loans which covered the costs of the investment. However, because these loans would, in the case of doctors, be substantial, many trainees would be reluctant to incur this level of debt. A variation on this would be to make the 'loan' conditional, to transform the loan into a grant made conditional on the trainee working for a stipulated number of years or hours, after they have completed training, in the publicly funded health care system. The number of years, or hours, required to provide government with an appropriate return on investment would need precise and careful calculation. Such an arrangement would make no difference to the majority of doctors, who train at public expense and then spend their career working in the publicly funded health service. It would, however, make an important difference where doctors train at public expense then proceed to work abroad or in the UK private sector after only a brief period working in the publicly funded health service. Such a scheme would increase the returns to government investment in health care human capital.

The scheme would be analogous to indenturing the trainee or in some other way 'tying' them to work for the public health care system which paid for their training. Indentured labour is labour that of its own free will has entered into a contract to stay with an employer. Though it is not called this, it is in effect what happens in the armed forces, where volunteers 'sign on' for a period which exceeds the time required to train them. The period in excess of the time required to train is a period during which the armed forces obtain a return on their investment in training.[20] If trainees leave before the time required for the government to obtain a return on their investment they incur a penalty.

At present the UK government shares the costs of human capital investment in training doctors with trainees. Government pays two-thirds of the costs of training doctors, which means that the scale of government investment is substantial. What the government appears to have done, consciously or otherwise, is traded off the investment in health care human capital it writes off each year as doctors leave the public service to work in the private sector and abroad against the increase in the pay bill that would be required to induce a sufficient number of these leavers to remain in public service and deliver the required return on its investment, judging that the costs of the former are less than the latter. Whether this is an efficient trade-off has not been established and a conditional grant scheme offers an alternative. What we observe is that each year government in the UK writes off

[20] An example of such a scheme in health care is the dental bursary scheme in Scotland. Undergraduates must agree to work a year as a dentist in NHS Scotland for each year they receive the bursary. The introduction of the bursary appears to have led to only a very small increase in the number of undergraduates who work in NHS Scotland, which is unsurprising given the modest (£4000) per annum) level of the bursary (NHS Education for Scotland 2018).

LABOUR SUPPLY TO FRONTLINE CARE   59

a not inconsiderable part of their, substantial, investment in training doctors, as the numbers of doctors entering the public health service fall short of those who completed training, while others leave the public sector to work in the UK private sector or abroad. The government should explore alternatives to the present arrangements.

2.8 The Number Training in the UK

Each year, nearly 7000 people enter medical training, around 25,000 start nurse training, and around 90,000 start apprenticeships in social care in the UK. Large numbers also train to enter the many AHP occupations, and around 1000 enter dental training each year.

The number training as doctors has increased substantially during this century. Between 2000 and 2010, several new medical schools were opened in England. and the number of doctors graduating from UK medical schools almost doubled, as shown in Figure 2.5. Since that time the numbers graduating each year have fluctuated around the 7000 mark. Figure 2.5 also reveals that, between 2000 and 2010, the supply of UK-trained medical graduates fell far short of the number required to meet demand. The Figure shows that, over that period, between 6000 and 14,000 foreign-trained doctors registered to work in the UK each year. Indeed, the number registering exceeded the number graduating from UK medical schools each year between 2000 and 2006, sometimes by a very substantial margin.

More recent data reveals that the number of foreign-trained doctors registering to work in the UK continues to exceed the number of UK medical graduates. Of the 17,000 doctors who joined the workforce in the year to end June 2019, around 45 per cent trained in the UK, while the balance of more than 9500 qualified outside the UK (GMC 2019). Dependency on foreign-born doctors to satisfy the UK demand for doctors has been a prominent and persistent feature of the UK labour market for doctors over many decades and will be discussed further in Chapter 5.

The UK has sought to contain its expenditure on training doctors by limiting the number of students at medical schools. In the later half of the decade from 2010, there were around 20,000 applicants each October to study medicine in the UK and, prior to the pandemic, around 7,000 entrants to medical school each year (Medical Schools Council 2018 and University and Colleges Admissions Service). The number of training places and their distribution between universities is decided in discussion with doctors' representatives by the administrations of the four nations of the UK and results in a set intake targets for each medical school. The resulting shortfall in the number of doctors emerging from UK medical schools is made good by hiring doctors trained abroad. The ease with which this latter can be done reduces the incentives for the UK administrations to increase the number of training places and produce more UK-trained doctors.

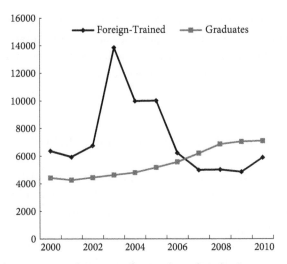

Figure 2.5 Changes in the Number of Medical Graduates and Registrations of Foreign-Trained doctors in the UK

Source: OECD 2015, Figure 3.22 StatLink 2 http://dx.doi.org/ 10.1787/888933261495

In contrast in the years immediately prior to the pandemic there were few government controls on the number of training places for nurses and AHPs, and none for social care workers. Colleges and universities were able to increase provision of training places as they judged appropriate, in the same way that they do for other subjects. The numbers training as AHPs each year in the four nations are not recorded in such a way as to allow the total to be easily distinguished, and though we know the numbers training in adult social care have increased in recent years, as the numbers employed in this sector have risen, the data recording this are not readily available. We know much more about the numbers training to become nurses and doctors.

The last twenty years have seen an increase in the number of nurses entering training in the UK, but in percentage terms the increase has been less than that of doctors. The numbers grew from just under 20,000 per annum at the start of this century to over 26,000 by 2008–2009. In 2009, the nature of nurse training changed; from that year all training was in universities and nursing became a degree profession. Thereafter, the numbers entering training fluctuated between 24,000 and 27,000 per annum over the years between 2010 to 2015, rising to just over 28,000 in 2016, before falling back sharply in 2018 for the reasons detailed in Box 2.1.

Attrition is a feature of most training programmes. Not all trainees complete their course and some who complete do not proceed to work in the occupations for which they have trained. Attrition, both during and after training, is a particular feature of nurse training. Data reveal that among those UK nursing students who began a three-year degree course which was due to finish in 2017, a quarter left or suspended their studies (Health Foundation 2018) while between 2013/14 and 2016/17 the number of newly qualified nurses who subsequently joined the nursing workforce fell by 17 per cent (NHS PRB 2018). Upon graduation, an increasing number of nurses chose either to delay working as a nurse or to do a different sort of work. For some, this would have been because their circumstances changed, however the transferability of nursing skills and the wide range of job opportunities available outside nursing also mean that nursing is particularly susceptible to developments in the wider labour market. Economic forces in the wider labour market exert a powerful influence on nurses' labour market decisions, as the research reported in Section 2.2 revealed.

Nor are doctors immune to such pressures. Workforce studies reveal that a declining proportion of UK junior doctors are now proceeding directly to specialist training, with many taking career breaks. The proportion of Foundation Year 2 (F2) doctors proceeding directly to specialist training declined from 71 to 50 per cent between 2011 and 2016. Doctors in training in the UK provide much of the resource to meet service demand, and so this contributed to short-term labour shortages. It appears that doctors taking a 'career break' constitute the largest category within this group, which suggests that many foundation doctors are choosing to delay the timing of their decision regarding choice of long-term specialty (Lachish et al. 2018).

2.9 Summary and Conclusions

In this chapter we have analysed the labour supply to frontline jobs in health and social care. The key points to take from this chapter are outlined below.

Pay matters, though it has been argued that frontline workers are differently motivated from other workers; that it is altruism which motivates them to work in frontline jobs; that they care less about pay and respond differently to financial incentives than other workers, the research evidence suggests otherwise. The research suggests that altruism was not the principal motivation of many frontline workers. This does not mean that it played no part in labour supply to frontline jobs, it may have been what attracted many people to the work in the first place. However, motivation can change through time. The initial motivation of these workers may have changed as they were confronted with the realities of what these jobs pay, by the challenges of workforce shortages, and the need to deliver care in a resource-constrained environment where they are not able to deliver the care they originally envisaged. We need research into how the motivation of frontline workers in different jobs may have changed over the years they have been working on the frontline.

Extensive research by economists has established that pay is of primary importance in both the short and the long-run labour market decisions of frontline care workers. Research has shown that in the short run the supply of nurses is affected by their relative pay and that doctors respond to financial incentives. It has shown that pay of jobs outside nursing and child care commitments play an important role in the short-run labour supply of nurses. Government therefore plays a central role in determining the supply of nurses and doctors in the short run, through its role in setting their pay.

In the long run, the number of people who invest in the human capital required to do frontline jobs will have a major impact on the supply of labour to frontline jobs. The number who invest is determined by the balance between the costs and benefits of such investment, and what frontline workers are paid is a central element of the benefits. Again, government policy has a significant impact on the long-run supply of doctors and nurses through its role in pay-setting. Government plays a further role in the long-run supply of doctors through subsidizing their training. Imprudent government policy can affect long-run supply by upsetting the balance between the costs and benefits of investment in health care human capital, as became evident when subsidies to nurse training in England were withdrawn in 2017 and the numbers willing to invest in this training fell sharply.

In the years before 2019, on average nearly 7000 people began medical training each year, around 25,000 entered nurse training, and around 90,000 started apprenticeships in social care in the UK. Large numbers also trained to enter the many AHP occupations, and around 1000 entered dental training each year.

The number of training places for doctors and their distribution between universities was decided in discussion with doctors' representatives by the administrations of the four nations of the UK. Both parties to this discussion have incentives to limit the number of training places. A shortage of doctors exerts upward pressure on doctors pay and limiting the number of students at medical schools contains public expenditure. The resulting shortfall in the supply of doctors can be made good each year by hiring doctors trained abroad. In contrast, prior to the pandemic there were few government controls on the number of training places for nurses and AHPs and none for social care workers. Colleges and universities were able to provide the numbers of training places they judged appropriate in the same way they do for other subjects.

Governments in the UK devote substantial resource to train doctors but very modest resource to train nurses and AHPs. Two-thirds of the cost of training a doctor in the UK is met from public funds, but this investment produces an uncertain return. Government investment in medical training is designed to produce doctors to work in the publicly funded health care sector. However governments cannot be confident this will happen because their investment produces transferable skills, and it is doctors not the governments which decide where, how, and when these skills are to be brought to the labour market.

When the private returns to working in the public health care sector decline, as occurred in the decade to 2019, and which is reported in Chapter 7, the returns to government investment in training doctors also decline. Increasingly during the years prior to the pandemic governments of the four nations had to write off part of their investment in training doctors. Each year, doctors who had trained at public expense choose to work in the UK private sector, to work abroad, and to work part time, all of which reduced the return on public investment in training doctors.

Economic theory makes clear that the costs of human capital investment which produces transferable skills should be borne by the worker, that the government should transfer the costs of training to become a doctor to the trainee. However, if the government only did this it would substantially reduce the numbers training to become doctors; the scale of investment would deter many from investing in training. To address this problem the government could offer conditional grants to medical trainees. A grant equal to the transferred training costs could be offered conditional on the trained doctor working for a stipulated number of years or a total number of hours in the publicly funded health care system. Such an arrangement would make no difference to the majority of doctors, who train at public expense and then spend their career working in the publicly funded health service. It would, however, make an important difference where doctors train at public expense then proceed to either work abroad or in the UK private sector after only a brief period working in the publicly funded health service. Such a scheme would increase the return on government investment in health care skills.

To an extent that differs across the four nations nurses bear the major part of the costs of investing in nurse training. In the years immediately prior to the pandemic there appears to have been a substantial write-off of this investment. In these years attrition during and immediately following nurse training appears to have been substantial. The appeal of nursing appears to have diminished as trainees learned more about what the work entails, and more about the rewards from working in jobs other than nursing. The greater part of this loss is borne by trainee nurses, and though government may therefore be relatively unconcerned, the impact of this on long-run nursing labour supply will be considerable. It is evident that if government wishes to see an increase in the numbers completing nurse training and proceeding to a career in nursing then it must increase the returns to nurses from investing in training: government must increase the relative pay of trained nurses. More generally government should conduct a review of policy toward nurse and medical training, it should commission research to identify policies which will increase the sustainability of long run supply and improve the returns to public investment in this training.

3

The Demand for Frontline Care Workers

Every market has two sides, buyers and sellers, and the labour market for front-line health and social care workers is no exception. In this market the sellers are the people who want to work in frontline care, and the buyers the organizations looking to employ people to deliver health and social care services. In the previous chapter we looked at the supply side of this labour market, here we look at the demand side.

In this chapter we will look at the determinants of the demand for health and social care workers. In the UK, the overall level of demand is primarily driven by what the UK spends on health and social care. The desired level of employment, called the establishment, in the NHS and other publicly funded non-commercial health and social care organizations, is determined by the budget they have available to spend on workforce. The composition of the workforce they employ is then determined by the way in which they spend their budget, by the procedures and interventions they deliver, and the care they provide. In this chapter we will detail what the UK spends on health and social care and how this compares to other countries. We will also use data for England to illustrate how this spending is distributed between health and social care and to detail spending on the NHS and hospitals.

Organisations demand labour because it produces output, how that output is produced is described in a production function. Each procedure and intervention that a health or social care organisation produces can be described in a production function. A production function describes the relationship between inputs and outputs, it identifies the inputs which produce the output, and shows how the level of the output changes as the quantity of the inputs change. In health and social care it shows the role that labour plays in delivering the procedures and interventions that constitute the output of the health and social care system and which improve the health and care provided to the population.

An organisations' demand for labour is described by a labour demand schedule. This schedule, taken together with the labour supply schedule, enables us to describe a labour market. We will describe the construction of the labour demand schedule and identify the information needed to do this.

In the final part of this chapter we will look beyond the labour demand schedule and consider the future demand for labour by health and social care organizations. We will explain why large health care organizations and some social care organizations believe they need to forecast their future demand for labour, and we then

The Economics of the UK Health and Social Care Labour Market. Robert Elliott, Oxford University Press.
© Robert Elliott (2024). DOI: 10.1093/oso/9780198883142.003.0003

review the methods they use to do this. We will also explore the impact of new technologies on the demand for labour by health and social care organizations.

3.1 Translating Need into Labour Demand

The demand for health and social care services in the UK arises from the needs of the UK population for health and social care and a large number of different organizations, hospitals, GP practices, and care homes exist to deliver this care. All of these organizations employ frontline workers to deliver care and therefore have a demand for frontline workers. We therefore describe the demand for frontline workers as a *derived demand*[1] because it is a demand which derives from the UK populations' need for health and social care.

Not all of the UK populations needs for health and social care services are met, and so not all give rise to a demand for labour. Only those needs that are recognized, and which translate into the provision of services, result in labour demand. There are three main reasons why some needs do not result in labour demand. Some go unrecognized because people fail to acknowledge they have a health condition which requires treatment, others are not translated into the provision of appropriate services because people fail to present for treatment, and still others are not translated into the provision of services because there is no funding available to provide the required services. All these result in 'unmet need', and in the UK there is considerable 'unmet need'.[2]

Frontline health and social care workers play a central role in translating need for health and social care into demand for courses of treatment, and packages of care. Doctors diagnose health conditions and identify appropriate courses of treatment, and by so doing, give specific form to the demand for labour, because different treatments require different frontline occupations. When doctors perform this role they act as the agent of the patient who, as the principal, delegates authority to the agent to identify an appropriate course of treatment.[3] This delegation hands considerable power to the agent; were they to be motivated by other

---

[1] The concept of 'derived demand' was introduced by Alfred Marshall in 1890.

[2] The European Commission estimated that, in 2019, 8.2 per cent of the UK population aged 16 and over had some form of unmet need for a medical examination or treatment. Of this 8.2 per cent, 4.5 per cent was due to either people judging that it was too far or too expensive to travel for treatment, or the length of the waiting list. The level of 8.2 per cent was one of the highest in Europe.
See https://ec.europa.eu/eurostat/statistics-explained/index.php?title=Unmet_health_care_needs_statistics

[3] This information advantage can result in what economists have identified as a principal–agent 'problem'. Where there is a conflict in priorities between the agent and principal a 'problem' arises because the agent, who is authorized to act on behalf of the principal, might act in a way that best serves their interests, but which is contrary to the best interests of the principal. The principal–agent problem occurs in many different contexts: between corporate managers and shareholders, between elected officials and constituents, between brokers and buyers and sellers in financial markets. In each of these examples the first is the agent and the second are the principals.

than the best interests of the patient they might propose treatments which primarily satisfied their own interests rather than those of their patient.[4] In the extreme, it could lead to 'over-treatment' or inappropriate treatment.

In the UK, this agency role is typically performed by GPs, the first point of contact for most people seeking diagnosis of a health care condition, but it is also performed by consultants recommending a course of treatment or surgical intervention, and to a smaller degree, by care managers, recommending a package of care.[5] This latter is perhaps the least recognized and most contested of agency roles in health and social care because here, the care manager—the agent—may have only a small information advantage over the principal, the elderly person seeking residential care. The agency role means that certain health and social care occupations also play a central role in determining what output the health and social care system produces and therefore what labour is required.

Diagnosis of a health condition or a requirement for social care does not always result in a demand for labour. The diagnosis might reveal a condition which is untreatable, or the required treatment might not be delivered due to lack of funding. Only those treatments and care packages which are supported by funding translate into a demand for frontline workers. Moreover where treatment is deferred, there is no immediate demand for labour, though if patients are placed on waiting lists, there will be demand in the future. The demand for health and social care workers results from the delivery of care, and that requires spending.

3.2 Spending on Health and Social Care in the UK

Spending on health and social care is the main driver of the overall level of demand for health and social care workers in the UK, and the distribution of that spending, between secondary, primary, and social care, is a driver of the relative size of the workforce in each of these sectors. Accordingly, in this section we look at what the UK spends on health and social care and how this is distributed.

---

[4] In the UK, checks on the abuse of power by the agent take the form of the opportunity to seek a second opinion, online diagnostic tools, and health care websites. NHS Choices advises that 'the NHS is working hard to improve opportunities for patients to make choices about their care. In the near future, NHS England wants all patients to be able to say: "I have discussed with my GP or health care professional the different options available to me, including the pros and cons and, where appropriate, whether to choose to not have treatment"'.

[5] The principal–agent problem has important implications for how we pay those health and social care workers who perform this agency role. We should avoid paying them in ways that might influence their recommendations for treatment or care. We should avoid creating what economists call 'perverse incentives'—incentives that have unintended or undesirable consequences such as inappropriate or overtreatment. This problem might arise if we pay those involved in diagnosis and treatment under a fee-for-service payment system because it might lead them to recommend those services which produce the highest fees, even though these might not be the ones which best meet the needs of patients and clients.

In financial year 2018/19, total spending on health and social care in the UK amounted to almost £220 billion. Spending by central government accounted for about 80 per cent of total spending on health care, and spending by central and local government accounted for around 60 per cent of total spending on social care. The balance of spending in each case was accounted for by private spending. Private spending on health care largely comprises spending on pharmaceuticals and private health insurance, while private spending on social care is across the entire range of provision.

The data required to distinguish the separate contributions of government and private spending on health and social care in the four countries of the UK are not easily accessible, and the data which is available do not allow for comparisons between the four countries. The most informative data is that compiled by The Health Foundation and The King's Fund (Gershlick et al. 2019) which reports total government spending on health care and government and private spending on social care in England.

The Health Foundation argue that 'the full DHSC budget remains the most accurate way to define [government] health care spending, as it provides the full picture of resources available for patient care' (Gershlick et al. 2019). The full DHSC budget, less the amount passed to local authorities as a contribution to funding social care, is shown in Table 3.1. In financial year 2018/19 this amounted to £130.1 billion.

By far the largest part of government spending on health care is spent on the NHS. The lower part of Table 3.1 shows how much of the total government spend in England went on the NHS. This spending comes out of the DHSC budget and totalled £122.9 billion in 2018/19. Of the total of £122.9 billion, £116.8 billion, or 95 per cent, was current spending[6] and just 5 per cent capital spend.[7] Of the £116.8 billion, £75 billion of NHS current spending was distributed to Care Commissioning Groups, and by far the largest part of this sum, nearly £60 billion, funded hospital activity (ONS 2018a).

Table 3.1 also shows that spending on social care in England in financial year 2018/19 totalled £33.5 billion. Spending on social care in England is done by local authorities and is decided, individually, by 152 local authorities.[8] A small part of the total they spent, £2.8 billion, came directly from central government, from the DHSC via the NHS budget. The largest part, £19.1 billion of the total spend of £33.5 billion, came from what are termed 'local authority resources'. Local authority resources comprise monies raised from business rates, council tax,

---

[6] In 2013 it was estimated that NHS England spent £4.5 billion or 4 per cent of NHS current expenditure on surgery. The majority were planned or 'elective' operations, but 18 per cent of procedures were for patients requiring emergency surgery (Foundation Trust Network 2013).
[7] Health visiting and training doctors and nurses are funded directly by the DHSC and are therefore included in the DHSC budget but not NHS Current Spending.
[8] The Health Foundation (2019) and The King's Fund (2021).

Table 3.1 Spending on Health and Social Care: on the NHS and Social Care in England in 2018/19

	England 2018/19 (Billions)	Share of Total Spending
DHSC budget, less contribution to local authorities spending on social care from NHS budget	130.1	79.5
Social care spending *including* client contributions, self-funding, and NHS contribution	33.5*	20.5
Total spending on health and social care identified above	**163.6**	100
NHS total spending out of DHSC budget	122.9	100
of which NHS current spending	116.8	95.0
and NHS capital spending	6.1	5.0

Sources: Gershlick et al. (2019) and The King's Fund (2019)
*£21.9 billion of the total spend on social care is by local authorities. This £21.9 billion includes an NHS contribution to local authorities of £2.8 billion (in this table it is excluded from the DHSC budget and included in social care spend) and £2.8 billion in 'client contributions'. The £21.9 billion, taken together with £11.6 billion self-funding, makes up the total of £33.5 billion. Private spending on social care totals £14.4 billion, comprising £11.6 self-funding and the £2.8 billion client contribution. The local authority total for 2018/19 was not available when this table was compiled and is estimated by taking the 2017/18 total reported by the King's Fund (op. cit.) and uplifting by 3 per cent. The self-funding total for 2018/19 is similarly estimated by taking the 2016/17 National Audit Office of £10.9 billion total reported by the King's Fund (op. cit.) and uplifting by 3 per cent in each of the following two years.

and specific government grants to local authorities, but they also include client contributions,[9] which amounted to £2.8 billion in 2018/19. Client contributions comprise means-tested contributions to their care by residents of care homes, and thus local authority spending out of their own resources was £16.3 billion. When this total is taken together with the £2.8 billion provided by the DHSC, total public sector spending on social care in 2018/19 amounted to £19.1 billion, or 57 per cent of the total of £33.5 billion spent on social care in England that year. This

---

[9] In England the elderly are required, where they can, to pay for their residential care until their resources are diminished, at which time the local authority assumes the cost of care. It is because there is this contingent local authority commitment to spend that this element of private spend is included under local authority resources.

means that public sector spending—spending by central and local government—in England on both health and social care amounted to £149.2 billion in 2018/19. Of this total, £130.1 billion was spent on health care and £19.1 billion on social care. Thus by far the largest part of public sector spending on health and social care in England, 87 per cent, was spent on health care.

Spending on health and social care in the UK is distributed between the three sectors that deliver care in the UK. Each of these sector delivers a very different type of care and so has very different workforce requirements, and thus the relative size of each sector will affect the composition of the overall health and social care workforce. The three sectors are secondary care (hospitals), primary care (GP practices, dentists, pharmacy, and optometry) and adult social care (long-term residential and domiciliary care). In 2018, spending on hospitals was six times greater than spending on either residential long-term care facilities or GP surgeries (ONS, 2018a).

Not all NHS and local authority spending on health and social care goes on workforce; how much is impossible to distinguish without extended research. However, the annual financial statements of hospital trusts and boards provide some insight, revealing that a typical hospital spends around 65 per cent of its operating budget on workforce; moreover, workforce costs are likely to account for a still greater proportion of GP practice and social care operating costs.

Part of this spending on workforce will be on workers who were not working on the front line, i.e., workers who were supporting those on the front line. Data for NHS England suggests that support workers accounted for around 23 per cent of all workers in NHS England in 2019 (NHS Digital 2019).[10] To know what this means for spend on frontline and support workers, we need to know how the average salaries of the two groups compare, and this data is not in the public domain. However, it seems reasonable to conclude that expenditure on frontline workers accounted for around 80 per cent of total expenditure on workforce in NHS England in 2019 and therefore that a typical hospital spent just over half of its operating budget on its frontline workforce.

---

[10] The NHS employs a different system to the ONS for coding occupations. As a result, it is impossible to identify all the frontline occupations in the NHS in the same way as was done for the UK workforce as a whole in Tables 1.1 and 1.4. NHS Digital produce monthly workforce statistics for England and these identify 'professionally qualified clinical staff', the vast majority of whom will work on the frontline. They accounted for 52.5 per cent of all workers in NHS England in 2019. In addition to these workers, NHS Digital data identify a further 24 per cent who are described as providing 'support to doctors, nurses and midwives'. Most of these workers, though not professionally qualified, also work on the frontline. Thus, as best can be determined from NHS Digital statistics, around 77 per cent of the workforce in NHS England in 2019 (counted on a headcount basis) were frontline staff and thus frontline staff likely accounted for almost 80 per cent of total expenditure on workforce in NHS England in 2019. Note that NHS England uses the term 'support' worker in a different way to this book, and this is discussed in more detail in Chapter 4 Section 4.5. They use the term 'support' worker to describe frontline staff supporting professionally qualified clinical staff. In Chapter 1 and throughout the book, the term support worker is used to distinguish workers in non-frontline occupations.

3.3 How UK Spending on Health and Social Care Compares

Though the UK spent some £220 billion on health and social care in 2018/19, as a share of national income this compared unfavourably to spending in many other high income countries. UK spending, expressed as a share of GDP, was above the average for all OECD countries, but below that of many other high income countries. Figure 3.1 shows that in 2018 the USA spent nearly 17 per cent of its GDP on health and social care, France, Germany, Sweden, and Japan spent around 11 per cent, Denmark and Norway spent over 10 per cent, while the UK spent 9.8 per cent. Wealthier countries typically spend a larger share of their national income on health and social care than do poorer countries, because the demand for health and social care increases as income rises and this is likely to be one explanation for the higher USA spend.

However, this doesn't explain the difference between the UK and most of these other European countries. It has been suggested that the lower UK spend is explained by the way the UK funds its health care system. In the UK, central government provides the major part of funding for health care, with the costs met by general taxation, and it has been argued this exerts downward pressure on spending. However, government is also the major provider of funding for health care in Australia, New Zealand, and Canada, where the costs are also met out of general taxation, sometimes called levies. While New Zealand and Australia spend the same or very similar shares of GDP on health and social care as the

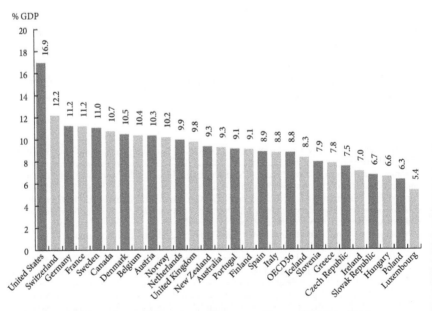

Figure 3.1 Health and Social Care Expenditure as a Share of GDP in 2018

Source: OECD (2019a) Figure 7.3 StatLink 2 https://doi.org/10.1787/888934016816

UK, Canada spends more. Canada's spending is only slightly lower than that of Germany and France, which fund health spending primarily through compulsory health insurance (King's Fund 2018). The funding of health care spending from general taxation undoubtedly exerts downward pressure on spending because of pressures to moderate taxation, though it is clear that there is no simple association between the system of funding health care and the share of national income that is spent on health and social care.

Figure 3.1 tells us the share of GDP that countries spend on health and social care, but it does not reveal what this means in terms of the level of spending per head of population, which is the more important statistic. Per capita income levels differ between countries, so even where two countries spend the same proportions of their GDP on health and social care, spending per head of population will be higher in the country with the higher per capita income. This is evident in the difference between the UK and the USA.

The USA has a much higher per capita income than the UK, and as we saw in Figure 3.1, it also spends a much higher percentage of its national income on health and social care than does the UK. In 2018, the United States spent almost three times as much on health and social care per head of population as the UK. In 2018, the US spent $10,586 (OECD 2019a) per head on health and social care, while the UK spent $3783 (ONS 2018a)[11] a difference of $6803. The largest part of this per capita difference, $4447, was accounted for by the greater share of national income the United States spent on health, 16.9 per cent of GDP as opposed to 9.8 per cent in the UK, but that still left a difference of $2356, which was accounted for by the higher per capita national income of the USA. If the USA had spent the same proportion of national income on health as the UK did in 2018, it would have spent $6139 per head that year, which is over 60 per cent more per head of population than the UK.

We might expect the share of the total workforce who are working in health and social care to be higher the greater the share of health and social care spending in GDP because spending on workforce is the single largest item of health and social care spend in all these countries. However, as a comparison of the ranking of countries reported in Figures 1.1 and 3.1 reveals, there is only a weak association

---

[11] The UK figure of $3783 is derived by taking the ONS reported per capita expenditure on health care in the UK of £2910 in 2018 and converting at the rate of 1.3 dollars to the pound, the average for that year. US expenditure is taken from OECD (2019a). This comparison ignores differences in purchasing power and price level differences in the two countries. If we are to distinguish the real differences in the level of spending we need to adjust using Purchasing Power Parities (PPP). The OECD (2019) reported that, in 2018, per capita spend on health and social care on a PPP basis, computed using a general price index, was $10,586 in the USA and $4070 in the UK. However, this is the wrong price index to use for such comparisons because the general price index does not reflect the relative price of health care in the two countries. Over a protracted period, health care inflation has been higher than general inflation in both the UK and USA. The OECD construct a health-specific PPP which shows the relative price of health care in the two countries. In this index the USA =100 and the UK = 83 in 2018. Adjusting using this index results in a smaller difference between the real per capita spend on health and social care in the two countries. Using this method, the USA per capita spend was $10,586 and UK was $4557. Using this index to calculate PPP narrows the per capita gap between the USA and UK from 2.8 times to 2.3 times.

between the two.[12] The reason for this is that it is not just how many we employ but also how well we pay them which determines the level of spend on workforce. Some countries have high spending on workforce because they pay these workers relatively well, though they employ relatively few. The more highly paid the health and social care workforce relative to the workforce in the rest of the economy, the greater will be the difference in rankings between Figures 1.1 and 3.1.

Changes in the share of GDP spent on health and social care provide an indicator of the relative strength of demand for health and social care workers. A rise in the share of national income spent on health and social care will generally indicate that the demand for health and social care workers is stronger than the demand for workers in the rest of the economy. However, this doesn't necessarily mean that employment will be increasing. If GDP contracts faster than health and social care spending (as happened during the pandemic) labour demand in health and social care is likely to be holding up better than in the rest of the economy, but employment in health and social care and the economy in general could both be diminishing.

3.4 Spending and Labour Demand in the Four Nations

The level of spending on health care differs between the four nations of the UK. Health and social care are devolved responsibilities; the four nations of the UK can each decide what to spend on health and social care.[13] What they decide to spend reflects the health and social care needs of their populations and the priority they attach to addressing these needs. In turn, what they spend, which needs they address, and how they meet these needs will determine the demand for health and social care workers in each country. Though it is difficult to distinguish with accuracy in the publicly available data, it would appear that in the decade up to 2019, Scotland, Wales, and Northern Ireland all spent a slightly larger percentage of their GDP on health and social care than did England.

The demand for health and social care workers in each country is shaped by decisions made at several levels. At the highest level it is affected by decisions about how much to spend on health and social care, how to organize health and social care, and the criteria to use when distributing funding to the organizations that deliver health and social care. In each of the four nations the structure and governance of health and social care is different.

In each nation, the distribution of funding to the organizations which deliver health and social care is determined by formulae which seek to estimate the populations need for health and social care services. These formulae take account of

---

[12] In Figure 1.1 the USA stands below the four Nordic countries, the Netherlands, France, and Switzerland. In Figure 3.1 it is in first place.

[13] Thus, for example in 2005/6, spending on the NHS per head of population was 23 per cent higher in Scotland, the highest spending of the four nations, than in Wales, the lowest spending (House of Commons 2006).

the size of the population served by each organization delivering care and the needs of this population for health and social care services. Needs are estimated by the age and gender composition of the population and the degree of economic deprivation. In England, the formulae are refined to include measures of differences between geographical areas in the cost of providing services to meet these needs.

In each of the four nations in the UK, the largest tranche of funding is delivered to hospitals. In hospitals, the demand for labour reflects the decisions of managers in the Health Boards and Trusts and clinical teams. Within a hospital, the number and the specialisms of clinical teams will determine the pattern of labour demand. Over time, the composition of these teams can change, either when people leave or the budget changes. Decision-making at this micro level therefore affects the pattern of labour demand.

Local authorities also affect the pattern of labour demand through the distribution of funds to residential and domiciliary care providers and in social care, the individuals who fund their own care affect the level and pattern of demand for adult social care workers through the choices they make. Thus government, local authorities, managers, and frontline workers, as well as the individuals who fund social care, affect the pattern of demand for health and social care workers.

3.5 The Production Function and Labour Demand Schedule

The next two sections detail the construction of the analytic device that labour economists use to identify how much labour an organisation should employ at different levels of the cost of labour, that device is the labour demand schedule. They detail how it is constructed and what information is required to do this. They detail a method the NHS can employ to measure and value its output and thus construct its own labour demand schedules. The central argument of these sections is that the NHS and other providers of health services should construct labour demand schedules, for these schedules convey vital information. They identify how much labour the NHS should employ in each different activity at each different level of the cost of labour. They identify the optimal levels of employment in each activity which is the level at which the value that labour produces in each activity is just equal to the cost of labour employed in that activity. This information is as central to the hiring decisions of the NHS and all the other non-commercial health care providers as it is to commercial organisations in the rest of the UK economy. These sections are necessarily detailed and not all readers may wish to dig as deeply into this as we do here, in which case they can jump to Section 3.7. It is however important they remember the central argument of these Sections.

Spending on health and social care finances the building of hospitals, surgeries, and care homes, the purchase of medical equipment and drugs, and the cost of employing health and social care workers. Each of these is an input to a production process, a process which produces a type of health or social care, and which can be described by a production function. Every clinical procedure undertaken, every type of social care delivered, is produced by combining different inputs and can therefore be described by a production function. A production function describes the relationship between inputs and outputs and reveals how output changes as inputs change.

The production function for most hospital procedures is specified in a protocol. This will detail how a specific treatment is to be delivered or a procedure undertaken and what type of equipment is to be used and by whom. Many leave room for discretion; the way in which a specific procedure or treatment is delivered can vary from hospital to hospital. Doctors' 'style' of treatment can affect the composition of the team that undertakes the procedure, and the hospital environment and judgements of peers can affect the way clinical interventions are carried out (Lee et al. 2019).

A typical production function is depicted in Figure 3.2, while the exact shape of the production function in each area of health and social care activity would be discovered by looking at the data on the inputs to and outputs produced by each activity. A typical short-run production function displays diminishing returns: each additional unit of labour, each additional person employed or hour worked, produces a smaller addition to output than the one before. Diminishing returns occur because, in the short run, labour is, by definition, the only variable input to production, the amount of capital labour has to work with hasn't changed, and there are clearly limits to how much extra output we can obtain by just increasing labour input. The shape of the production function in Figure 3.2 displays diminishing returns, as we increase the amount of labour we use, we move along the production function, and in doing so we encounter successively shallower regions of the production function until eventually we encounter a region where the function is flat, where additional labour input produces no extra output.

The addition to output is called the marginal product and the size of the marginal product produced by each additional unit of labour employed can be depicted in a Figure. In the region of the production function, where the slope of the production function is flattening, the increments to output are becoming smaller and so the line we draw to depict this relationship slopes downwards like that in Figure 3.3. Because the increment to output has been produced by labour the increment is called the *marginal product of labour*. In Figure 3.3 the marginal product of labour is declining.

We demand labour because it produces output, and therefore understanding how much extra output we will get if we employ more labour will be an important driver of our demand for labour. However we also need to know that the additional output we get will be valued by those who might use or consume it. There is no point producing more output if the output is judged to be of no benefit, if it is not

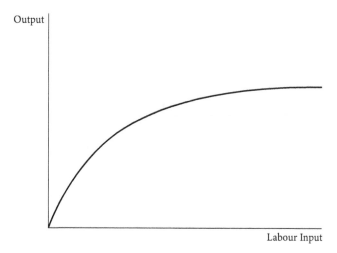

Figure 3.2 The Production Function

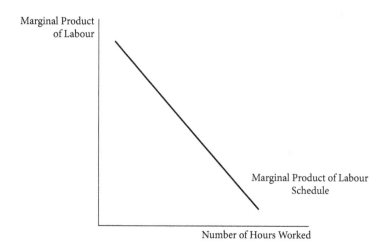

Figure 3.3 Marginal Product of Labour Schedule

valued. If nobody wants or values the additional output that will be produced, we should not produce it.

Furthermore, we need to know not just whether the output is valued, but how much it is valued. This is because we have paid labour to produce the additional output. We therefore want to know how the value of the additional output produced by labour compares to what we have to pay labour to produce it. If the value of the output is greater than what we have to pay labour to produce it, we should produce more because each additional unit of output adds more to value than it does to costs. If on the other hand the cost of the labour which produces the additional output is greater than the value we ascribe to the output, we should produce less. It should be clear from this that the optimal point, the point at which we have the right balance between what it costs to produce the additional output and how much we value that output, is where the two are equal. These points of equality between the value of the extra output that is produced by employing more labour and the cost of the labour which produced the extra output at different levels of the cost of labour can be mapped in a schedule.

The line drawn in Figure 3.4 does this. It details the set of points at which the value of the additional (the marginal value of the) output produced by labour is just equal to the cost of the labour which produced it. The line maps all these points of equality at different levels of the cost of labour, at different levels of pay. If pay was P_1, we should employ N_1; if pay was P_2, we should employ N_2, and so on. The line we have drawn in Figure 3.4 is the *labour demand schedule*; it describes how much labour is demanded at each level of pay. In Appendix 3.1 to this chapter, we show in greater detail how we derive the labour demand schedule from the production function.

Appendix 3.1 details how the commercial organization distinguishes the value of the output it produces. For the commercial organization this is straightforward, it sells its output in a market, and what the public is willing to pay for the output determines its value to the organization. The commercial organization therefore employs labour up to the point at which the revenue generated from selling the additional output produced by employing more labour is just equal to the cost of that labour. The commercial organization can identify the optimal level of employment and the optimal level of output to produce by employing labour up to the point at which the marginal revenue generated by employing more labour is equal to what it has to pay that labour.

However, it is rather different for non-commercial health and social care providers. They do not sell their output in a market, no market tells them the

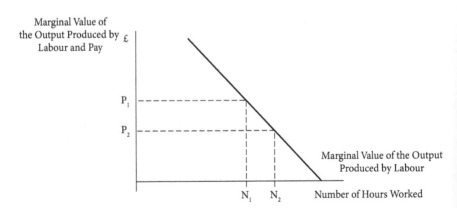

Figure 3.4 The Labour Demand Schedule

value of the output they produce and so they must find a different way of valuing their output. Nonetheless the concept of an optimal level of employment is no less important to the NHS and other non-commercial health and social care providers than it is to the commercial organization. We would not want them to waste resources, to produce output of less value than it costs to produce, nor fail to produce output which we would value greater than it cost to produce it.

We therefore need to find a method which will allow us to identify the value of the output of the different activities undertaken by non-commercial health and social care providers. Moreover, because labour costs are specified in monetary terms we need to find a method of assigning a monetary value to the output because only then will they be able to compare the value of their output to the cost of the labour. This might appear to present a considerable challenge, not least because the dominant producer of health care in the UK, the NHS, produces many different types of health care using many different production methods. It has several different types of hospitals—providing acute, general, and mental health care—and a range of different establishments producing community care. No other organization in the UK employs such a diversity of production processes or operates from as many different sites as the NHS.

Yet all of these different processes, all the different procedures and interventions the NHS delivers from its many sites, ultimately aim to produce the same type of output, which is improvement in the health of the UK population. Every one of the procedures and interventions it delivers is intended to contribute to improvement in the health of the UK population. Indeed, the Constitution of NHS England makes this clear,[14] and though this is articulated slightly differently by the health services in the other three nations of the UK, the purpose of each is the same.[15]

Though there might be argument about whether this is exactly the right label to describe the ultimate output of the health care sector, what cannot be disputed is that it is neither the procedures, interventions and care, nor any advice for prevention and self-care, which constitute the ultimate output of health care organizations, all of these are intermediate outputs.[16] They are all inputs to the intended ultimate output of the health care sector, which is improvement in the health of the

---

[14] See the NHS Constitution for England at https://www.gov.uk/government/publications/the-nhs-constitution-for-england/the-nhs-constitution-for-england and, for a more general statement of the mission of health care systems, the World Health Organization, which states that the ultimate and intended outputs of a health care system is the 'change [improvement] in the health of an individual, group of people, or population that is attributable to an intervention or series of interventions'.

[15] It can similarly be argued that the many different sites and organizations producing social care have a common aim, to improve the well-being of those they care for, though in this case it matters less because the output of much of this sector, in particular the residential care sector, is priced and so the market enables producers to identify the marginal value of what they produce.

[16] Throughout the book we will typically describe the activities of the health care system as undertaking 'procedures or interventions'. This should not be taken to ignore that frontline health care workers also deliver services in the form of advice for prevention of ill health and for self-care, the contraction is simply for concision.

UK population. In all four nations of the UK, the purpose of the different types of health care they deliver is to produce improvement in the health of the populations they serve.

A single hospital will deliver a large number of different health care procedures and will seek to produce improved health of the population it serves, using many different production processes. To illustrate, a typical acute hospital (a hospital in which a patient is treated for a severe episode of illness) in Scotland will normally deliver some 350 different health care procedures. Among the most frequently delivered procedures will be: epidural injections and spinal puncture, mastectomy, cataract procedures, appendicectomy, coronary angioplasty/stent, varicose vein procedures, urinary tract endoscopy, vasectomy, hysterectomy, osteotomies, amputation through to chemotherapy for neoplasm, to name just a small number of the more familiar. Supporting the production of these different procedures are intermediary processes such as CT scanning, radiology, and phlebotomy. The purpose of all these different activities is to produce improvement in the health of the population the hospital serves.

It is informative to look at the different ways in which the NHS measures its' output, and we do this in the next section. The NHS uses a variety of 'output' measures to illustrate its contribution to society. For many years it measured intermediate outputs, only latterly has it sought to articulate and measure its contribution to improving population health. In the next section we will also detail a more appropriate method for measuring and valuing the output of the NHS and indeed, other non-commercial health care providers.

3.6 Measuring and Valuing NHS Output: An NHS Labour Demand Schedule

The NHS measures its output in many different ways. It reports the volume of different activities, such as the number of hospital discharges each quarter,[17] the number of attendances at accident and emergency (A&E), the number of consultant-led referrals to treatment, and the number of diagnostic tests. Some of these measures, such as attendances at A&E, alongside measures of NHS process, such as waiting times and length of stay, have a strong hold on the public imagination and attract considerable media attention.

However, the contribution of the NHS to improving population health is only partly determined by the volume of its' activities, it also depends on the quality of those activities and none of the above measures capture this. The NHS therefore

---

[17] Reporting in the very early years focused on the number of hospital discharges though it was recognized that volume measures alone were a poor measure of contribution and that the quality of the activity was also important. One measure which sought to measure the quality of treatment was the number of deaths per acute hospital bed (Cutler 2010).

also reports a number of measures of quality, principal among them are readmission rates to hospital (an indicator of an unsatisfactory outcome) and standardized mortality and survival rates for major diseases (cancer, cardiovascular, and liver are examples). The NHS also asks patients about their experience of, and satisfaction with, certain NHS services such as A&E and access to GP services. Measures of activity, process, the success of outcomes, and the satisfaction of patients today all form part of a broad set of indicators which the four administrations in the UK use to provide an overview of how the NHS is performing in each of the four nations.

While the successful delivery of a procedure or intervention is an important indicator of the contribution of the NHS, this still does not tell us all we ought to know. The absence of readmission, though reassuring, does not tell us by how much the health of the patient improved after the procedure was completed. The NHS seeks to measure this through questionnaires, patient-assessed health-related quality of life (HRQoL) and in England, Patient Reported Outcome Measures (PROMs) which are administered to patients. Both of these seek to measure the improvement in a patient's health through the completion of a short, self-completed, questionnaire which is administered to patients pre- and post-procedure. In the questionnaire, health status is scored on a scale and health improvement calculated by taking the difference in scores on the pre- and post-procedure questionnaires.[18]

Health economists have also developed a number of methods which can be used to measure the contribution of different procedures and interventions to health improvement. The two most widely used are Quality Adjusted Life Years (QALYs) and Disability Adjusted Life Years (DALYs) (Drummond et al. 2015). The QALY measures a person's health in terms of the quality of each of their (estimated) remaining years of life following a treatment or intervention. Quality is measured by an assessment of the person's ability to carry out the activities of daily life, and their freedom from pain and mental disturbance, and is scored on a 0 to 1 scale where 1 is equal to one year in perfect health and 0 is death.

QALYs constitute numeraires, generic measures of improvement in health (Milton et al. 2009), which enable the improvement from different procedures and interventions to be measured and compared. The health improvement achieved by two different interventions, for example, hip replacements and surgery to insert stents, can be measured and compared by calculating the number of QALYs each

---

[18] There are of course limits to the extent to which health improvement can be attributed to the activity of the NHS. Improvement can be affected by factors outwith the control of the NHS. The success of a surgical intervention is affected both by the skill and effectiveness of the surgical team and by the extent to which the patient engages with the prescribed post-operative regime. If the improvement in health the patient expected is not achieved it might have been due to the poor quality of the NHS procedure or it may have been due to the lack of engagement with the post-treatment regime on the part of the patient.

produces. QALYs enable improvement in health to be identified by a simple count of QALYs, and the number of QALYs produced by an intervention can be calculated from the responses of patients to questionnaires.[19] QALYs are now widely used to inform public policy and to identify the improvement in population health that results from different policies. QALYs can be used to measure the output of the health service and to measure the change in output that results from a change in the amount of labour used to produce different procedures and interventions. QALYs can be used to quantify the marginal product of labour in different procedures and interventions.

QALYs can also be given a monetary value and they are used to distinguish the monetary benefits of a range of different public policies, they therefore allow the benefits of these policies to be compared to the costs of the policies. Considerable research effort has been devoted to distinguishing whether a year of life in perfect health, a QALY, can be assigned the same monetary value in all settings.[20] Currently, the answer seems to be no—the monetary value of a unit of health improvement differs according to the context in which it was delivered. The Treasury Green Book (HM Treasury 2018) recommends that UK government departments and agencies which are conducting cost–benefit analyses of non-health care projects value a QALY at £60,000, while the National Institute for Health and Care Excellence (NICE)[21] when appraising the cost-effectiveness of new medicines and medical procedures, judges that the value of a QALY falls within the range of £20,000–£30,000 (NICE 2022a).

NICE currently appears to judge that new medicines and procedures which have been developed to produce an improvement in health and which can be produced at a cost to the NHS of £30,000 or less per QALY gained are cost-effective and can therefore be adopted by the NHS. They are judged cost-effective because the cost, at £30,000 or less, of producing one unit of health improvement as measured by one QALY is less than the monetary value of the benefit when the QALY is valued at £30,000. However, NICE also recognizes certain special circumstances which warrant an even higher threshold, and this allows them a considerable margin of discretion.[22]

---

[19] One way of doing this is by use of the EQ-5D-5L, which is a self-assessed, health-related, quality of life questionnaire. The scale measures quality of life on a five-component scale including mobility, self-care, usual activities, pain/discomfort, and anxiety/depression.

[20] A detailed and very thorough review of research into the valuation of risks to life and health is to be found in the report and accompanying appendices and annexes of the study by Chilton et al. (2020) and an equally authoritative discussion of the application of the NICE cost-effectiveness threshold in a resource-constrained environment like the NHS is to be found in Claxton et al. (2015).

[21] The role of NICE is 'to improve health and wellbeing by putting science and evidence at the heart of health and care decision making' (NICE 2022b).

[22] Much of NICE's documentation identifies £20,000–£30,000 as the threshold range, though if certain conditions are satisfied they will use a threshold of £100,000 per QALY, with the highest threshold employed for specialized technologies (NICE 2022a, pages 103 and 110). At the time of writing, the

It has been argued that QALYs have weaknesses because they miss aspects of care that patients attach value to, and which could be identified by asking patients what they would be willing to pay for the intervention which produced the health improvement. The proposition here is the same as that made when evaluating market behaviour, namely that the price people are willing to pay for a successful treatment or intervention tells us the value they place on the improvement in health that results. Accordingly, researchers have developed a number of methods which distinguish patients' willingness to pay, using questionnaires administered to patients.

Some of these methods seek to identify value by offering patients a choice from a list of monetary values; others known as discrete choice experiments present patients with a set of different scenarios and elicit the 'implicit' price that patients are willing to pay from the choices they make. The strength of the latter is argued to be that it embeds the concept of opportunity cost within the experiment and recognizes that a patient's willingness to pay must be understood within the context of the resource constraints they face. The strength of these approaches is that they directly attribute a monetary value to the improvement in health—they do not require the intermediary stages of counting QALYs and then agreeing a monetary value of a QALY.

However, QALYs are now used to quantify health improvement across a wide range of health care activity,[23] and they can be used to quantify the marginal product of labour across the range of health care activity. If there is moreover, agreement on the monetary value of a unit of improvement in health, as measured by a QALY, then QALYs can be used to derive labour demand schedules. Constructing labour demand schedules for each of the different procedures and interventions, will then enable the NHS to identify the optimal level of employment, and output, for each of the procedures and interventions it delivers.

In the same way that the commercial organization asks, 'does the addition to revenue that will result from employing more labour exceed the cost of that labour?', so the NHS would ask 'does the monetary value of the health improvement that results from employing more labour, to produce more procedures, exceed the cost of the labour that produced the improvement?'. If employing more people to produce more procedures produces an improvement in health which, when valued in monetary terms, is greater than it cost to produce, then the NHS

threshold most commonly adopted was £30,000. An alternative approach would be to identify a single monetary value for a QALY and then take account of the circumstances in which NICE currently exercises discretion through a system of weighting the QALY. Yet another view might be that there should be no exceptions, no account should be taken of the circumstances because the value is in the output, counted in terms of Quality Adjusted Life Years, not in the input, the way in which the QALY was produced. One QALY should be valued the same as another QALY regardless of how they were produced.

[23] QALYs are now widely used as a measure of the benefits of surgical interventions (Rios-Diaz et. al. 2016).

should increase employment. However, if employing more people produces an improvement in health which, when valued in monetary terms, is less than the cost of the labour which produced it, then employment should not be increased. The NHS hospital, seeking to maximize the improvement in the health of the patients it cared for, would employ health care workers up to the point where their cost was equal to the monetary value of the health improvements they produced. The marginal NHS worker would be the one whose contribution to health improvement was valued equal to their cost.[24]

The labour demand schedule for a procedure produced by a non-commercial health care provider would look like that depicted earlier in Figure 3.4. At any given level of pay, employment would be taken to the point at which the monetary value of the additional QALYs produced by employing more labour was just equal to the cost of that labour. At pay level P_1 employment would be N_1, and at P_2 it would be N_2, and so on. The set of these points at different levels of pay would constitute the NHS labour demand schedule for the procedure. These labour demand schedules would enable the NHS to identify the optimal level of employment and output in each area of activity[25] (in Appendix 3.1 this is discussed in greater detail).

All organizations should compare the value that is produced by labour to the costs of the labour which produced that value. Just as NICE compares the cost to the NHS of a new drug or procedure to the value of the improvement in health that is produced by that drug or procedure to determine whether it should be adopted by the NHS, so the NHS should compare the cost of additional labour to the value of the health improvement that labour will produce.

Such an exercise conducted for an organization such as the NHS[26] which is subject to severe budget constraints might of course reveal that any new hires

---

[24] Alongside the NHS and private for-profit health providers there are private not-for-profit providers, and the situation is further different for them. They exist in both health and adult social care. They will value the health improvement workers produce but, because they are also likely to pursue other objectives, including the generation and retention of a surplus (profit) to further their organizational goals, the value of the contribution of the marginal worker may differ from that of the NHS or the government. Yet although they are making a different calculation, these providers will also wish to continue employing health workers up to the point where the weighted value of their contributions (to health and other things) just equals their pay.

[25] The proposition that health care providers should weigh the costs and benefits of different interventions is well established. Among the most widely used methods for doing this are cost-effectiveness analysis (CEA), cost–benefit analysis (CBA) (see Culyer and Chalkidou 2019), and programme budgeting and marginal analysis (see Mitton and Donaldson 2003). All have been developed to provide an economic framework for resource allocation in health care. Methods of quantifying benefits differ between the three methods, the differences between CBA and CEA in seeking to quantify the value of health care interventions are illuminatingly discussed in Culyer and Chalkidou (2019).

[26] The application of this method to NHS procedures and interventions would also likely require weighting to take account of the initial health status of the patient presenting for treatment. Because these vary, some patients require much greater labour input to produce a unit of health improvement than others. Patients presenting with multiple comorbidities and babies in neonatal intensive care units (NICU) require greater labour input to produce a unit of health improvement. To avoid penalizing these patients, QALYS might be weighted according to initial health status. In this way the benefit–cost approach could be employed as a method for incorporating society's values into decisions about the optimal level of frontline employment.

would add more to value than they would add to costs, and so it would follow that employment should be expanded in all lines of activity. Under these conditions, devoting resource to deriving labour demand schedules might be thought wasteful and unnecessary. However, the application of this 'benefit–cost calculus' to areas of current NHS activity still makes sense.[27] It would reveal those areas which should be considered as the priorities for expansion—those areas where the greatest value of improvement in health could be achieved relative to cost. Further, by applying this calculus to all areas of current NHS activity it would enable the NHS to distinguish how it might reallocate labour within existing budgets to achieve greater contribution to health improvement; it would enable it to identify those margins of current activity where it should reallocate from lower-value–high (labour)-cost activities to higher-value–low (labour)-cost activities.

3.7 The Interdependence of Labour Demand Schedules

Labour demand schedules identify optimal levels of employment, they identify the level of employment at which the cost of labour is just equal to the value that the labour produces. They also tell us how, in order to sustain optimality, the demand for labour must change as the cost of labour changes. The downward sloping labour demand schedules we have derived above inform us that if the price of labour rises we will, all else the same, demand less labour, and that if it falls, we will demand more. However, in important areas of the NHS, such as hospitals, some of the procedures and interventions which produce improvements in health result from team work and where occupations work in teams their labour demand schedules are interdependent. Just how the demand for labour for any particular occupation in a team changes as the pay of team members changes will depend upon whether the health care occupations are complements in the production process or substitutes.

Where occupations are complements in production, their demand schedules will be interdependent and any increase in the demand for one occupation will result in an increase in the demand for all other occupations in the team. Conversely, a reduction in demand for one occupation results in a reduction in demand for the other occupations. Occupations can be complements because particular skills are required to operate the technology used when delivering a procedure and only specific occupations have those skills, or they may be

---

[27] The optimization of hospital output currently focuses on the efficient use of inputs; the use of hospital beds, the allocation of hospital beds to different specialties, and the allocation of operating theatre time to different specialties, etc. See Humphreys et al. 2022 for an overview of hospital capacity planning and optimization. Nowhere is optimization conceived of in terms of contribution to or improvement in population health nor the contribution of labour to that improvement quantified.

complements because regulations and protocols require specific occupations to undertake particular tasks.

Where occupations are complements in production, the demand for one occupation is affected by the pay of the other occupations. If nurses, anaesthetists, and surgeons work in a clinical team then the demand for nurses and anaesthetists is sensitive to what surgeons are paid. If surgeons were awarded a large pay increase and there was, as a result, a reduction in the demand for surgeons, there would also be a reduction in the demand for nurses and anaesthetists, even though they had received no pay rise; the reverse would hold if there were a fall in the pay of surgeons. The demand schedules for complementary occupations are interdependent due to their complementarity in the production process.

Occupations can also be substitutes in production—different occupations are able to undertake the same tasks. Where occupations are substitutes in production, their demand schedules are again interdependent, but now the effects run in a different direction. A rise in the pay of one occupation which leads to a fall in the demand for that occupation will now result in an increase in the demand for those occupations which are substitutes. Suppose that GPs and Advanced Nurse Practitioners (ANPs) are equally proficient at examining and diagnosing patients in GP practices and that salaried GPs receive a significant pay rise while ANPs working in GP practices do not. Then the GP practice seeking to contain costs would reduce its demand for salaried GPs and increase its demand for ANPs. Where occupations are substitutes, their employment is again linked, but now the pay rise of one occupation is no longer to the detriment of the other occupation, as happened when they were complements.

It would evidently be very helpful if we could measure the nature and degree of the interdependence of the demand schedules between any two occupations, and Appendix 3.2 describes how this can be done.

In recent years, the skill sets of different health care occupations have overlapped to an increasing extent, and as a result the range of tasks which can be performed by more than one occupation has grown and the opportunities for substitution have increased. The skill sets of doctors and Physician Associates (PAs) and ANPs overlap, as do those of ANPs and Qualified Nurses, and those of Qualified Nurses and Nursing Assistants. The increase in overlapping is the result of the increased scope of practice of some occupations, such as Qualified Nurses, which has occurred in recent years—the scope of practice of a health care occupation describes the activities they are permitted to undertake consistent with the terms of their professional license. It is also due to the emergence of new intermediate occupations, such as ANPs and PAs though, as yet their numbers are small, around 6000 in total across the UK in 2019. ANPs are predominantly to be found in GPs surgeries, while PAs predominantly work in hospitals, though the ambition of the NHS in England is to increase the number of PAs working in general practice to address GP shortages.

Overlapping skill sets offer opportunities for task substitution. PAs and ANPs now undertake some of the tasks previously done by doctors in hospitals and GPs surgeries (Maier et al. 2018). In some areas, task substitution has been driven by pressures to contain health care costs (substituting less expensive labour), in others it has been motivated by the desire of some occupations to extend their roles. One reason for the increase in the number of PAs is that it offers a way of addressing doctor shortages.

The substitutability of occupations differs between different areas of health and social care because of differences in the scope for substitution and the ease of substitution. There appears to be less scope for substitution in hospitals than in either primary or social care because hospitals are both more capital intensive—they employ more capital relative to labour—and they employ more advanced technology than community health and social care organizations. Advanced technology is likely to require particular skills to operate it, and only some occupations will have those skills. A second reason there is less scope for substitution in hospitals than in primary and social care is that in hospitals protocols are more likely to specify which occupation is permitted to perform which tasks, and while protocols also exist in primary and social care, the protocols that govern practice appear less prescriptive than those in hospitals.

The ease of substitution between occupations is affected by the supply position of substitute occupations. Where the supply of substitutes, such as PAs and ANPs, is restricted, perhaps because there are few places where they can train, this will reduce the ease with which PAs and ANPs can be substituted for doctors. Where it is difficult to attract qualified nurses back into working for the NHS, this will make it more difficult to hand over some of the tasks previously done by ANPs to qualified nurses.

The degree of substitutability between occupations will be greater in the long run than in the short, and this adds to the difficulty of forecasting the future demand for specific occupations. Yet forecasting future labour requirements is essential for an organization the size of the NHS, both because of its dominance of key occupational labour markets and because of the lead times involved to train essential staff. We turn to the subject of forecasting future labour demand in the next section.

3.8 Forecasting Future Labour Demand: Workforce Planning

Over the longer run, technology can have a substantial on the demand for labour, though this is less the case in health and social care, than it is in other areas of the economy. Technology can, nonetheless, change both the pattern and the level of labour demand in health care. It will change the pattern of labour demand when new treatments and drugs, which improve treatment of existing conditions and enable the health service to treat previously untreatable conditions, result in a demand for new skills and reduce the demand for some existing skills. It will also change the level of labour demand where new drugs and treatments reduce individuals' good management of their own health, as for example when people pay less attention to managing their diet and weight because drugs to regulate cholesterol and diabetes are available, because labour will be required to address the increase in these conditions. Moreover, in the UK there is considerable pressure for adoption of new technology because drugs and new procedures once approved are provided free at the point of use.

Technology can also reduce labour demand, as, for example, where it enables greater self-care, the remote monitoring of long-term conditions, or remote consultation with specialists and GPs (Mason et al. 2019). Throughout much of the rest of the economy, in manufacturing and in some parts of the service industry, new technology has reduced labour demand because it has improved worker productivity. This has also happened in some areas of health care—surgery and diagnostics are examples, and indeed in Chapter 4 it will be reported that, in the decade after 2005, labour productivity growth in health and social care outstripped that in the rest of the economy.

However, technology will not displace labour in the same way as it has in some other sectors of the economy. This is because health and social care is predominantly a personal service industry, which means that the output it produces is by definition a service delivered in person, and the scope for reducing the personal contribution to the delivery of these services is quite limited. Moreover, in health and social care the effectiveness of the treatment or care, and thus the improvement in the health of the patient or the care delivered to the elderly, depends to a considerable degree upon the quality of the interaction between the frontline worker and the recipient of care. High-quality, empathetic, patient-centred care is critical to the quality of health outcomes.

The result is that the scope for reducing frontline employment through productivity gains is severely limited in health and social care, and, on balance, new technologies appear to have increased the demand for health and adult social care workers in the UK. This makes the task of forecasting the composition of labour demand in the future somewhat less difficult than in some other industries.

Forecasting future labour demand is the task of workforce planning, which involves forecasting future workforce requirements and then developing workforce policies designed to meet those requirements. Most large organizations undertake some form of workforce planning because they wish to avoid their business being disrupted by labour shortages in the future. Forecasting involves predicting future demand for output and the labour required to produce it. Forecasting aims to enable organizations to identify the numbers they need to train and the budget required to do this.

The purpose of workforce planning is to balance future labour supply and demand. Workforce planning is particularly important for the NHS because of the prominent role it plays on both the demand and the supply sides of the occupational labour markets in health care. On the demand side it dominates the UK demand for doctors, nurses, and most AHPs. On the supply side it plays a prominent role in the production of doctors through subsidies to the direct costs of training and the provision of on-the-job training places. In the absence of planning, there might not be sufficient trained personnel to satisfy the NHS's requirements, and the resulting shortages would disrupt the provision of health care.

The principles which underpin all workforce planning models are the same. Because the demand for labour is a derived demand, all organizations start by forecasting the future demand for their product. They then marry these forecasts to the production processes which will produce the required output and through these production functions distinguish the occupations and the number in each that will be required to produce the output. These stages are shown in Figure 3.5. Models differ in their sophistication and detail according to modelling capacity and data availability, but the underlying principles are essentially the same regardless of the industry or sector of the economy.

Some organizations stop at this point because, though they have identified their future labour requirements, they have no instruments with which to affect labour supply. Other organizations, those which require large numbers of highly skilled labour, usually proceed to the next step and develop a strategy to either train or attract the required labour.

The approach to workforce planning in health and social care in the UK is essentially the same. The first step is to model the future demand for health and social care.[28] Typically, this involves forecasting the population's future health and social care needs, in which case the next step should be modelling future expenditure on

Figure 3.5 Forecasting Future Workforce Requirements

---

[28] Where health care providers are paid under fee-for-service it may not be possible to arrive at an 'independent' forecast of future workforce requirements. In this chapter, we have discussed the principal–agent problem. People rely on their agents to advise them on their health care requirements, but if these agents also play a role as care provider and earn incomes from providing that care, the future demand for health care may be affected by the number of these providers in the future. Future supply

health and social care because, as we stated earlier, it is only those needs which are matched by expenditure which constitute the (effective) demand for health and social care workers. In fact this second step is rarely undertaken; it is either, implicitly, assumed that the required expenditures will be provided or that funding will cover the same proportion of health and social care need as they have in the past.

The next step is to marry projections of the demand for health and social care to health care production functions in order to understand what labour and capital are required to meet these needs. The focus in workforce planning is on the labour requirements which then need to be broken down into the different occupations that are involved in production. Once this has been done, policies on the supply side can be developed in order to meet those workforce requirements.

The very simplest, at least conceptually, and most often reported method of workforce planning is to take current health care workforce to population ratios and apply them to forecasts of future population size. In this way, the number of health care workers required to meet the estimated populations future health care needs can be identified. A variation on this is to apply health care workforce to population ratios from other countries, under the implicit assumption that future health care needs might be better met by producing health care the way that some other countries do. Countries with 'better' health outcomes or lower-cost health systems might be chosen. Data from WHO and OECD can be used in this approach.

The health care workforce to future population approach to workforce planning is perhaps most appropriate for specific health initiatives; an example illustrates this. Suppose the forecast health care need is to vaccinate all adult women against a particular disease at some time in the near future. The number of women to be immunized could be forecast with some confidence; the women have been born and the number surviving to the age of vaccination could be found by applying appropriate death rates to the total. Workforce requirements could then be easily calculated from the production function for the procedure, which will identify who does the procedure and how many they can do each day. If the procedure is undertaken by a nurse, then the number of nurses required is simply found by dividing the total population to be immunized by the number of vaccinations that can be done by each nurse.

A much more sophisticated approach is required when we go beyond a single procedure and attempt to forecast the workforce required to meet the health or social care needs of a whole country. Here, what is called 'needs-based forecasting' is the most common approach. This approach uses epidemiological and population data to estimate a country's future health care needs by forecasting

---

and demand may be interconnected. This could result in the over-expansion of some services, which could sit alongside unmet need for other types of care if overall expenditures on care are restricted.

the incidence of diseases and adverse health conditions. This is then combined with aggregate production function data, in order to identify the size and occupational composition of the workforce required to treat these conditions. A further, still more advanced variant of this approach is to disaggregate the required workforce in terms of skills and competencies rather than occupations. This method, the competency approach to workforce planning, allows for the fact that some of the tasks can be undertaken by more than one occupation. Thus, it allows for substitution between the health care professions and for the least-cost combinations to be identified.[29]

In between the two approaches outlined above are a variety of intermediate methods. A widely used variant of needs-based forecasting employs proxies for epidemiological need—proxies such as age, gender, geographical location, and deprivation—because these are all associated with different health care needs. These proxies are then used to generate forecasts of demand which can be combined with production function data to distinguish the occupations required to meet this need.

Workforce planning is data intensive and requires simplifying assumptions. The weaknesses of workforce planning are evident to all in this post Covid-19 world. It assumes that we know the diseases of the future and that we can estimate their incidence. It assumes that the way we treat these diseases, where they are known, will be the same or very similar in the future to the way we treat them now. It also involves assumptions about workload: about the number of cases a health care worker could treat in a year and, with the exception of the version that builds on skills and competencies, makes no allowance for the substitution of one health care group by another. Covid-19 will have shaken all of these assumptions.

Currently, workforce planning in health and social care suffers from a number of weaknesses. Models often assume no funding constraint and that forecast health care needs will be met; that health care need translates into effective health care demand. We know that this often does not happen; that funding constraints restrict treatment numbers. We also know that health care needs may not translate into effective demand for health care even though funding has been provided to meet those needs because some people, particularly those in low-income and deprived communities, fail to present for treatment (McCartney, et al. 2011).

A significant weakness is that they take no account of the concept of optimality and therefore employ no criteria to allow them to identify optimal levels of employment. They fail to recognize that for each procedure and intervention, there is a point at which the value of the improvement in population health, resulting from producing more of the procedure or intervention, is equal to the cost of the labour which produced it. More generally, they make no attempt to quantify the

[29] An illuminating application of this approach to pandemic influenza is provided by Murphy et al. (2017).

improvements in population health which are expected to result from employing more staff.

Workforce planning models also make no use of key labour market data; data on the relative costs of the different occupations which are inputs to the production of health care. This means that the costs of different workforce configurations are seldom considered. Data on vacancy rates, which reveal how far health care labour markets are from equilibrium, and data on the returns to human capital investment in health care occupations, which is the key driver of long-run labour supply, are seldom used. Vacancy rates are required to inform the initial starting point for the forecasts, and the competitiveness of health care workers' pay is required to inform the likely supply response of key occupations and therefore the likelihood of realizing the required workforce numbers.

Workforce planning in health care in the UK is undertaken by the NHS and by the Health Departments of the four governments in the UK.[30] In social care it is undertaken by local authorities and independent charities.[31] In the NHS, workforce planning is largely focused on qualified nurses and doctors and seeks to inform both short- and long-run policies on the supply side of the labour market. Long-run policies address issues in training and migration; short-run policies focus on working hours and participation.[32] In England, workforce planning is undertaken by Health Education England, which comprises a national board and thirteen regional local education and training boards (LETBs). It has an annual, ring-fenced training budget of £5 billion. In Scotland, NHS Education supports workforce planning for nurses, midwives, and doctors.

In both countries, the approach builds from the bottom up; it might be best described as 'tell us what you think you need'. In both countries, senior clinicians and managers in Trusts and Health Boards try to predict future workforce needs (numbers and skills). The government health departments then translate these forecasts into training needs and in England inform the postgraduate deaneries who sit within the LETB structure. In England, the deaneries then contract for education and training, within a tariff-based system to enable national consistency in the funding of all clinical placements (both medical and non-medical) and postgraduate medical programmes.

The approach assumes that those on the front line are best placed to forecast future health care needs and to decide how they should be met. In England there is also a body tasked with oversight of the process to ensure its coherence. It does this by interrogating and testing LETB plans, collating inputs from national workforce

[30] For an example of an approach to workforce planning which integrates health and social care see NHS Scotland, COSLA, and Scottish Government (2019).

[31] See Skills for Care (2015).

[32] Recent short-run initiatives in England have aimed to encourage nurses, who had left the workforce for retirement or career breaks, back to work and to encourage GPs to return to practice. See Health Education England (2015).

advisory groups, strategic advisory groups and patient advisory groups, and other stakeholders. Persistent labour shortages suggest that the assumptions on which the current approach rests are far from realistic.

Yet for all the evident weaknesses of workforce planning, it is necessary. When a policymaker decides how many training places for nurses and doctors to create today, they are taking a view about the number of doctors and nurses we will require in the future. The alternative to planning, which is to leave it to the market, means we must accept the risk that there will be even more severe workforce shortages and shortfalls in service delivery in the future.

3.9 Summary and Conclusions

In this chapter we have analysed the demand side of the health and social care labour market and considered the drivers of the demand for frontline health and social care workers. The key points to take away from this chapter are outlined below.

The demand for frontline workers is a derived demand; it derives from the needs of individuals and households in the UK for health and social care services, though it is only those needs which are supported by spending which result in the effective demand for frontline workers. In the UK, most spending on health and social care is by government and therefore the level of effective demand for frontline workers is largely determined by government.

The UK spends a smaller percentage of GDP on health and social care than France, Germany, and Scandinavian countries, and in Purchasing Power Parity terms the UK spend is less than half the per capita spend of the USA. In 2019, the UK spent nearly 10 per cent of its GDP on health and social care, and government spending accounted for most of this. In 2019, over 80 per cent of all spending on health care in the UK was by central government and almost 60 per cent of spending on social care in the UK was by central and local government. In England, 87 per cent of government spending on health and social care went on health care.

Spending on workforce is the largest item of spend: in 2019 it accounted for around 65 per cent of the annual operating expenditure of a typical hospital and a larger, but unknown, percentage of social care spending. Not all spending on workforce was on frontline staff. As best can be determined, about 80 per cent of all NHS spending on workforce was on the frontline workforce and so just over half of the annual operating expenditure of a typical hospital was on the frontline workforce.

The purpose of spending on health care is to improve the health of the population of the UK, and the purpose of spending on social care is to improve the well-being of those cared for. These improvements constitute the outputs of the health and social care sectors and represent the benefits of employing labour in these sectors. These benefits must, however, be judged relative to their costs. In each area of activity in health and social care there will be an optimal level of employment at which the additional benefits produced just equal the additional costs of producing them. Much of the chapter was devoted to detailing the information and the methods that health and social care organizations require to allow them to identify this point.

The level of spending on the output of an organisation in the commercial sector of the economy also determines the demand for labour by the commercial organisation. However in the commercial sector spending also provides the organisation with a direct measure of the value of its output. The market price signals that value and the labour demand schedule for the commercial organisation maps the value that the market puts on each additional unit of output it produces. When this is taken in conjunction with the cost of the labour which produced the additional output, it enables the commercial organization to identify the optimal level of employment. The point at which the additional value that labour produces is just equal to the cost of that labour is the optimum for the commercial organization; taking employment beyond this point means paying labour to produce output which the public does not value as highly as it costs to produce, which reduces profits, while operating with employment below the optimum means that output which the public values more highly than it cost to produce it, is not being produced, more profit could be earned.

This concept of optimality, identifying the point at which the additional value that labour produces is just equal to the cost of that labour is of equal importance to the NHS and other non-commercial health and social care providers. The principal challenge for them is to find a way of valuing the output they produce. In order to do this, they need both a generic measure of the output produced by the many different activities they undertake, and a way of assigning a monetary value to the measured output.

QALYs constitute a generic measure of the output of organizations in health and social care. QALYs measure the output of the health and social care sectors in terms of units of improvement in health and constitute a measure which has gained acceptance across many areas of activity. They constitute a valid measure of the output that results from the many different procedures and interventions delivered by health care organisations. Moreover, each unit of output, each unit of improvement in health measured by a QALY, can be assigned a monetary value. QALYs are presently assigned monetary values and these values are used to inform policy across a wide range of different areas of public policy.

Assigning a unique monetary value to a unit of improvement in health would enable health care organizations to distinguish the incremental value of the improvement in health they were producing, and compare it to the cost of the labour which produced the improvement. Thus, health care organizations, such as the NHS, would be able to distinguish labour demand schedules for each of

THE DEMAND FOR FRONTLINE CARE WORKERS 93

the different procedures and interventions they delivered. Just as NICE compares the cost to the NHS of a new drug or procedure to the value of the improvement in health that is produced by that drug or procedure to determine whether it should be adopted by the NHS, so the NHS would be able to compare the cost of additional labour to the value of the health improvement that labour will produce.

The NHS hospital deciding how many more nurses to employ would be able to estimate the monetary value of the health improvements these additional nurses would produce and set this against the addition to workforce costs that would result. Conceptually, they would be able to identify the marginal worker, the one whose contribution to health improvement was valued equal to their pay. In this way, the NHS or indeed any other health or social care provider which did not charge fees for their services would be able to engage in the same calculus of benefits and costs as the commercial firm when taking on additional employees.

There would be different labour demand schedules for each procedure and intervention delivered by the NHS because of the different production processes that underpinned them. NHS recruitment would need to be grounded in an understanding of these underlying production processes and of the complementarity and substitutability of the different occupations which contribute to production. The calculus of benefits and costs would need to recognize that there are NHS procedures and interventions which are delivered by teams and that where the occupations are complements labour demand will need to be specified in terms of the team, and the measure of labour input adjusted accordingly. Where doctors work in a team, recruiting more doctors will only produce more output if more nurses and more of the other occupations that constitute the production team are recruited. Simple targets for recruitment of one occupation, doctors, ignoring their complementarity with other occupations in the production of some procedures would frustrate ambitions to increase the output of the health care system.[33]

Finally, we looked at labour demand over the longer run and at how health care organizations seek to identify their future labour requirements. We saw that workforce planning was necessary in health care, because of the time it takes to train doctors and nurses. How appropriately workforce planning was currently undertaken appeared open to question. The bottom-up approach, which underpins the current approach, derives strength from reflecting different production processes, but lacks the broader perspective of changing health care needs and changing ways of meeting those needs. There is effectively no workforce planning in social care,

---

[33] The Conservative Party website for August 2020, under 'Strengthening Our NHS', promised '50,000 more nurses', '6,000 more doctors in general practice and 6,000 more primary care professionals, such as physiotherapists and pharmacists. This is on top of the 7,500 extra nurse associates and 20000 primary care professionals that we have already announced'. See: https://www.conservatives.com/our-priorities/nhs

and the short lead times involved in training adult care workers argue it is not necessary.

There are significant weaknesses in current workforce planning. They take no account of the concept of optimality and therefore employ no criteria to allow them to identify optimal levels of employment; they make no attempt to quantify the improvements in population health which are expected to result from employing more staff. Moreover, they make no use of key labour market data; data on vacancy rates, which are required to inform the initial starting point for the forecasts, and data on the competitiveness of health care workers' pay which is required to inform the likely supply response of key occupations and therefore the likelihood of realizing the required workforce numbers.

4

The Labour Market for Frontline Care Workers in the UK

In this chapter we bring the supply and the demand sides of the health and social care labour market together in order to consider the market as a whole and to discuss the way in which it achieves balance. We use the now familiar 'scissors' figure introduced by Alfred Marshall[1] to depict the market and we discuss how competition within labour markets can bring the two sides into balance. This simple model of the labour market is then adapted to more accurately reflect conditions in health and social care labour markets.

This methodological approach of building a simple model which focuses on the key relationships and holds constant other factors known to affect the relationship distinguishes economics from that of other branches of the social sciences. Constructing a simple model of the labour market allows us to focus on the variables that most influence the behaviour of buyers and sellers in the market. Models of this type are constructed under clearly stated, simplifying assumptions, and their strength is that the assumptions can be relaxed in an ordered way to reveal how each of them influences the outcomes. The model can also be extended by introducing 'real-world' features and increasing levels of complexity. This is the approach we adopt in this chapter.

In the chapter, we explore what is meant by the health and social care labour market. This market is an aggregate of several different occupational and spatial labour markets, and we employ the tools of economics to analyse and discuss the most important differences between these labour markets. We discuss the concept of equilibrium, or balance, in the labour market and the role that competition, local and international, plays in establishing this balance. We examine important features of this market when it is in balance and distinguish the concepts of the normal rate of turnover and the normal rate of unemployment. The NHS is a dominant player in the UK health care labour market, and it has an important influence on the social care labour market; we explore the consequences of this. Finally, we discuss how the performance, or productivity, of the workers in this market has changed in recent years.

---

[1] Marshall (1920: 228, footnote 1).

The Economics of the UK Health and Social Care Labour Market. Robert Elliott, Oxford University Press.
© Robert Elliott (2024). DOI: 10.1093/oso/9780198883142.003.0004

4.1 What Is Meant by the Health and Social Care Labour Market

A market is a place where exchange takes place. It is an arrangement where buyers and sellers interact to agree the price and quantity of a commodity they are to exchange. Markets are mechanisms for matching the supply of a commodity to the demand for that commodity and therefore for allocating resources. In the labour market the commodity is labour, and in this market buyers and sellers interact to agree employment and pay. The actors in the labour market are the firms and organizations who wish to buy labour and the people, or their representatives, who wish to sell labour. Labour is a heterogeneous commodity, there are many different types of labour, and in most labour market transactions the different types are primarily distinguished by occupation. These occupations are bought and sold in many different geographical labour markets and when these markets are working efficiently, they allocate labour to its most productive use.

The health and social care labour market is the title given to the aggregate of all the occupational markets that match labour supply to labour demand in health and social care. On the supply side are the people who have the skills required to work in health and social care and who want to work in this sector. On the demand side are all the organizations who are seeking to employ people to produce health and social care. Though we talk of the market as a whole, the aggregate market consists of many different labour markets. On occasion, labour markets are viewed through the lens of the type of care provided, as happens when the health care labour market is distinguished from the social care labour market. However, it makes no sense to do this for those occupations which can be employed to deliver either social care or health care. Health care and social care organizations often recruit in the same occupational and geographical labour markets, and the suppliers of labour often move between jobs in the two sectors.

Labour markets are distinguished along occupational and spatial lines. The occupational title describes the expertise and skill of the people in the market. Examples of occupational labour markets are the labour markets for doctors, for qualified nurses, anaesthetists, care assistants, and all the occupations listed in Table 1.1. Some of these labour markets, those for nurses and doctors, can be further subdivided by specialty. The labour market for qualified nurses consists of separate markets for Advanced Nurse Practitioners (ANPs), midwives, other specialisms, and for the generalist qualified nurse. The labour market for doctors can be subdivided into separate markets for the different specialties, paediatric consultants, oncology consultants, etc. The different training and resulting skills and expertise are the distinguishing features of these separate markets. In some cases these labour markets are sector specific, for example consultant oncologists work only in secondary care, but in others they are not, for example ANPs are to be found in both primary and secondary care while qualified nurses work in both these sectors as well as in social care.

The spatial dimension describes the geography of the market. Geography identifies the physical boundaries to the market in which the sellers and buyers interact.
The geographical boundaries of a labour market are given by the area within
which people are willing to travel to take up employment and the area from which
employers are willing to recruit people to work for them. Here a distinction must
again be made between the short and the long run. In the short run people will
generally only be willing to take a job in an area they can travel to and from within
a day, while in the long run people may be willing to move considerable distances
to take a job; to move between different regions of the UK or even internationally. Moving costs can be substantial and are best understood as investment costs.
Human capital investment and investment in changing geographical location are
the two main types of labour market investment that individuals make. We shall
discuss location investment in more detail in the next chapter.

In the short run, it is seldom the preferences of employers which determine
the geographical boundaries of the labour market. If employees can turn up for
work on time and are prepared to incur the costs of commuting from their place of
residence, most employers are unlikely to be concerned about where an employee
lives. The geographical boundaries of the labour market will then be determined
by how far people are willing to travel to work and, in turn, this will be determined
by people's income and the coverage, efficiency, and cost of the transport system.
People in high-paying jobs can afford to spend more on travel and thus to travel
further; they will on average commute over longer distances.

The efficiency of the transport system affects the time spent commuting.
Employers in cities which are served by efficient and cheap transport systems will
draw their labour from a large geographical area. The greater the coverage of an
efficient, reliable, and cheap transport network, the larger the labour market. The
distance over which people are prepared to travel to work is also affected by the
time at which they are required to work. If travel is more difficult or more haz-
ardous in the evenings and at night, and the job involves shift or night work, people
may prefer to live closer to work, and the geographical boundaries of the market
will then be more tightly drawn. Because there are substantial differences between
what different health and social care occupations are paid, and because some of
these occupations involve shift work and some require night work, there are substantial differences between the geographical boundaries of the labour markets for
different health and social care occupations.

The labour markets for adult social care workers and nursing auxiliaries cover
quite small geographical areas. These occupations are among the lowest paid in the
health and social care workforce and many of them work night shifts. Adult social
care workers and nursing auxiliaries who work in hospitals, care homes, and the
organizations which deliver domiciliary care, are therefore likely to live relatively
close to their place of work. They are likely to live closer than do either the qualified
nurses or doctors who work in these same premises. The more highly paid will have

greater choice over the means of transport to work. Thus a geographical labour market for doctors will cover a larger area than one for nurses, and a geographical market for nurses a larger area than those for either adult social care workers or nursing auxiliaries.

A fundamental consideration underpinning all of this discussion is that frontline health and social care workers cannot work from home, they cannot 'attend' their place of work remotely. While many workers in other industries now work from home several days a week, those in frontline health and social care cannot. Frontline health and social care workers must deliver care in person, each working day they must travel to the surgery, the hospital, or the care home. Increased homeworking has extended the geographical boundaries of the labour markets for many occupations. The boundaries have been extended because people are required to attend the office less frequently and as a result are prepared to commute over longer distances on the, fewer, occasions this is required. Because this has not happened for frontline workers; frontline health and social care workers, save perhaps for some GPs, the geographical boundaries of the labour markets for frontline occupations are diverging further from those of other occupations.

This change in the boundaries of labour markets has important implications for the relative attractiveness of frontline jobs. The willingness of people in jobs outside frontline care to commute over longer distances has offered them an expanded choice of residential location and enhanced the attractiveness of these jobs. Because there has been no similar expansion of choice for frontline workers, there has been a reduction in the relative attractiveness of working in frontline jobs. We shall return to consider the implications of these developments in later chapters.

4.2 Equilibrium in the Labour Market

When we marry a labour supply schedule, as detailed in Chapter 2, to a labour demand schedule, as detailed in Chapter 3, at the level of an occupation and for a specified geographical area, we depict a labour market. For doctors, this is most appropriately done at the specialty level, for nurses at the grade and specialty level, while for adult social care workers we need make no such distinction. In each case the geographical area will be a local labour market and the boundaries will differ between occupations for the reasons discussed in Section 4.1 above. The boundaries of the local labour market will be smaller for nurses than for doctors and smaller again for social care workers than for nurses.

The labour market we depict will either be in balance, equilibrium, or in disequilibrium. A labour market is said to be in equilibrium when the number of people who wish to work just matches the number that organizations require to do the work, and while these conditions exist there will be no pressures for change.

Diagrammatically, this is the point at which a labour demand and a labour supply schedule intersect, as depicted by the intersection of labour supply schedule LS_1 and labour demand schedule LD_1 in Figure 4.1.

The concept of equilibrium is an important one. At the equilibrium rate of pay, the number of people that organizations wish to employ and the rate they are willing to pay them is just equal to the number who wish to work at that rate of pay. The equilibrium rate is therefore that unique rate of pay at which what employees require to attract them to work matches what employers are willing to pay them to work, and it produces a unique level of employment. The equilibrium rate of pay uniquely balances the supply of labour to the demand for that labour and is illustrated at P_1 in Figure 4.1.

If the number of people willing to work at each rate of pay increases, the equilibrium rate of pay will change. An increase in the number willing to work at any given rate of pay is depicted by an outward shift of the labour supply schedule, as in the shift from LS_1 to LS_2 in Figure 4.1. Before the shift when labour supply was described by the schedule LS_1, only N_3 were willing to work at the rate of pay P_2. The shift in the schedule reveals that for some, unspecified, reason N_2 are now willing to work at this rate of pay. The labour demand schedule makes clear that employers are only willing to employ N_2 people if they can pay them a lower rate than they did when employment was N_1. In Chapter 3 we explained the reasons for this.

From Figure 4.1 we can also identify the size of the pay bill—this is given by the area under the point at which the schedules intersect. In Figure 4.1 the pay bill at level of employment N_1 is given by the rate of pay at that level of employment, P_1, multiplied by the number of people employed at this rate of pay, N_1. If labour supply increases to LS_2 the equilibrium rate of pay will change, and the size of the pay bill will change to P_2 multiplied by N_2.

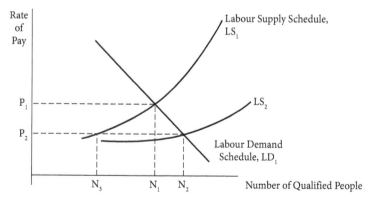

Figure 4.1 The Labour Market for a Health or Social Care Occupation

The concept of the equilibrium rate of pay does not mean that the labour market is static. At the equilibrium rate of pay there is still be labour turnover—people are still leaving organizations—but in equilibrium they are matched by an equal number who are joining, so that the level of employment remains unchanged. At the equilibrium rate of pay the number of people joining the organization is sufficient to replace all those who left. All organizations experience some labour turnover, irrespective of what they pay and how attractive the working conditions they offer. Workers leave for family reasons, because they are moving to another area, or because they are retiring, and workers are recruited on a regular basis to fill the resulting vacancies. This level of labour turnover is termed 'normal' turnover and has a counterpart in a 'normal' number of job openings, or vacancies. These 'normal' rates are sometimes called 'natural' rates.[2]

The equilibrium rate of pay is therefore also the rate which generates 'normal' labour turnover, and which is associated with a 'natural' rate of vacancies. The natural rates of turnover and vacancies are likely to differ between health and social care providers, between health and social care occupations, and between geographic areas because they are driven by such things as the age of the workforce and the ease with which workers can access jobs. Thus hospitals with older workforces are likely to have higher natural turnover and vacancy rates because they will have more retirees, and hospitals in cities which are served by efficient and cheap transport systems will have higher natural turnover and vacancy rates because of the ease with which employees can change jobs. In Chapter 6 we shall explore these issues further and give practical content to the concept of the natural rate of vacancies. Below we discuss how balance in a labour market is attained; how the equilibrium rate of pay is established.

4.3 Establishing Equilibrium in Health and Social Care Labour Markets

One way in which an equilibrium rate of pay is established is through competition in the labour market. Consider how this might work. Suppose there are a large number of organizations looking to hire workers from a particular occupation while at the same time there are also a lot of people from this occupation who are looking for work, also suppose that on balance the number of people organizations

---

[2] The natural, in the sense of normal, vacancy rate is the rate of vacancies that will emerge once labour supply and demand are in balance, taking into consideration the institutions which affect the efficiency with which labour supply and demand are matched. Institutions such as employment agencies, which gather data on and advertise job vacancies, affect the efficiency of matching. Employment agencies improve efficiency because they improve people's understanding of the characteristics of the jobs that are being advertised and so produce a better match of people to jobs. In the absence of institutions like employment agencies, labour supply and demand would balance at a higher overall rate of vacancies; the natural rate would be higher.

want to hire exceeds the number looking for work. We have described a position where labour demand exceeds labour supply, as it would at all points along LS_1 to the left of N_1 in Figure 4.1 if pay were only P_2. Organizations would seek to attract skilled people to work for them by making work more attractive, and they could do this by increasing what they pay. As pay was increased and more people were attracted to work for these organizations, we would move up LS_1 toward N_1 and P_1 in Figure 4.1, and as a result the vertical distance between the labour demand schedule and the labour supply schedule would shrink. This process would continue until the vertical gap was eliminated and we reached the equilibrium rate of pay P_1.

If, on the other hand, there had been more people seeking work at rates of pay higher than organizations were willing to pay, we would be on LS_1 at a point to the right of N_1 in Figure 4.1. At all points along LS_1 to the right of N_1, there would be people seeking work at rates these organizations were unwilling to pay. Receiving no job offers at the rates they wanted, people would leave this labour market and so we would move down the labour supply schedule until labour supply equalled labour demand at N_1.

In these examples both the price - the rate of pay - and quantity - the number of people seeking work - adjusted to establish equilibrium. If this had not happened, we would not have reached an equilibrium. The size of the quantity adjustment, as measured along the horizontal axis, relative to the size of the pay adjustment, as measured along the vertical axis, reflected the slopes of the labour supply and demand schedules, it reflected the elasticities of labour supply and demand. It should be evident that, starting from any particular position out of equilibrium, to the left or right of N_1, the less pay changes the more that employment will have to change to secure equilibrium and vice versa.

The above is a description of what happens in competitive labour markets, and we can deduce from the foregoing that for an occupational labour market to be described as competitive it must exhibit certain properties. The skills that distinguish this occupation must be transferable skills, they must be skills that several organizations want to employ, and there must also be a large number of organizations competing to hire people with these skills. Organizations must also be able to vary the pay they offer people and so pay must be flexible. Further, people must be willing to change employers, to move from one job to another. Finally, in order to ensure that the matching of employees to organizations is an equilibrium—that organizations have recruited the right people for the job and people have found the right employer—both parties must have high-quality information. Organizations need to know whether the applicants match the job specification, while applicants need to understand the characteristics of the jobs they take. These are quite demanding requirements, and it is not surprising that many labour markets do not satisfy them; however, the more they are satisfied, the more competitive the labour market will be. The question for us is: to what extent do health and social care labour markets in the UK satisfy these requirements? Are the labour markets in health and social care competitive?

First consider the labour market for hospital doctors in the UK. The requirement that skills are transferable is satisfied: most doctors have skills which can be used in several different hospitals, health care settings, and countries. Only a very small number have skills which are so specialized that they can only be deployed in one health care establishment. Even doctors who have acquired the highly specialized skills which can only be deployed in National Centres of Excellence, those specialized medical centres which provide the most expert and highest levels of care, are likely to be able to work in a number of different centres and countries. It is also likely that the requirement that people are mobile is satisfied, there is no reason to suppose that doctors are any less willing to change hospital than the working population in general is to change employer. Furthermore, it is likely that both doctors and potential employers have, or can relatively easily obtain, reliable information about the jobs on offer and the applicants for jobs. Professional associations and networks, both formal and informal, transmit high-quality information about jobs and the characteristics of applicants for jobs, to doctors and potential employers respectively. Therefore, the market for doctors exhibits several of the characteristics required for a competitive labour market.

However, we have left until last, judgement as to whether there are a large number of different employers with a demand for these skills who compete to hire doctors by adjusting what they pay. There are hospitals abroad and in the UK private sector[3] which recruit UK-based hospital doctors, but our view about the competitiveness of this market must turn on how we view the NHS hospitals which dominate this market. Does their behaviour mean we should view them as separate employers?

Most doctors in the UK are employed by NHS Hospital Trusts in England, Wales, and Scotland and by Health and Social Care Trusts in Northern Ireland, and while these Trusts compete for the services of doctors, they are constrained in the degree to which they can entice doctors away from other Trusts by offering higher pay because they are restricted to pay doctors under national pay scales (we shall explore this in greater detail in Chapter 7). They therefore compete on other parts of the compensation package—research opportunities, working conditions, and opportunities for private practice—but here the scope for manoeuvre is also limited. The consequence is that, because there is limited scope for changing pay and other parts of the compensation package, the burden of adjustment in NHS hospitals falls on employment. In the language of markets, because prices are slow to adjust, because prices are 'sticky', the burden of adjustment falls on quantities.

---

[3] UK private hospitals offer a narrower range of procedures than do most NHS hospitals and they are concentrated in particular geographical areas. The intensity of competition in medical labour markets therefore differs between specialties and geographic areas.

This means that any vacancies that arise in NHS hospitals from changes in either labour supply or demand can take a long time to fill. In summary, the labour market for hospital doctors is competitive, but very far from perfectly competitive; further research is required to establish just how competitive it is.

Not all doctors working in the UK work in hospitals; a large number work in general practice but the labour market for general practitioners is very different from that for hospital doctors and other frontline workers, because most GPs are not employees. Most GPs are principals, partners in a practice, they do not receive a salary but as small business owners they take a share of the practice's profits. The 'pay' of GP principals is their share of practice income after the costs of running the practice have been deducted. GP principals can increase their income by either reducing practice costs or increasing practice income, and sometimes they can do both. Sole practitioner practices can work on both these margins to increase income, while some of the principals in multi-practitioner practices also have scope to increase their income through bargaining for a larger share of practice profits. The scope for increasing practice income will depend upon the payment system for GP practices, and this scope may be limited.; we shall discuss the payment systems that have operated in the UK in Section 6.3.

In this labour market the burden of adjustment has historically fallen on GPs incomes, because principals were highly immobile. They were immobile because they were the sole owners or partners in a business which is geographically anchored, the practice served the population of a particular geographical area. If a principal wished to work in a different geographical area they had to sell their share in the partnership, and if they wanted to continue as principal buy into another practice. Until recently the costs of doing this were high, because partnerships owned the capital, the buildings and equipment, used by the partnership. This meant that partners had substantial money invested in a partnership and buyers of their share had to raise a considerable sum of money. Unsurprisingly this was difficult and so once a GP had become established as a partner in a practice in one area they seldom moved. A degree of competition entered this market when practices sought to recruit new partners. They competed by offering different levels of partnership income, and other advantage, but this was at the margins, and overall competition in the labour market for GP principals was muted.

However, the labour market for GPs is changing. In recent years many Hospital Trusts have become owners of the capital, the premises and equipment, GPs use in their businesses, and this has substantially reduced the costs of either becoming a partner or leaving a partnership. Moreover in recent years an increasing number of GPs have opted to become salaried employees rather than partners. One reason for this development is that an increasing number of those entering general practice no longer wish to spend the whole of their career working in one geographical area. Some wish to retain the freedom to change the area in which they work as their circumstances change, while others judge that tying themselves to one area may reduce the employment and career prospects of other family members. Another reason is that the shortage of GPs has led practices to offer higher pay to the temporary replacements, locums, who fill these vacancies and this has encouraged an increasing number of newly qualified GPs to select this route.

The market for salaried GPs is more competitive than that for either GP principals, and even hospital doctors, because practices seeking to recruit salaried GPs are not constrained by national pay scales as to what they can pay. We should therefore expect the labour market for salaried GPs to clear more quickly than that for GP principals or hospital doctors. The market for salaried GPs has introduced much greater flexible into the GP labour market and together with the increasing mobility of GP principals means that the labour market for GPs is among the more competitive frontline labour markets in the UK.

The labour markets for qualified and auxiliary nurses exhibit some of the same characteristics as those for hospital doctors, but they are much more competitive than those for either hospital doctors or GP principals. This is because these occupations have general, transferable skills which can be productively employed by employers in other sectors of the economy. There is much evidence from the employment histories of nurses that they are quite willing to change employer and to take jobs in other sectors of the economy. There are large numbers who trained as nurses who are working for employers who are providing neither social care nor health care (Elliott et al. 2007, Table 1). There is also competition for qualified nurses between organizations providing adult social care and those providing health care. Here too, there are professional associations and networks, formal and informal, which transmit high-quality information about the jobs on offer and about applicants' qualities to, respectively, the sellers and buyers of labour in health and social care. The labour markets for the vast majority of qualified and auxiliary nurses are highly competitive. The exception to this is the labour markets for highly specialized and advanced nursing skills; these labour markets are more comparable to those for hospital doctors.

AHPs are different in that there is a substantial demand for their skills, which the NHS is unwilling to meet. As a result. many AHPs have left the NHS to set up their own business or to work for health care providers in the private sector. In the case of some occupations, such as podiatry and physiotherapy, the vast majority work outside the NHS.

Organizations outside the NHS have pay flexibility—they are free to adjust rates of pay as market conditions require—and AHPs in private practice can alter the fees they charge. This might have been expected to have encouraged the NHS toward greater flexibility in the way it paid nurses and AHPs, yet the pay structures for nurses and AHPs still working in the NHS exhibit substantial pay rigidity. Both nurses and AHPs working for the NHS are paid under national pay scales within the UK-wide agreement titled Agenda for Change. The pay rigidity that results places the NHS at a competitive disadvantage in some areas of the country because it pays less than nurses and AHPs can earn elsewhere.

The labour market for adult social care workers is again different from that for nurses. The demand side of this market appears to be highly competitive. There were estimated to be around 9500 long-term care homes in the UK in the first decade of this century, with 90 per cent of residential capacity provided by the private sector. Among these providers there were many single home providers and small multi-home organizations, and around 85 per cent of these providers were for-profit (Forder and Allan 2011). There were also some large commercial chains, and their presence has grown in recent years.

We would expect to see substantial competition for labour between the owners of different care homes, and because these employers are not constrained by national pay agreements, we would expect rates of pay to adjust to clear the market and for turnover and vacancy rates to be at their natural rates. However this is not the case; as we shall see in Section 6.7, both turnover and vacancy rates are substantially above their natural rates. Moreover, the National Minimum Wage, which sets a UK-wide floor under rates of pay across all sectors of the UK economy, plays a prominent role in this labour market, setting the effective rate of pay for workers in residential and domiciliary care in many areas of the country (Allan and Vadean 2017; Vadean and Allen 2021). When turnover and vacancy rates are substantially above their natural rates this signals pay rates are too low, and although we would expect employers operating in competitive labour markets to bid up rates of pay as they compete for labour, this does not appear to happen.

We can depict what we expect to happen in the labour market for adult social care workers with the help of Figure 4.2. If pay is below the level required to clear the market, as illustrated by P_1, organizations find themselves desperately short of labour because, though they would like to employ N_2, they are only able to hire N_1 workers. When only N_1 workers are employed, they are producing output with a value to employers which is much higher than the wage they are being paid. The value in excess of the wage they are being paid is given by the vertical distance between the labour demand schedule and the labour supply schedule at the non-market clearing rate of pay, P_1, between A and B above N_1.

We would expect organizations to respond to the labour shortage by offering to pay more than P_1 to encourage people into employment. We would expect the organizations seeking to recruit social care workers, most of whom are in business to make profits, to compete for labour, and for pay to increase to the market clearing rate. Indeed, we would expect organizations to increase pay until the rate they were paying was equal to the value the workers they were hiring were producing, as illustrated by the intersection of the labour supply and demand schedules at N_3 P_3. Yet the high turnover and vacancy rates for adult social care workers reveal that this is not happening: pay is not bid up as we would expect in a well-functioning labour market. The social care labour market presents something of a puzzle, since

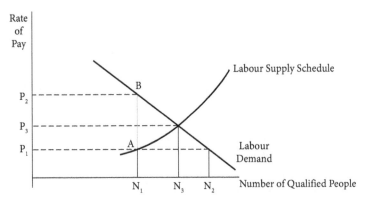

Figure 4.2 The Labour Market Out of Equilibrium

it is characterized by wage rigidity not as a consequence of the system of pay set-ting but by the reluctance of employers to pay what is required and the inability of market forces to compel them to do so.

4.4 The International Dimension

The UK labour markets for frontline health and social care workers cannot be considered in isolation from the labour markets for these same occupations in other countries, and in recent years global labour markets have had an increas-ing impact on UK markets. Global markets affect the UK labour market because they increase both the job opportunities of UK workers who have transferable skills, and the hiring opportunities of UK-based organizations. They increase UK workers job opportunities because they introduce new buyers of their labour, organizations based in other countries, while they increase UK-based organiza-tions' hiring opportunities because they introduce new sellers of the labour they require by introducing foreign-based workers. These two effects work in opposite directions. The introduction of new buyers of labour exerts upward pressure on domestic rates of pay, while the introduction of new sellers moderates this effect. However, their impact is affected by the ease with which foreign-based organiza-tions can recruit UK-based health and social care workers and by the ease with which UK-based health and social care organizations can recruit workers from abroad.

Health and social care are not unique in operating in global labour markets. The labour markets for many, though certainly not all, academic occupations (disciplines), as well as those for IT specialists, the players in elite sports, and some occupations in the fields of finance and management are also global. A global labour market can emerge where there is a general, transferable skill, multi-country labour demand and substantial inter-country labour mobility. In a global labour market organisations and workers from a large number of countries will be active on both the demand and the supply sides of the market. The intensity of competition in these global markets will differ between occupations because in some of these markets, labour flows are inhibited by language barriers and restrictions on migration. The labour market for workers in frontline health and social care occupations is likely to be among the largest global labour market. It appears to encompass a greater number of countries spread across more continents than any other labour market, and the flows of labour between countries are larger than in other markets. It is also a market in which labour flows are among the least inhibited and as a result it is perhaps the most competitive of all global labour markets.

The UK is one among many high income countries which compete in the global market for frontline health and social care workers. While this participation enhances opportunities for both organizations and workers, it also increases risk. It increases risk because it introduces new, less well-understood, players into the market and requires both buyers and sellers to process information from less familiar sources.

Organizations seeking to recruit in global markets have to process information from an extended range of institutions training and certifying the successful completion of the training of health and social care workers. Workers have to evaluate pay and benefits offered in different currencies. Each country has a unique cost of living and its own tax and benefit system. Salaries, tax, and benefit systems need to be understood and adjusted for the cost of living. The resulting net benefits need to be converted into a common currency if the benefits from different jobs are to be compared. None of this is straightforward, and so it may be difficult for the sellers of labour to distinguish the real rewards that are offered by organizations in other countries.

Some of the risks to UK organizations recruiting foreign-trained workers have been mitigated through the UK's membership of international organizations. A number of Commonwealth countries have medical schools established along similar lines to those in the UK, train to standards similar or equal to the UK, and award qualifications recognized in the UK. Recruiting from these countries substantially reduces the risks to UK organizations of recruiting foreign-trained workers. Until 2021, the UK was a member of the European Community. The EC required the free flow of labour between member states and developed a system for mutual recognition of professional qualifications. The UK's membership of both the Commonwealth and the EC increased the transparency of overseas training and qualifications and reduced the risk to UK employers of recruiting from these areas.

Globalization has provoked considerable controversy; some people judge the increase in competition which results from the globalization of health and social care labour markets to be a good thing; others judge to the contrary. Increased choice is generally judged by economists to enhance welfare and productivity. Competition among employers should improve workers welfare by exerting upward pressure on pay and providing employers with incentives to improve other non-monetary characteristics of jobs. Competition among workers for jobs should mean that employers are able to hire the most productive among them.

Globalization will have exerted upward pressure on the pay of UK-based health care workers because it increased the demand by foreign-based organizations for UK-trained frontline workers. This occurred at a time when there was an increased willingness on the part of UK-based workers to work abroad. The number of UK-based doctors, nurses, and AHPs who moved to work abroad has increased in recent years.[4] However, this upward pressure has been more than offset by the increased opportunities that globalized markets have afforded UK organizations to satisfy their labour requirements by recruiting abroad. In the next chapter, we report the large number of doctors, and increasing number of nurses, care workers, and AHPs that the UK has recruited from abroad. On balance, globalization is likely to have exerted downward pressure on the pay of frontline workers trained in the UK.

4.5 The Dominance of the NHS

A distinguishing feature of the UK labour market for health care workers is the dominance of a single buyer of labour: UK labour markets for frontline health care workers are dominated by the NHS. The unified UK health system has resulted in the NHS becoming one of the largest employers in the world indeed the NHS was once the second largest employer in the world, after Indian Railways. Today, McDonalds, Walmart, the People's Liberation Army of China (PLAC), the China Railway Construction Corporation (CRCC), and the Department of Defence (DoD) in the USA all employ more people than the NHS (Nuffield Trust 2019). That the NHS is compared to these organizations reminds us of the sheer size of the NHS, but this fact is of little relevance to an analysis of labour markets. Employment numbers alone provide little guide to dominance because they ignore the context in which these other large employers operate, which is completely different to that of the NHS.

McDonalds and Walmart are large multinational companies which employ people throughout the world, and their labour requirements are very different from those of the NHS. They employ predominantly low-skilled workers across

---

[4] Nine thousand doctors who left the UK between 2012 and 2014, when aged between 32 and 43, had not returned by 2019. The largest group among them were doctors who originally trained abroad, though UK trained doctors numbered nearly 2000 among this total (General Medical Council 2019).

THE LABOUR MARKET FOR FRONTLINE CARE WORKERS IN THE UK   109

Table 4.1 NHS Workforce in the UK in 2018 (Thousands)

Total NHS Employment	England[*]	Scotland[**]	Wales[***]	N Ireland[****]	Total
Full-Time Equivalent	1227	140	79	50	1,503
Headcount	1375	163	90	57	1,693

Note: * = Health Workforce Statistics, England March 2018, NHS https://digital.nhs.uk/data-and-information/publications/statistical/healthcare-workforce-statistics/march-2018-experimental
** = Staff directly employed by the NHS in Wales, at 30 September 2018 https://gov.wales/staff-directly-employed-nhs-30-september-2018 per cent
*** =NHS Scotland Workforce https://www.isdscotland.org/Health-Topics/Workforce/Publications
**** = Northern Ireland Health and Social Care Workforce Census March 2018 https://www.health-ni.gov.uk/sites/default/files/publications/health/hscwc-march-18.pdf

a narrow range of occupations. The PLAC, CRCC, DoD, and Indian Railways are, on the other hand, national organizations like the NHS, and they have more sophisticated labour requirements than either McDonalds or Walmart. However, they are all located in countries with populations several times larger than that of the UK; twenty-one times in the case of China, twenty times in the case of India, and five times in the case of the USA. It is not surprising that in these much larger countries we find organizations of equivalent size or larger than the NHS.

The NHS is distinguished from all these other large employers by its size relative to the domestic market in which it operates, by its dominance of certain occupational labour markets, and by its presence in every geographical labour market. In March 2018, the NHS employed almost 1.7 million people, some of whom worked part time. When adjusted onto a full-time equivalent basis, the total number of people working for the NHS in 2018 was 1.5 million. These data are reported in Table 4.1. In that same month, the total number of people working in the UK was just over 32.3 million (ONS September 2018). Thus in 2018, 1.7 million from a total of 32.3 million people, or one in every nineteen people working in the UK, worked in the NHS.

Most of these 1.7 million will be frontline workers, though it is impossible to distinguish the number precisely because NHS Workforce data does not employ the system for classifying occupations developed by the ONS. It is therefore impossible to distinguish the occupations listed in Tables 1.1 and 1.4 in the NHS Workforce data. However, NHS England workforce data distinguish two groups of workers which are likely to be on the frontline (NHS Digital 2019).[5] From these data it

---

[5] The first is 'professionally qualified clinical staff' and the second a group described as providing 'support to doctors, nurses and midwives'. However these are not support workers in the sense that we have used the term earlier. Elsewhere it is explained that these are 'clinical support staff [who] work with nurses, midwives, doctors and allied health professionals to *deliver* (authors italics) high-quality care' and who 'are involved in *looking after* (ibid) the general well-being and comfort of patients' (NHS Health Careers, 2020). These are workers who, though not professionally qualified, are also working on the frontline.

would appear that professionally qualified clinical staff accounted for 52.5 per cent and other frontline workers a further 24 per cent, a total of almost 77 per cent of all workers in NHS England in 2019.

The annual reports of NHS hospitals provide a route for distinguishing the share of frontline staff in this area of NHS activity. These reports give a breakdown of the staff they employ, though they use a different classification system to that used by NHS Digital. As can best be determined from these reports, around 70 per cent of the staff of a typical hospital work on the frontline.

The dominance of the NHS has significant regional and occupational dimensions. Most other large organizations in the UK, save perhaps for some of our largest supermarkets, concentrate employment in a small number of geographical areas. The NHS, in contrast, employs people in every geographical area of the UK. Moreover, the NHS is by far the largest employer of skilled labour in the UK. In 2018, around one in every six people in the UK working in an occupation which could be called a profession worked for the NHS (ONS September 2018).

The presence of the NHS in every geographical labour market in the UK has an impact on other employers in these labour markets. What the NHS does, in terms of the rates it pays and the numbers it recruits, or indeed discharges, will affect other employers in these markets, sometimes quite profoundly. The labour market activities of the NHS impose costs on other employers over which they have no control. If the NHS increases its rates of pay, it will exert upward pressure on rates of pay in those labour markets in which it has a prominent presence.[6] These pressures will be greatest in those occupational labour markets in which these other organizations and the NHS compete directly for labour. Thus, for example, though the retail industry does not require nursing skills, some who have trained as nurses are to be found working in retail. They may only be there temporarily, perhaps seeking some relief from the demands of frontline work, but the attractions of this work will be affected by the relative rates of pay in retail and the NHS. Thus, a rise in NHS rates of pay will affect the ability of these other employers to attract and retain workers, and vice versa. The external effects of NHS pay increases have not been studied and are little understood, but they may be profound.

The NHS also has an impact on the labour markets in which adult social care providers operate. In some occupational labour markets, social care providers compete directly with the NHS. Social care providers employ qualified nurses and so compete with the NHS in this labour market. They also compete directly in the auxiliary nursing/care assistant labour markets, for these two labour markets

---

[6] An increase in NHS rates of pay will increase the incomes of NHS employees, which will exert upward pressure on the price of goods that are in inelastic supply in the local area. Goods such as housing would likely rise in price. An increase in NHS rates of pay, the rates paid by other employers remaining the same, will result in people leaving jobs in other organizations to work for the NHS. In turn this would likely lead other employers to respond by increasing pay.

overlap. Other than the NHS, there is no dominant presence in the labour markets in which adult care homes operate.

4.6 Frontline Worker Productivity

In a competitive labour market, the equilibrium rate of pay will reflect the value of the marginal workers output. In Chapter 3 we saw that employers seek to equate what they pay for labour to the value it produces and that in equilibrium, the value that a worker produces determines what they get paid. Moreover, the growth in the value they produce determines the growth in what they are paid. In competitive labour markets, the forces of competition ensure that pay growth and productivity growth are aligned, and though in the health and social care labour markets these competitive forces are muted, this relationship is still of great importance. What health and social care workers produce and what they are paid is of great importance to the employers of these workers, and so, therefore, is the productivity of these workers.

Labour productivity is calculated by measuring the change in output relative to the change in labour input, and it is depicted by the slope of the production function which we discussed in Chapter 3. Labour input can be measured in terms of either the number of employees or hours. An indication of how the productivity of frontline workers in NHS hospitals in England may have changed over the decade between 2010 and 2020 is presented in Figure 4.3. The Figure uses Hospital Episode Statistics to report the growth in the number of Outpatient Attendances and Finished Consultant Episodes (FCEs), over half of which included some form of procedure, between January 2010 and January 2020. Both constitute measures of hospital activity, and alongside them is shown the growth in the number of clinical workers in NHS hospitals, where this input is expressed in terms of FTEs. All three series are expressed as indices, with 2010 equal to 100. Figure 4.3 reveals a steady increase in both FCEs and Outpatient Attendances at English NHS hospitals over the decade from January 2010 to January 2020. Over this decade, Outpatient Attendances increased by over 60 per cent and FCEs by nearly 40 per cent. In contrast, clinical workers' input increased by just 13 per cent. The strong suggestion emerges that the productivity of clinical workers has increased over this period, activity is up sharply, and workers' input has increased more modestly.

However, in order to attribute any change in output to a change in labour input, we must also be able either to measure the change in all other inputs or to assume, with evidence to support the assumption, that other inputs have not changed. To do otherwise might lead us to wrongly attribute the change in output to a change in labour input, when in fact it was due to a change in some other input. The growth in output might have been due to a huge programme of capital investment. Evidently, if we are to measure labour productivity we need to be able to measure

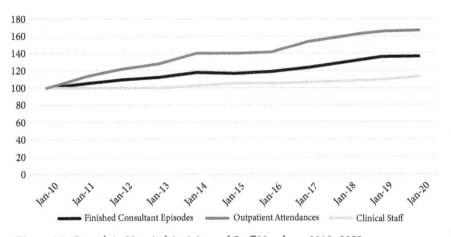

Figure 4.3 Growth in Hospital Activity and Staff Numbers, 2010–2020

Source: NHS Digital, Hospital Episode Statistics for Admitted Patient Care and Outpatient Data. NHS Digital, NHS Workforce Statistics, January 2020

the growth in outputs and all inputs. Ideally, we would measure output in terms of the improvements in health not in terms of the volume of activity, but we do not yet have the data we require to do this; the current state of play is as follows.

The most general measure of productivity is multifactor productivity (MFP) growth. MFP measures both the rate at which each input has grown and the change in the contribution (the share) of each input. The growth rate in all the inputs, after adjusting for any change in their shares, is then deducted from the growth rate in output, and the residual—the increase in output that cannot be explained by changes in inputs—measures MFP growth. The contribution of each input must be measured using a common unit of measurement, a numeraire, and the most obvious to use is the monetary value of each input. However, such a measure could include both a change in the volume of an input and a change in its price, and therefore monetary values must be deflated by a measure of price change so that only the change in the volume of inputs is being measured.[7] UK health and social care productivity is estimated using this method by the Office for National Statistics (ONS 2018).

The ONS measure UK health and social care productivity by comparing the growth of output to the growth of inputs used. Health and social care output is measured as the volume of health and social care that is provided after standardizing for the quality of delivery. The volume of output is measured as the cost-weighted number of individual health and social care activities performed, while the quality of delivery is measured using a combination of different indicators,

---

[7] For a comprehensive review of approaches to measuring productivity in health care, see Sheiner and Malinovskaya (2016)

among which are measures of waiting times and the results from National Patient Surveys.

The ONS estimated that between 1995 and 2015 the average annual rate of productivity growth for publicly provided health and social care was 0.8 per cent a year. They arrived at this estimate by calculating average annual output growth, which they found to be 4.7 per cent and deducting from it the average annual input growth, which was estimated at 3.9 per cent. The ONS also estimate the rate of productivity growth for the whole of the UK economy. Over the period 1980 to 2007, the period prior to the 2008 financial crisis, the annual rate of productivity growth in the UK economy as a whole was 2.3 per cent. Thus, in the period prior to the financial crisis, productivity growth in health and social care was much lower than the average for the economy as a whole. However, whole economy productivity growth slowed markedly after 2008. The average annual rate of productivity growth after 2008 was a mere 0.4 per cent. ONS estimates therefore suggested that, in the period after the financial crisis up to 2015, productivity growth in health and social care, measured by MFP growth, was around double the rate for the whole economy.

Embedded within these MFP estimates is labour productivity growth, which is what we really want to know, but it cannot be 'stripped out' of the ONS estimates; the ONS do not produce separate estimates of labour productivity in the health and social care sectors. However, the University of York do—they produce estimates of both MFP and annual labour productivity growth for the NHS in England (NHSPRB 2019, para 3.30). They estimated that, between 2005/6 and 2015/16, average annual MFP growth in the NHS in England was 1.2 per cent per annum, which is higher than that of the ONS estimate. Over that same period, they estimated that average annual labour productivity growth in the NHS was 2.5 per cent. Both seem to have slowed toward the end of the period, MFP growth was estimated to have been zero and labour productivity growth 1.3 per cent in 2015/16.

The University of York estimates of annual labour productivity growth in the NHS can also be compared to ONS estimates of annual labour productivity growth in the economy as a whole. At 2.5 and 0.6 per cent per annum respectively for the period 2005/6 to 2015/16, labour productivity growth in the NHS was four times greater than in the economy as a whole. The conclusion both the ONS and York reach is that in recent years the performance of the NHS has been considerably better than the performance of the economy as a whole.

Delivering health and social care is a labour-intensive activity and so it might be thought more difficult to improve productivity in this sector than in others. Other service industries that were once labour intensive have achieved sharp improvements in productivity by replacing labour with capital. In banking for example, counter clerks were replaced by ATMs, raising the productivity of the remaining employees, as measured by the number of transactions completed or cash dispensed per hour. Further productivity gains are now being realized in banking as ATMs are replaced by contactless payment, which further raises the productivity of bank workers by removing cash as the intermediary to completing transactions. Contactless payment also saves both the buyer and seller time (no need for the seller to tramp to the bank to deposit the cash) and so raises the productivity of both parties to the transaction.

In different ways, the use of advanced technology and the use of more capital have also improved productivity in health and social care. They have improved the productivity of support workers in health care by enabling more rapid and accurate radiological and laboratory-based diagnosis. There have also been improvements in surgical productivity due to the use of advanced technology, such as keyhole surgery. Further improvements in surgical productivity have been achieved by concentrating surgical activity in centres of excellence, where advanced surgical procedures can be undertaken using the most recent technology by the most skilled practitioners at volumes of activity which allow them to refine and develop their skills. Even modest technology, such as the introduction of hand sanitizers, can produce general improvements in health. The widespread use of hand sanitizers has reduced hospital-acquired infections and improved outcomes across a wide range of hospital activity.

In health care, there is also scope for productivity improvements through task substitution, or task shifting. Task shifting involves reallocating responsibilities to workers who require less, but still appropriate, training and who are paid accordingly. Examples of this were given in Chapter 3 at Section 3.7, where we discussed labour substitution.

However, in one important respect, the scope for substituting input from frontline health and social care workers by technology is limited. Personal input by the care worker is a central element of much health and social care, and the quality of the personal input is often critical to the outcome. The essence of frontline health and social care is personal delivery, which is hard to replace by technology. Successful care outcomes often depend both on the quality of the care that is delivered and on its reception by the recipient of care. Improved health, the intended outcome of the care, often depends upon the patients' engagement in their treatment, and their engagement is affected by the presence and behaviour of the health care worker.

Frontline activity requires the bedside attendance of the doctor and nurse or the presence of the social care worker. People deliver frontline health and social care services, and this restricts the scope for improving productivity by replacing labour with capital. The consequence is that, if we demand more frontline health and social care services, then we will need to employ more frontline workers, and this is of course what has happened. In Chapter 1 we saw that the share of the UK workforce employed in frontline health and social care has grown steadily through time, and this seems likely to continue.

4.7 Summary and Conclusions

In this chapter we have explored what is meant by the health and social care labour market. We have seen that this labour market is an aggregate of several different occupational and spatial labour markets and we have employed the tools of economics to discuss and analyse what distinguishes each of them. We have discussed how these markets clear, detailed the degree of competition in them, and discussed the impact of globalization. We have looked at the dominance of the NHS, assessed the impact of technological change, and reported the productivity growth of health care workers. The key points to take away from this chapter are as follows.

The health and social care labour market is an aggregate of many different labour markets, each distinguished along occupational and geographical lines. The geographical boundaries of labour markets differ substantially between occupations and in the short run are determined by how far people are willing to travel to work. This in turn is determined by people's income, the number of occasions on which they need to attend the workplace, and the efficiency, cost, and coverage of transport systems. The labour markets for nurses and social care workers cover smaller geographical areas than those of doctors, and there are accordingly a greater number of these labour markets within the UK.

The pandemic has expanded the geographical boundaries of the labour markets for many non-manual occupations. More working from home, and its corollary, fewer journeys to work, has extended the distances that many people who are not working in frontline care are prepared to travel to work on the few days they now have to. Their willingness to travel longer distances has increased housing choice, because people can now search over a wider area than before, and this has increased the attractiveness of these non-manual jobs.

There has been no comparable development in frontline health and adult social care: frontline workers cannot work from home, they are required to deliver their services in person and each working day they must travel to their place of work. The boundaries to their labour markets have not changed and neither, therefore, has choice of residential location. This development has therefore reduced the relative attractiveness of health and adult social care jobs. This will have important consequences for the recruitment and retention of frontline workers and for what they should be paid.

Labour markets are in equilibrium when the number of people willing to work just matches the number of people that organizations require to work. When a labour market is in equilibrium there are no pressures to change, and labour turnover and vacancy rates are at their natural rates. Competition in labour markets is a mechanism for realizing equilibrium, but the degree of competition in each of the largest occupational labour markets in frontline care differs substantially.

The labour market for hospital doctors is far from a perfectly competitive market in the short run, but there is competition. There is competition for hospital doctors, from the private sector, and from hospitals abroad, and there is muted competition between UK hospitals. Competition between hospitals in the UK is muted because hospital doctors are paid on national pay scales and rates of pay in this market are sticky, they change slowly, and so the burden of adjustment toward equilibrium falls on employment. This means that when vacancies arise they take a long time to fill. How much time it takes for the labour market to clear is an empirical question, and research is required to provide the answer.

The labour market for GP principals is very different to that for other frontline workers. This is because a majority of GPs are principals, partners in small businesses which are geographically anchored, and until recently this meant partners were relatively immobile. However the reduced costs of buying into a partnership and the growth in the number of salaried GPs have increased the degree of competition in the GP labour market, which is now among the more competitive frontline labour markets in the UK.

The labour markets for qualified and auxiliary nurses are different from those for hospital doctors and GPs in one important respect; there is substantial demand for these occupations from employers outside the health and social care sectors. These employers are not restricted as to what they can pay, and large numbers who have trained as nurses and care workers are to be found working for employers providing neither health care nor adult social care. The labour market for AHPs is different again because there is a substantial demand for their skills, which the NHS is unwilling to meet at competitive rates of pay. As a result, many AHPs have left the NHS to set up their own businesses or to work for health care providers in the private sector.

These features of the labour markets for nurses and AHPs might have been expected to have encouraged the NHS toward greater pay flexibility to enable it to respond to pay developments among competitors. Yet as we shall see in Chapter 7, the rates of pay for these occupations exhibit substantial rigidity, and they put the NHS at a disadvantage when it competes for labour.

The labour market for social care workers would be expected to be a competitive labour market because the demand side of this labour market is populated by a large number of different organizations who are not constrained by national pay agreements. We would therefore expect to see substantial competition for labour and rates of pay which cleared the market, yet this did not happen. The National Minimum Wage, which sets a UK-wide floor under rates of pay, set the effective rate of pay for a sizeable part of the workforce in the residential and domiciliary care sector. Organizations in this sector appeared to lack either the capacity or the will to raise rates of pay to the market clearing level.

Globalization has affected the UK labour market for frontline health and social care workers. It has increased opportunities and risk for both health and social care organizations seeking to recruit in this market and for frontline workers selling their labour in this market. Globalization reduces labour market transparency by introducing new, less well understood, players to the market, which requires buyers and sellers to process information from less familiar sources. It has increased the risk that organizations will make the wrong hiring decisions and that health and social care workers will make the wrong job acceptance decisions.

The globalization of health and social care labour markets affects the pay of frontline workers in the UK. It does this by introducing new buyers of labour, which exerts upward pressure on UK rates of pay, and new sellers of labour, which exerts downwards pressure on UK rates of pay. On balance, it was judged that globalization had exerted downward pressure on the pay of frontline workers in the UK.

The labour markets for frontline workers in the UK are profoundly affected by the presence of the NHS. It is the dominant player in the health care market and has a substantial impact on the adult social care market. In March 2018, almost 1.7 million people worked for the NHS, and the vast majority of these were frontline workers. It was by far the largest employer of skilled labour in the UK, with around one in every six people in the UK working in a professional occupation working for the NHS. As best could be estimated, around 77 per cent of people working in the NHS were frontline workers.

The prominence of the NHS in many geographical labour markets in the UK resulted in spillover effects. What the NHS paid affected what other employers had to pay and thus the reward and recruitment strategies of the NHS resulted in externalities. These effects have not been studied and are little understood but may be profound.

Estimates of productivity growth suggested that the performance of the NHS over the period from the financial crisis in 2008 to 2015 was considerably better than that of the economy as a whole. The average annual rate of multifactor productivity growth in health and social care was double that in the rest of the economy. Estimates for the period 2005/6 to 2015/16, produced by the University of York, revealed that at 2.5 per cent per annum, labour productivity growth in the NHS was four times greater than in the economy as a whole over this period.

The scope for improving productivity in health and social care by substituting capital for labour appears limited. Personal input by the care worker is a central element of frontline care, and this personal input is often crucial to the care outcome. The essence of frontline health and social care is personal delivery, and successful outcomes often depend upon the patient's engagement in their treatment. This engagement is affected by the presence and behaviour of health care workers.

5

The UK and the Global Health and Social Care Labour Market

The UK health service is heavily dependent on doctors and nurses born and trained abroad, and the adult social care sector is also reliant on foreign-born workers. Each year, large numbers of foreign-born workers enter the UK to join the health and adult social care workforce, and every year a smaller number leave this workforce to work abroad. These flows provide evidence that the UK labour market is part of a larger global labour market in health and social care. In the years prior to 2019 these flows increased, and the impact of global health and adult social care labour markets on UK markets intensified.

Without migrants, health and adult social care in the UK would be seriously understaffed and the delivery of health and social care seriously impaired. In this chapter we detail the scale of this dependency and the increasing globalization of health care labour markets. We explore the economic explanations for this dependency, distinguish the reasons health and social care workers come to the UK, and examine some of the impediments to their migration. We consider the impact of migration on the UK labour market and what this might mean for the pay and employment prospects of native workers.

5.1 UK Dependency on Foreign-Born Workers

Foreign-born workers make up a significant part of the UK labour force. In the final quarter of 2019 they accounted for 17.6 per cent of the total labour force (ONS 2019) or nearly one in every five workers in the UK. At the highly educated end of the workforce, the UK is even more dependent on foreign-born workers; in 2016 they accounted for 22.1 per cent of this workforce (OECD 2019b).

Health care is more heavily dependent on foreign-born workers than the UK economy as a whole. In 2019, 29 per cent of all doctors working in NHS hospitals were foreign-born, while across the health service as a whole one in three doctors, 33.1 per cent, were foreign-born (ONS 2019b). Foreign-born nurses account for around one in five of the nursing workforce. In 2019, 18 per cent of all nurses working in NHS hospitals and 21.9 per cent of nurses working in the UK health care system as a whole were foreign-born (ONS 2019b). Social care is only slightly

The Economics of the UK Health and Social Care Labour Market. Robert Elliott, Oxford University Press.
© Robert Elliott (2024). DOI: 10.1093/oso/9780198883142.003.0005

less dependent; it is estimated that in 2019 around 17 per cent of all social care workers were foreign-born (Charlesworth and Gershlick 2019).

The UK's dependence on foreign-born workers is of long standing, and the UK health care sector has long sought to solve shortages in key occupations through active recruitment abroad. As early as the 1950s, foreign-born doctors were an important part of the UK medical workforce, and by the 1970s around a quarter of this workforce had been trained abroad (Bach 2010). This dependency increased still further over the years to 2000, by which time almost a third of the NHS medical workforce had been trained abroad, and since then it has changed little (OECD 2019b).[1] This stands in contrast to the nursing workforce, where the UK's dependence on foreign-born nurses has increased during this century. In 2000, the share of foreign-born nurses working in the UK was 15.2 per cent and by 2016 it had risen to 21.9 per cent (OECD 2019b).

The number of foreign-born doctors and nurses joining the health care workforce varies from year to year and depends, among other things, on the intensity of UK recruitment. In some years they account for the majority of new hires. Between 2001 and 2003, international recruitment accounted for 73 per cent of the growth in the number of nurses and 80 per cent of the increase in the number of doctors (Pond and McPake 2006).

Foreign-born need not mean foreign-trained, though the vast majority of foreign-born doctors and nurses practising in the UK were trained abroad. During the period 2015 to 2017, 28.5 per cent of all doctors and 15 per cent of all nurses practising in the UK were trained abroad. That there are more foreign-born than foreign-trained doctors reveals that some foreign-born doctors and nurses came to the UK to train and then stayed on to work. Though to date very few UK born doctors and nurses working in the UK have trained abroad, these numbers are likely to increase. Training, and in particular medical training, is becoming increasingly internationalized, and in some countries—Norway is an example—large numbers of native-born doctors trained abroad.

5.2 How UK Dependency on Foreign-Born Workers Compares

Developments in the UK are part of a broader, global phenomenon. OECD migration data reveals that in recent years high income countries have increasingly resorted to global labour markets to satisfy their labour requirements. The OECD data reported in Figure 5.1 shows that while the UK is one of the more heavily dependent countries on foreign-born, highly educated workers, it is not alone in this respect. The foreign-born share of the highly educated workforce in 2015/16

---

[1] In 2000, 33.7 per cent of the NHS medical workforce had been trained aboard, while in 2016, the percentage stood at 33.1 (OECD 2019b).

was 39.9 per cent in Australia and 32.1 per cent in Canada, while among large European countries it was 15.6 per cent in Germany and 15.7 per cent in France, compared to 22.1 per cent in the UK.

Health systems are more heavily dependent on foreign-born workers than is the economy in general. Figure 5.1 also shows that the share of foreign-born doctors in the medical workforce was considerably greater than the share of foreign-born in the highly educated part of the workforce in most OECD countries. Foreign-born doctors accounted for 33.1 per cent of all doctors in the UK in 2015/16, 38.5 per cent of all doctors in Canada, 41.1 per cent in Ireland, 47.1 in Switzerland, 53.9 in Australia, and 55 per cent in Luxembourg.

These same countries were also heavily reliant on foreign-born nurses, though in general they made up a smaller share of the nursing workforce than did foreign-born doctors in the medical workforce. Figure 5.2 reveals that foreign-born nurses accounted for 24.4 per cent of all nurses in Canada, 26.1 per cent in Ireland, 31.6 in Switzerland, 35.3 in Australia, and 29.1 per cent in Luxembourg, while they accounted for 21.9 per cent in the UK.

The dependence of the health care services in OECD countries on foreign-trained doctors and nurses has been increasing in recent years. The OECD report that over the decade to 2016 the number of foreign-trained doctors working in OECD countries increased by 50 per cent to reach a total of nearly 500,000, while over the shorter, five-year, period to 2016 the number of foreign-trained nurses working in OECD countries increased by 20 per cent to reach a total of nearly 550,000 (OECD 2019b). The greater part of this migration was permanent, but

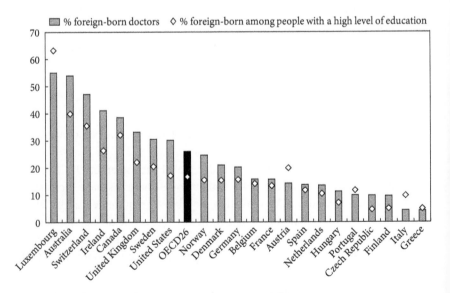

Figure 5.1 Percentage of Foreign-Born Doctors, 2015/2016

Source: OECD (2019b) Figure 1.3 StatLink 2https://doi.org/10.1787/888933969905

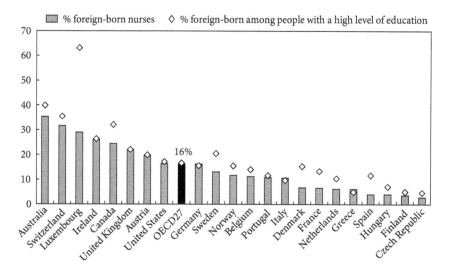

Figure 5.2 Percentage of Foreign-Born Nurses, 2015/2016
Source: OECD (2019b) Figure 1.4 StatLink 2https://doi.org/10.1787/888933969924

there were sizeable flows of temporary migrants between the health and social care systems of some OECD countries. This temporary migration was greatest between high income English-speaking OECD countries (Mullan 2005 and OECD 2019b).

Among the large European countries, the UK was the most heavily dependent on foreign-born doctors and nurses as Figures 5.1 and 5.2 have shown. The UK was more heavily dependent on foreign-born doctors and nurses than France, Germany, Italy, and Spain. In Europe, only Ireland, Luxembourg, and Switzerland, which all had much smaller populations than the UK, had a heavier dependency than the UK. Moreover, in Switzerland and Luxembourg, the position is rather different from that of UK or Ireland. In these two countries, many foreign-born health care workers are non-resident. In both countries, a significant proportion of the foreign-born labour force live in bordering countries and commute to work each day, crossing the border to get to work. For these foreign-born workers the costs of accessing the Swiss and Luxembourg health care labour markets were much lower than they would have been had they been required to migrate.

The UK's long-standing and heavy dependence on foreign-born doctors and nurses means that a significant proportion of all foreign-born doctors and nurses resident in OECD countries live in the UK. Thirteen per cent of all foreign-born doctors, and 11 per cent of all foreign-born nurses resident in OECD countries in 2016 lived in the UK. Figure 5.3 reports the distribution of foreign-born doctors and nurses by country of residence in the OECD area in 2016 and shows that only the United States and, in the case of nurses, Germany, accounted for a larger share than the UK.

In 2016, 42 per cent of all foreign-born doctors and 45 per cent of all foreign-born-nurses resident and practising in OECD countries were practising in the USA. That the United States accounts for by far the largest share is not a surprise. The US health and social care labour market is by far the largest of any OECD member state, it is over four times the size of that in the UK, and it spends a larger share of its GDP on health and social care than any other OECD country. Moreover, it pays its health care workers some of the highest salaries in the world. It would therefore be expected to have a substantial presence in global health care labour markets. The UK's prominence is, perhaps, more surprising.

In Section 5.1 above we noted that foreign-trained need not mean foreign-born. One recent development has been the increasing proportion of native-born workers in health and social care in high income countries who trained abroad.[2] While there have long been flows of people from low and middle income countries to high income countries in order to train, and there still are, in recent years an increasing number of people from high income countries have gone abroad to train. An increasing number of students from high income countries are availing themselves of lower cost medical training opportunities abroad. An extreme example is Norway, where around half of the foreign-trained doctors working in Norway were born in Norway (OECD 2017: 164). Another example is that of Caribbean-trained doctors who applied for US certification to practice. Between 1995 and 2008, 80 per cent were USA and Canadian nationals (WHO 2019). As yet, the number of UK-born doctors and nurses who train abroad is small, but this is expected to grow as training becomes increasingly globalized and lower cost training opportunities abroad become more accessible and recognized.

5.3 Why Do Foreign-Born Workers Come to the UK?

The UK's dependence on foreign-trained health and social care workers results from its failure to train sufficient numbers of doctors, nurses, and care workers to meet its requirements. There has long been an excess demand for trained nurses, doctors, and care workers in the UK, and foreign-born workers have satisfied part of this demand. Foreign-born workers migrate to the UK for a variety of pecuniary and non-pecuniary reasons. They come for better pay and employment conditions, for professional reasons and for family and social reasons.

Migration is costly, it takes time, and it involves expenditure. Voluntary migration should be viewed as an economic decision, one which is conceptually

---

[2] The OECD record that 'the number of medical students pursuing their education abroad has soared in recent years' (OECD 2015: 107). They attribute this to generally increased international student mobility, the internationalization of medical training, and the wider accreditation of skills. These developments have certainly facilitated such movements, but the increased number training abroad is also a result of a shift in the burden of payment for training from the public purse to the individual resulting in students seeking lower cost training options abroad.

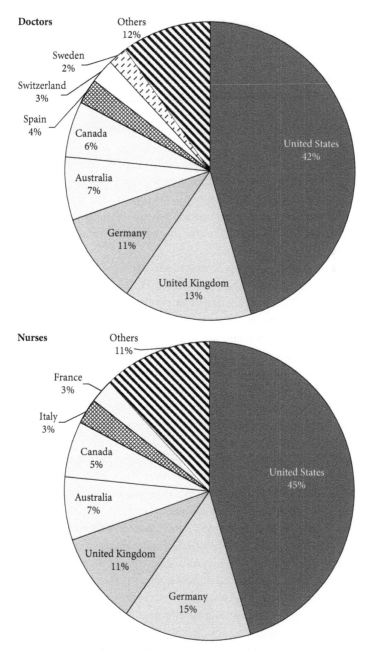

Figure 5.3 Distribution of Foreign-Born Doctors and Nurses by Country of Residence in the OECD Area, 2015/2016

Source: OECD (2019b) Figure 1.5 StatLink 2https://doi.org/10.1787/888933969943

the same as the decision to invest in human capital. Both involve an evaluation of costs and benefits, costs which are incurred in the present and must be weighed against benefits accruing in the future. There are two important differences between human capital investment and migration. First, the benefits of migration start to accrue almost immediately, because the physical act of migrating, unlike training, is completed in a very short time. Second, the magnitude of costs and benefits in relation to migration are more difficult to estimate with any accuracy and so the cost–benefit calculation cannot be as finely calibrated as in human capital investment.

This said, in the case of migration, precision is often unnecessary because the value of one key parameter is such as to overwhelm the other elements of the calculation. The difference between pay in the origin and destination countries is often of such an order of magnitude as to overwhelm the differences between other factors, and as a result it makes the fine calculus of other costs and benefits unnecessary.

The costs of migration comprise both initial and recurring costs. The initial costs are the costs of travel and relocation, and they are relatively easy to distinguish and quantify. The recurring costs are those which are experienced after arrival in the destination country, and they are more difficult to quantify because a significant part of them are emotional and psychological costs. They are the costs which result from severed family and social ties, adapting to a new culture, and forming new friendships, and these costs can be experienced over a lengthy period subsequent to migration.

As with costs, so with benefits: some are enjoyed immediately, and others accrue over a much longer period. Again, the pecuniary benefits are likely to be relatively easy to distinguish and quantify. Improved pay is probably the major benefit for most people migrating to the UK because NHS rates of pay for doctors and nurses are much higher than in most origin countries (Bach 2003; Stilwell et al. 2004; Connell et al. 2007). Working conditions and access to technology and medicines are also likely better in the UK than in most countries in which migrants trained (Bach 2003). Health systems in many of the origin countries are less well resourced than in the UK, and in recent years declining investment in health sectors has increased these differences. Less easy to distinguish are the benefits realized over the longer period such as enhanced career opportunities (Kerry et al. 2011) and the non-pecuniary social benefits of migration such as new social ties, the opportunity for new friendships, and access to a new culture.

As with any investment decision, information is key, and the reliability and accuracy of the information is critical for informed decision-making. Migrants obtain information on the costs and benefits of migration through both formal and informal channels. Formal channels, the written and oral statements of the prospective employer, provide information on pay and other pecuniary benefits, while informal channels are likely to be the main source of information about working conditions and the wider social environment in the destination country.

Well-established informal channels which provide reliable information go a long way toward explaining the patterns of migration to the UK.

For many migrants, the informal channels comprise family and friends. Their presence in the UK increases both the volume of information and its reliability. Moreover, their presence in the UK is likely to reduce initial transaction costs through the provision of accommodation and access to social networks. Informal channels often generate information networks (Price 2009), which in turn produce migration chains where migrants follow friends and relatives to a particular destination. These chains help explain the patterns of migration to the UK by foreign-born doctors and nurses.

A majority of foreign-trained doctors working in the UK come from Commonwealth countries. Doctors trained in just two Commonwealth countries, India and Pakistan, accounted for 43 per cent of all foreign-trained doctors working in the UK in 2017, while a further 5 per cent were trained in Nigeria. Figure 5.4 shows the countries where foreign-trained doctors working in the UK in 2017 were trained.

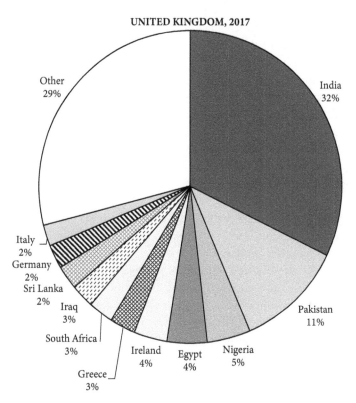

Figure 5.4 Main Countries of Training of Foreign-Trained Doctors in the United Kingdom, 2017

Source: OECD (2019b) Annex Figure 1B1 StatLink 2https://doi.org/10.1787/888933970171

Institutions created in imperial times and more recent political and economic arrangements facilitated the flow of migrants to the UK. Two in particular were important: the Commonwealth of Nations and the European Community. In 2018, one in every seven doctors working in the NHS came from an Asian Commonwealth country (ONS 2019) and a large number of nurses working in the UK came from India and Jamaica. Until 2021, membership of the EC also facilitated the recruitment of foreign-trained workers. The ONS report that in 2018, 6 per cent of those who were providing health and social care services that were of direct benefit to patients came from other EC countries (ONS 2019), while the OECD report that 15 per cent of foreign-trained doctors in the UK in 2017 came from other EC countries. (OECD, 2019b)

The decision to migrate and the decision to invest in human capital are often linked. This is evidently the case where migration is to undertake training, and though it is less clearly the case where training precedes migration, there is often still a link. This is because the initial investment in human capital is often motivated by the desire to migrate, and training is undertaken to improve the chances of migration (Connell et al. 2007). In many low and middle income countries there is substantial private investment in health care human capital, and in some of these countries the demand has been such that it has led to the growth of a private for-profit training industry for health professionals (McPake et al. 2015). Many people in low income countries view the acquisition of transferable human capital as a passport to migration. This is particularly true of health care human capital because the excess demand for trained health and social care workers in high income countries means that this form of human capital investment offers the best prospects of migration. In many low and middle income countries the motivation for investment in health and social care human capital is the enhanced prospects of migration that are expected to result.

However, migration imposes costs on low and middle income countries where either investment has been at public expense or high income countries hire people who are working in health and social care. The latter lowers the costs of high income countries because the workers are both trained and have gained experience through working in a frontline setting. The practice has depleted the health service workforces of several low and middle income counties and adversely affected the delivery of health care in a number of them (Stilwell et al. 2004; Connell et al. 2007). Agreement to mitigate these costs led to the development of a Code of Practice for overseas recruitment, although this appears to have had little impact (Buchan et al. 2009).

5.4 The Impact of Migration on the UK Labour Market

The presence of large numbers of foreign-born workers in health and social care in the UK is the result of factors on both the supply and the demand sides of these labour markets. On the supply side are the choices of people born outside the UK to invest in transferable health and social care human capital and migrate to the UK. On the demand side is the persistent excess demand for key health and social care occupations in the UK. Migration allows the UK to satisfy a demand for health and social care that would otherwise go unmet and so makes a vital contribution to the health and well-being of the UK population. However, international flows of labour can also affect the pay and employment of native-born workers, and we explore the economics of this here.

The impact of migration on the pay and employment prospects of native-born workers will depend on the degree of competitiveness in the domestic labour market, the state of that market prior to migration, and the degree of complementarity between the skills of native-born and migrant workers. Migration will reduce the pay of people in the occupations which migrants join if native-born and migrant labour are perfect substitutes, if the labour market in the destination country is perfectly competitive, and if it was in equilibrium prior to migration. Such a position is illustrated in Figure 5.5. Initially, the labour market is in equilibrium at P_1 and N_1. Migration to this country increases labour supply, which shifts the labour supply schedule to the right. The resulting competition for jobs exerts downward pressure on pay, and this continues until a new equilibrium position is reached at a lower rate of pay P_2 and N_2.

However, this simple model is not an appropriate representation of the UK health care labour market, as will be evident when we read Chapter 7. The main occupational labour markets in health and social care in the UK are in not equilibrium, but are characterized by labour shortages. Furthermore, health care labour markets are not perfectly competitive, and in many health care settings, the skills of native-born and migrant labour are complements rather than substitutes. We can illustrate what happens in a labour market characterized by labour shortage by again using Figure 5.5

In Figure 5.5 at the pay level P_2 there is an excess demand for labour equal to N_2–N_3. The labour market is therefore in disequilibrium, there is a labour shortage due to a pay rate, P_2, that is too low to 'clear' the market. Migration will shift the labour supply schedule to the right, and thus will reduce the labour shortage; if it continues, it can eliminate the shortage. Migration is one way in which supply and demand can be brought into balance at N_2. In this example, the level of employment and the rate of pay of native-born workers were unaffected by migration; migration could be said to have 'bailed out' those who had set pay at P_2.

Migration could, however, be judged to be at a cost to native-born workers if it was thought that in the absence of migration the labour market would eventually adjust, and pay levels would have risen to P_1. This would be expected to happen in a perfectly competitive labour market, but in a labour market like health, where pay is set through an administrative process, this seems very much less likely. Migration would also be at a cost to native-born workers if the scale of migration exceeded that required to address the labour shortage, and as a result migrants displaced native-born workers, though why health care organizations in the UK

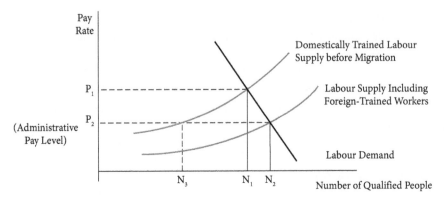

Figure 5.5 Excess Demand Resulting in Migration

would do this is unclear because they must pay native-born and foreign workers of the same skill level the same.

Native-born workers will benefit from migration if they and foreign-born workers are complements in production, because employing foreign-born workers will increase the demand for native-born workers. If doctors and nurses are complements in production, employing migrants to fill vacancies for doctors will create jobs for nurses.

In practice, migration is far from the unimpeded process implied in the above discussion. Migration to the UK is regulated, and there are controls on the number of health and social care workers that are permitted to migrate to the UK. The system changes frequently and is the subject of much political debate. At the time of writing, the number of migrants who could enter the UK was determined by a points-based system regardless of country or region of origin. The number of points awarded depended on whether migrants met specific requirements. Higher points were awarded for higher skills, and the ability to command a salary above the specified threshold facilitated the migration of doctors and nurses to the UK (NHS Employers 2019). In this system, doctors and nurses were also listed as shortage occupations, which meant that, provided an offer of employment in the UK was accompanied by a salary offer on 'the national pay scale rate for the job', migrants could enter through this route (Home Office 2020). Initially, adult social care workers were not listed as a shortage occupation because the average pay for the occupation was below that required to enter the list (The Conversation 2020), though this was subsequently changed.

Some of the countries from which people wish to migrate to the UK impose restrictions on migration, and they have good reason to do so. Where the government has funded the investment in training, the migration of the trained worker will mean the government receives no return on its investment, and in a low income country the opportunity cost to the government of funding the investment will have been substantial. Origin countries have therefore created several different systems to penalize and deter the migration of health care workers. They have made funding for training conditional on an agreed period of service in the investing country, they have required trainees to post bonds, with the money returnable only after an agreed period of service, and they have concluded no-poaching agreements with potential recruiters. However a large volume of research has revealed that, to date, such policies have met with limited success both because the arrangements are difficult to enforce and because the private returns to migration are often so substantial that bonds are willingly forfeit (Grobler et al. 2015; Dolea et al. 2010; Ozegowski 2013; Mbemba et al. 2013; Frehywot et al. 2010; and Elliott and Scott 2004).

5.5 Summary and Conclusions

In this chapter we have looked at the impact of the global labour markets for health and social care workers on labour markets in the UK. The key points to take away from this chapter are outlined below.

Foreign-born workers accounted for nearly 18 per cent of the total UK labour force in 2019 and for 22 per cent of the most highly educated part of that labour force. Like the rest of the economy, UK health and social care also relied heavily on foreign-born workers. Eighteen per cent of all nurses and 29 per cent of all doctors working in NHS hospitals in 2019 were born abroad. Seventeen per cent of all social care workers in the UK in 2019 were born abroad, and across the health service as a whole, a third of all doctors and just over a fifth of all nurses practising in the UK in 2015/16 were born abroad. Among large European countries, the UK was the most heavily dependent on foreign-born doctors and nurses. Thirteen per cent of all foreign-born doctors and 11 per cent of all foreign-born nurses resident in an OECD country in 2016 lived in the UK.

UK recruitment of foreign-born workers has been concentrated within the Commonwealth of Nations and particularly in the countries of the Asian subcontinent. Doctors from India and Pakistan together accounted for 43 per cent of all foreign-trained doctors working in the UK in 2017. Migration from these countries to the UK has been facilitated by the existence of migration chains, which reduce the transaction costs associated with migration, and by institutions in the Asian subcontinent providing training similar to that in the UK.

The UK's dependence on foreign-born workers is of long standing, and in recent years has become a subject of some debate. The evidence suggests that in health and social care there is little if any displacement effect. Foreign-born workers come to the UK to fill positions that would otherwise remain vacant. Indeed, foreign-born workers help create jobs for native-born health and social care workers when they supply skills that are complementary to those of native-born workers. Controversy arises because the vast majority of foreign-born workers have trained abroad. It is argued that recruitment by high income countries depletes the health workforce in low and middle income countries, and this has led to the development of the WHO Global Code of Practice on International Recruitment of Health Personnel.

There are two features which are often overlooked when migration from low income countries is discussed. The first is the growth of the private for-profit industry offering training in health and social care skills in many low and middle income countries. This industry has a large presence on the Asian subcontinent. The growth of this industry reflects the demand to invest in health care human capital in low and middle income countries, where it is seen as the passport to migration. The excess demand for health and social care workers in high income countries in Europe, Australasia, and North America incentivizes this investment.

The second is the low level of demand for health care skills in many origin countries. In 2018, spending on health care amounted to 3.5 per cent of GDP in India, 3.2 per cent in Pakistan, and 2.3 per cent in Bangladesh (World Bank 2020), with government spending accounting for around a third of the total in each country (Economic Survey 2020/21). Such low levels of demand for health care will provide very weak incentives to invest in health care human capital if the domestic health service is the only source of employment.

Migration provides an important incentive to invest in health care human capital in many low and middle income countries. By erecting barriers to migration, high income countries reduce the private incentives to invest in health care human capital and health care human capital formation in low and middle income countries. Barriers in high income countries also reduce the knowledge transfer which results when health care workers from low and middle income who have worked in high income countries return to work in their countries of origin.

The migration of health care workers is at a cost to low and middle income countries where these workers have been trained at public expense or where they worked in health care before migrating. Economic theory makes clear the risks that attach to public investment in producing transferable skills, and to date, low and middle income countries have been unable to develop policies to substantially reduce these risks.

Voluntary migration should be viewed as an economic decision, one which is conceptually the same as the decision to invest in human capital. The migration of health and social care workers to the UK is largely driven by the difference between what health and social care workers are paid in the UK and what they are paid in the origin countries. This same calculus has informed migration to the UK from the EC. Membership of the EC lowered the costs of migration to the UK, and mutual recognition of professional qualifications was one of the ways it did this. Fifteen per cent of foreign-trained doctors working in the UK in 2017 came from another EC country, while the ONS has estimated that in 2018, 6 per cent of those who were providing health and social care services that were of direct benefit to patients in the UK came from other EC countries.

The departure of the UK from the EC in January 2021 has increased the costs to workers from EC countries and as a result many who had been working in the UK have left. Moreover, as the rate of pay growth in the UK falls below that in EC countries, due to weaker economic growth in the UK, the salary advantage that the UK offered is eroded. As a result, the UK health service will become even more heavily dependent on the migration of foreign-trained nurses and doctors from outwith the EC, a dependence which is unlikely to reduce substantially any time soon.

The UK can be confident of a continued supply of foreign-trained workers from low and middle income countries provided three conditions are met. First, the willingness and the ability of people in low and middle income countries to invest in health care human capital continues. Second, and partly motivating the first, the differences in pay between the UK and the origin countries are of an order of magnitude sufficient to cover both the monetary and the social and psychological costs of this investment and migration. Third, the UK is perceived to be an open, accessible, and welcoming place to work. None of these can be predicted with confidence.

6

The Theory of Pay Setting and Its Application to Frontline Care Workers

For most workers, pay is much more than 'just another price'. For the vast majority, it is the most important price of any they encounter. Pay is the main source of income for most working people, and what they are paid determines what goods and services they can buy. Beyond enabling them to buy basic goods and services, pay provides people with the means to enhance and enrich their lives, it determines their lifestyles, social standing, and affects their peace of mind and well-being. What we are paid is of central importance to us all.

How workers are paid also matters, because it can affect how intensively they work and how carefully they work. Workers can be paid under a system of payment-by-results or a time rate payment system. Both systems relate payment to contribution, where this is defined in terms of what is produced in the first case, and the amount of time spent at work in the second. Which of these systems of payment is most appropriate for health and social care workers will be discussed in this chapter.

In health care labour markets, pay is set through an administrative process. In these labour markets, a very small number of sellers, trade unions representing workers, often acting in concert, negotiate a rate of pay with representatives of health care employers. The process is intermediated by institutions which interpret the state of the labour market using data, and recommend rates of pay that they judge appropriate to their interpretation of these data. This process is very different from the way that pay is set in the social care labour market.

However, common to both health and the social care labour markets is the underlying driver of labour supply, which is what workers believe they should be paid for doing the jobs they do. What they believe they should be paid is determined by the characteristics of the jobs they do, and if their pay does not reflect these characteristics then it is not an equilibrium rate, and there will be pressures for the rate to change.

In this chapter, we discuss the economic theory relevant to setting the pay of frontline health and social care workers. We will detail the basic economic principles which should underpin how health and social care workers are paid, and we will identify the very distinctive characteristics of the jobs they do which should affect what they are paid. We will discuss whether frontline workers' pay should be related to what they produce or the time they spend at work, we will explain why

The Economics of the UK Health and Social Care Labour Market. Robert Elliott, Oxford University Press.
© Robert Elliott (2024). DOI: 10.1093/oso/9780198883142.003.0006

the pay of these workers should increase incrementally during the first few years of work, and we will explain why it is important that frontline workers' pay varies according to the area of the country in which they work. We start by discussing how job characteristics affect pay and how the particular characteristics of health and social care workers' jobs should affect what they are paid.

6.1 How the Characteristics of Jobs Affect Pay

All jobs have characteristics, features of the work and the conditions under which it is carried out. Among the most important are the skills required to do the work, the number of hours that have to be worked each week, the timing of those hours, the distinguishing features of the workplace, and its location. These characteristics will affect what the jobs pay because they affect people's willingness to do these jobs, they affect labour supply. In this section we outline the economic theory which explains how the characteristics of jobs affect pay, while in the next section of this chapter we detail how the specific characteristics of jobs in health and social care should affect what health and social care workers are paid.

The proposition that job characteristics affect pay was first advanced by Adam Smith in 1776. In *An Inquiry into the Nature and Causes of The Wealth of Nations*, published that year, he advanced the theory of net advantages to explain differences in pay between different occupations and between people in the same occupation who were working in different areas of the country. He argued that differences in pay were neither random nor haphazard but were logical and systematic; they reflected the characteristics of jobs. He argued that characteristics affected pay because they affected the supply of labour to different jobs, and where pay was set within competitive labour markets, differences in pay could be explained by differences in the characteristics of jobs.

The theory which Smith developed, the theory of net advantages, is still the appropriate conceptual framework for understanding why jobs pay differently, and for this reason it should sit prominently in the minds of people involved in pay setting today. Smith identified five different sets of characteristics which affect the supply of labour to jobs.[1] Some of these characteristics people would find attractive; others they would find unattractive. Smith called the characteristics of jobs

---

[1] In Book 1, Chapter X, of *An Inquiry into the Nature and Causes of The Wealth of Nations*, published in 1776, Adam Smith elaborated the 'theory of net advantages' and detailed the five principal features, characteristics, of jobs which explain pay differences. They were:

the costs of learning the business; the higher the costs of learning, the greater post-training pay,
the agreeableness of the job; the less agreeable the job, the higher the pay,
the constancy of employment; the less permanent the job, the higher the pay,
the trust reposed; the greater the trust, the higher the pay, and
the probability of success; the lower the probability of success, the higher the pay.

which people find attractive, the advantages of jobs, and the unattractive characteristics, he termed the disadvantages. Smith's fundamental insight was to recognize that it was the balance of these advantages and disadvantages, the net advantages of different jobs, that affected what different jobs paid. Jobs in which, on balance, the disadvantages outweighed the advantages would need to pay more than jobs in which, on balance, the advantages outweighed the disadvantages.[2]

To illustrate this let us take two examples from industries other than health and social care, coal mining and deep-sea fishing. Both of these industries have some jobs that are unpleasant and potentially dangerous. The number of fatalities per annum, among coal miners and deep-sea fishermen, once standardized by the size of the coal mining and fishing workforces respectively, testifies to the dangerous nature of these jobs. Danger is of course only one of the characteristics of these jobs; they are also done in conditions that most people would consider unattractive: in coal mining, deep underground; in fishing, on high, often turbulent, seas. The disadvantages of the jobs coal miners and deep-sea fishermen do will therefore need to be compensated by higher pay than in jobs which are, in other respects similar, if people are to be attracted to work in them.

Indeed these two occupations, coal miners and deep-sea fishermen, are both relatively high paying; they pay above the average for jobs that require the same levels of skill and effort.[3] In both cases, the higher rate of pay compensates for the dangerous and unpleasant nature of the work. It should also be noted that the higher pay that has to be offered to attract people to dangerous jobs also incentivizes employers to make these jobs safer: if they can make the jobs safer they can reduce what they pay.[4]

These pay differences will only exist if people have a choice of jobs. If this is the case, they will avoid those with unattractive characteristics and choose jobs that have attractive characteristics. Employers with jobs that have unattractive characteristics will find that they have to offer higher pay to attract people to their jobs

The theory is an equilibrium theory and it has been described as 'the fundamental (long run) market equilibrium concept in labour economics' (Rosen 1986) because it describes the forces at work which are tending to produce, balance, equilibrium, in labour markets. These forces are the responses of workers to differences in what they perceive to be the advantages and disadvantages of different jobs. The principal mechanism within labour markets which will propel them toward equilibrium is adjustments in pay, but if there are impediments to this adjustment then other compensating adjustments will be set in motion to restore equilibrium.

[2] A more advanced development of this theory, titled the theory of equalizing differences, recognizes that employers will trade off pay and the attributes of the working environment in order to accommodate workers' preferences. See Rosen (1986: 641–692).

[3] It is interesting to note that in Smith's time, fishermen were poorly paid, because most were not deep-sea fishermen. Smith wrote, 'Hunting and fishing, the most important employments of mankind in the rude state of society, become in its advanced state their most agreeable amusements, and they pursue for pleasure what they once followed from necessity. In the advanced state of society, therefore, they are all very poor people who follow as a trade, what other people pursue as a pastime. Fishermen have been so since the time of Theocritus' (1776: Book 1, Chapter X, Part 1).

[4] The importance of this characteristic has steadily reduced due to the passage of health and safety legislation, which has done a great deal to equalize the safety of different workplaces,

than employers who have jobs that have attractive characteristics. Jobs that are attractive and safe will therefore pay less than jobs which are judged dangerous and unattractive.

Through the workings of competition in the labour market, the pay of all jobs would adjust to reflect their non-pay characteristics. Left unimpeded, the process of adjustment would continue until an equilibrium had been established at which the pay for every job was at a level which reflected the advantages and disadvantages of the job. Indeed, it follows that once we include pay as an advantage of a job, competition would ensure that the whole of the advantages and disadvantages of every job would be equalized because pay would adjust to balance them.

It follows from this line of reasoning that the pay of jobs with the same non-pay characteristics must tend toward equality, and equally logically, that where there are differences in pay between jobs, these must be due to differences in the non-pay characteristics of these jobs. The theory of net advantages is therefore also a theory of pay inequality: according to Smith, pay inequality is explained by differences in the characteristics of jobs. An extensive research literature provides empirical support for Smith's theory of net advantages (Viscusi and Aldy 2003; Maestas et al. 2018; Lavetti 2020).

Most large organizations recognize that the characteristics of the jobs their employees do affects how they view their pay, and so they conduct surveys of their employee's job satisfaction. These surveys should be understood as surveying the advantages and disadvantages of jobs, and Smith's theory provides us with the relevant framework for interpreting the results of these surveys. If the advantages and disadvantages of the different jobs surveyed are fully compensated by what they pay, each job should generate the same level of satisfaction. If, on the other hand, the survey reveals that some workers on a particular rate of pay report higher levels of satisfaction than others on the same pay, then the jobs these workers do must have different characteristics, and they should be paid differently. Rates of pay should be adjusted to equalize levels of satisfaction; either the rates paid in the jobs with the higher level of satisfaction should be adjusted down, or the rates paid in the jobs with the lower levels should be adjusted up.

Moreover, it would be reasonable to predict that if rates were not adjusted and these differences were sustained, then people would try to switch from the jobs which generated the lower levels of satisfaction into the jobs with the higher levels of satisfaction. In a competitive labour market this would exert upward pressure on pay in the former jobs and downward pressure on pay in the latter, and these pressures for adjustment would persist until the level of satisfaction was the same in all jobs.

However, the pay of health care workers is not set through a competitive process. Even so, these same forces are at work in health and social care labour markets. Failure either to adjust pay or, if possible, to improve the characteristics of jobs with lower levels of satisfaction, will cause people to leave these jobs and take jobs with the higher levels of satisfaction. If they are unable to move, they will be discontented and likely to perform less productively. The characteristics of jobs are the source of job satisfaction, and if satisfaction levels differ between jobs, organizations should seek to adjust either pay or other characteristics of the jobs to bring satisfaction levels into equality.

Smith's theory is based upon the reasoning of a rational person, reflecting on the characteristics of the jobs they do. The characteristics of the jobs people do determine whether they judge they are being fairly paid; they capture the fundamental differences between jobs that drive people's perceptions of what constitute fair differences in pay.

6.2 The Net Advantages of Frontline Jobs

Smith's theory provides the theoretical framework which should inform the setting of frontline workers' pay. The theory of net advantages provides the conceptual framework required to explain why there have to be different rates of pay between occupations in health and social care and between them and occupations in other industries. The theory makes clear that the characteristics of jobs in health and social care will determine what people believe these jobs should pay. An understanding of these distinctive characteristics must therefore lie at the heart of any attempt to set the pay of health and social care workers, and so in this section we identify what these are.

The most important distinguishing characteristic of jobs in health and social care is the training required to do these jobs. The training required to work in health and social care distinguishes these occupations from those in other parts of the economy. In Chapter 2 we explored the theory of human capital investment and saw that pay should be understood as a return on this investment. Smith described investment in human capital as 'the cost of learning the business'. People will only invest in human capital if jobs which require investment pay more than the jobs which do not. Differences in the levels of human capital investment required by different jobs are a major reason for differences in pay between jobs.

Doctors make a greater investment in human capital than do either nurses or AHPs, and therefore we should expect doctors to be paid more than nurses and AHPs. In turn, nurses invest more than do adult social care workers, and thus we would expect nurses to be paid more than adult social care workers. Differences between occupations in the private costs of human capital investment represent the first and most important explanation for differences in pay between health and social care occupations. The substantial human capital investment made by doctors is also one of the main reasons we would expect them to be amongst the most highly paid among all occupations.

Jobs in health and social care have other distinguishing characteristics which affect what they should pay. These characteristics can be grouped under four headings which correspond closely to the headings identified by Smith, they are: the type of work done; the working environment; the geographical location of work; and the rank of the job. We consider each of them in turn below.

The *type of work done* by frontline health and social care workers is evidently very different from that done by other workers. An important distinguishing characteristic of frontline work is that it requires intimate contact between the carer and the recipient of care. Moreover, frontline workers care for and treat people at some of the most challenging and distressing stages of their lives. In acute care, the interventions can be short and dramatic; in primary care workers support people who live with life-threatening and terminal conditions; and in social care, workers support people unable to care for themselves. These characteristics of the work can result in the carer becoming deeply and compassionately involved in the condition and progress of individual patients and clients.

The work requires mental resilience coupled with compassion and empathy. It may be for this reason that these jobs have been found to be particularly stressful. Recent research has recoded high rates of suicide among nurses and doctors (Nursing Standard 2019; Lancet Editorial 2017; West et al. 2016), and though this was recognized prior to the recent pandemic it appeared to increase stress levels and brought the issue to the attention of the wider public. Moreover, it was widely reported during the pandemic that the work done by residential and domiciliary care workers also generated high levels of stress. Stress is an unattractive characteristic which we would expect to find compensated by higher pay.

Yet this same characteristic, intimate contact between the carer and the recipient of care, can also generate high levels of job satisfaction. Work which restores the sick to good health or improves the condition or comfort of the infirm and frail can be satisfying and rewarding and generate levels of satisfaction seldom matched in other jobs. High levels of job satisfaction resulting from this characteristic of work might be expected to attract some to this work and thus might exert downward pressure on pay.

The nature of the *working environment* is an important distinguishing characteristic of frontline jobs. In frontline health and social care, work has to be undertaken at the designated place of work, in the residential care home, the GP practice, or the hospital. In all but a few special cases, care cannot be delivered remotely, and therefore the characteristics of the designated place of work matter. Like other people, health and social care workers prefer to work in pleasant, clean, and safe surroundings. If work is undertaken in conditions that are dirty or dangerous, we would expect the work to be compensated by higher pay rates. It has long been recognized that some jobs expose medical workers to danger (Fearns et al. 2006), although, given the range of different working environments in which frontline workers operate, exposure to health risk and danger will vary greatly between frontline jobs. Exposure to health risk will be an important consideration, exerting upward pressure on pay in some, but not all, jobs in health and social care.

The safety of the working environment is monitored and regulated through health and safety legislation, and we might therefore expect workplace safety to play a modest role in explaining pay differences. Yet during the early months of the pandemic, nurses and care workers were not supplied with the personnel protective equipment they required for safe working. This increased the exposure of frontline workers to this health risk and may have reduced their confidence in the safety of the workplace. The safety of the working environment may become an important consideration exerting upward pressure on pay in the future.

The *geographical area* where the job is located is an important driver of pay in all sectors of the economy but is of particular importance when setting the pay of health and social care workers because we find them working in almost every area of the country. There are likely to be some people from the two largest occupations, nurses and social care workers, working in almost every geographical area of the UK. The geographical area in which people work will exert a powerful influence on what they believe they should be paid for two main reasons. First, if they work in a high-cost area of the country, they will require higher rates of pay to compensate for the higher cost of living. The evidence shows that people working in high-cost areas such as capital cities are typically paid more (Elliott et al. 1999). Second, if the workplace is located in an unattractive, perhaps unsafe, locality, people will need to be paid more to attract them to work there. The location of the workplace is an important consideration when setting the pay of frontline care workers, and it seems likely it will increase in importance. This is because in jobs outside frontline care there is now increased home working and correspondingly fewer journeys to a designated place of work, but these same opportunities for home working are not available to frontline health and social care workers. We will discuss the implications of this characteristic in much greater detail in section 6.5 below.

The *status of the job* is the last of the four. Smith explained the link between the pay of a job and the status or rank in society that a job afforded as follows. 'We trust our health to the physician' and 'Such confidence could not safely be reposed in people of a very low or mean condition. Their reward must be such, therefore, as may give them that rank in society which so important a trust requires' (Smith 1776: Book 1, Chapter X, Part 1). In Smith's view, high rank was required for patients to trust physicians, and that rank resulted from what they were paid.

Here, Smith advances a rather different argument from the one which underpinned his discussion of the other characteristics. Smith argued that the other characteristics affected labour supply and through competition in labour markets would affect what jobs pay. In this case, Smith appears to be arguing that, no matter what rate of pay is warranted by the net advantages of the jobs doctors do, they should be well paid because this is a requirement for our confidence in them. Today, our confidence in the competence of doctors is conferred by their registration at the General Medical Council, and while the pay of doctors might influence our judgement of the profession, their rank in society does not determine our trust. However, the status, the rank, of an occupation will affect the appeal of an occupation,[5] and therefore affect labour supply. High status and high appeal will increase labour supply and so exert downward pressure on pay.

The status of an occupation, the position of an occupation in the ranking of occupations by level of pay, may affect the appeal of an occupation for a further reason, which is that the ranking of an occupation in the pay hierarchy determines access to scarce goods. Some goods, such things as rare paintings, rare books, antiques, seats at the leading orchestral or opera performances, period housing in desirable neighbourhoods, are in finite supply. Access to these goods is determined by what a person is paid relative to others. Put simply, access to the most desirable 1 per cent of the housing stock is afforded to the 1 per cent at the top of the income distribution: relative income and relative pay determine access to scarce goods. Occupations at the top of the ranking are able to access scarce goods more easily than occupations further down the ranking. If an occupation should slip down the ranking, accessing these goods will become more difficult, and this may be an important consideration with respect to the labour supply to some health care occupations, doctors and perhaps nurses, yet it has been little studied. In recent years, doctors[6] and nurses have slipped down the pay ranking, and declining status is likely to reduce labour supply.

In summary, the theory of net advantages directs our attention to those characteristics of jobs in health and adult social care which distinguish them from other jobs, and which must inform our judgement about what the workers doing these jobs should be paid. Some of the characteristics of frontline jobs enhance their appeal and therefore increase labour supply to these jobs, others diminish their appeal and reduce labour supply. Reviewing the above discussion, it is judged that on balance the characteristics of the jobs that frontline workers do which exert upward pressure on pay outweigh the characteristics which exert downward pressure. In competitive labour markets, pay would adjust to take account of these changes, but when pay is set by an administrative process this is much less likely to happen.

Workers in frontline jobs will have an understanding of the changes in the characteristics of the jobs they do and will take a view about how they should affect

---

[5] The link between the status of an occupation and the appeal of the occupation is also recognized in the sociological literature (Wootton 1955: 68).

[6] The New Earnings Survey reveals that in 1970, when ranked by median earnings, doctors were the third highest paid occupation for men: only company chairmen and company managers were paid more. In 2019, doctors were ranked tenth, with lawyers, pilots, CEOs, marketing managers among the occupations paid more. We should exercise some caution in interpreting these statistics, because the SOC used in 2019 provides a much finer breakdown and therefore identifies many more occupations than the system that NES used in 1970. However, this appears a very fair representation of what has happened. The same detail is not available for women doctors or nurses.

what they are paid. If they judge that their pay does not compensate them for the disadvantages of the job they are doing they will become dissatisfied and look for work elsewhere. High levels of dissatisfaction will produce high vacancy rates and, as we shall see in Section 6.7, by 2019 the vacancy rates for frontline occupations were substantially above their natural rates.

The theory of net advantages helps us understand what frontline jobs should pay. It distinguishes the characteristics of these jobs which explain why their pay should differ from that for other occupations. However, it leaves open how these jobs should be paid, and we therefore discuss this in the next section.

6.3 Paying for Output or Input: Payment-by-Results or Time Rates?

Organizations seek to link what they pay workers to a measure of the value they judge that workers produce, or put another way, what they judge workers contribute to the output of the organization. There are two main ways of measuring this contribution. The first is in terms of the output workers produce, the second is in terms of the time they spend at work. Where an organization links a worker's pay to what they produce, the payment system is called a payment-by-results (PBR) system,[7] and where they link a worker's pay to the time they spend at work, they are paying them under what is called a time rate of payment system. The former links pay directly to output, the latter links pay to a proxy for their expected output, their labour input. Labour input can be measured in terms of, hours, days, or weeks worked.

The way people are paid can have a powerful effect on their behaviour, because people respond to financial incentives. If pay is linked to what workers produce, this can encourage them to produce more. Delivery drivers are paid according to the number of deliveries they make and fruit pickers the amount of fruit they pick in order to encourage them, respectively, to make more deliveries and to pick more fruit. PBR is widely used in organizations outside health and social care, particularly in some of the newer service industries, and it was once extensively employed in UK manufacturing.

Payment-by-results has also been used in a number of important areas of frontline care in the UK. In the 1980s, England introduced a range of financial incentives to encourage GPs to meet public health objectives such as cervical screening. These payments led to a steep increase in GP activity in the targeted

---

[7] PBR is used in labour economics to describe a system for paying employees, but in health economics and health services research it is often used interchangeably with pay for performance to describe the payment system for English hospitals. Under this system, hospitals are rewarded for the volume of activity, the number of procedures they complete. PBR as discussed here should not be confused with the system for paying hospitals.

areas (Hughes and Yule 1992). In 2004, the UK introduced the Quality and Outcomes Framework (QOF) to pay GPs. This was a blended payment system which incorporated a substantial element of PBR. In the private health care sector, fee for service is a common form of payment, and PBR is still used in adult domiciliary social care in the UK.

The suitability of PBR to health and adult social care will depend on the way that health and adult social care are produced; that is, on the nature of the underlying health and social care production functions. For PBR to be effective it must be possible to measure the output that workers produce and to attribute the outputs to the efforts of one person or a small group of people. If many people are involved in producing a procedure or treatment and it is difficult to distinguish exactly how each person's contribution has affected the volume of output that has been produced, then the conditions for PBR do not exist. An example will serve to illustrate the points at issue here.

Consider the suitability of PBR for people undertaking surgical procedures such as coronary angioplasty, an operation to insert a stent. These operations are performed by teams, comprising a cardiologist, anaesthetist, and nurses. Though this is a relatively simple surgical procedure, it would be extremely difficult to distinguish the contribution to a successful operation of each individual team member. Moreover, in addition to the team in theatre, there are those involved in the pre-ops preparation of the patient and at the post-ops stage. All are important contributors to the successful outcome of the operation, though the skills of some, for example the surgeon, are more important than others. In this example, it would be difficult to identify the individual contributions to a successful outcome and therefore to relate the pay of each member of the team to their individual contribution.

Now consider a much more straightforward case, the suitability of PBR for a nurse whose only task is to give flu vaccines. The nurse could be paid a fixed fee per vaccination administered. This would encourage the nurse to administer the largest number of vaccinations possible in the time they had available. In these circumstances, PBR might appear a suitable method of payment.

However, the suitability of PBR does not mean that it is appropriate. Consider the appropriateness of PBR if giving flu vaccinations was only part of the nurses job and they had other tasks to undertake, such as dressing wounds, changing bandages, and advising on medication. In this case, a PBR scheme paying a fee for each vaccination would create a perverse incentive: it would encourage the nurse to focus on this activity to the neglect of their other duties.

Both of these examples illustrate different aspects of why PBR as a method of payment may be inappropriate in large areas of hospital care: because individual contribution cannot be distinguished and because it creates incentives to focus on the tasks that attract additional reward to the neglect of others. Now let us look at two more concrete examples where PBR schemes have been introduced in health and social care but are now widely regarded as inappropriate.

The first is that of adult social care workers employed in domiciliary care. Some organizations which provide domiciliary care services pay their workers according to the number of clients they visit but do not pay them for travel between different domiciles (Para 7.46, Low Paid Commission 2020). They do this to encourage workers to make the maximum number of visits possible in the time they have available to work. However, this also encourages them to spend the minimum amount of time feasible on each visit or, put another way, it penalizes those workers who spend more time with each patient. It also encourages workers to prioritize clients living in close proximity to one another and it discourages the care of those clients who live more remotely or inaccessibly. To counter this, organizations specify the tasks that care workers have to undertake on each visit and in some cases the elements of each task and the time that should be spent on each task. Specifying tasks in this detail and monitoring compliance requires substantial managerial input, and this has an opportunity cost; it consumes resources that could have been employed elsewhere, that might have been used to hire more care workers or pay them more. Moreover, even these refinements will not be sufficient for appropriate care because the range of tasks, their duration, and intensity will vary from one patient to another. It is difficult to see how PBR can be judged as either an efficient or effective way of paying adult social care workers.

The second example comes from primary health care in the UK, and is the QOF, which introduced an element of PBR into the GP contract in 2004. The QOF introduced payments for completing specific activities that represented either good quality care or resulted in outcomes that were in line with best clinical evidence. Payments were made for achievement against a large number of indicators, initially there were 146. Two such examples were 'the percentage of patients who had influenza immunization between September and March of the preceding year', and 'the percentage of patients with a record of measured cholesterol'. Payments were triggered when a 'threshold', a percentage of eligible patients, was achieved.[8] QOF was combined with payments to GPs which were unrelated to performance, GPs received a capitation fee, a payment for each patient registered with them, to produce a blended payment system.

Research revealed several disadvantages of the QOF. Prioritizing the attainment of targets lead to distortion of activity and the neglect of non-targeted aspects of care. In particular, it appeared to have resulted in the neglect of those aspects of care which were difficult to measure and quantify. Researchers found evidence that linking financial reward to the achievement of the pre-specified targets narrowed the focus of activity and gave rise to unintended and what was described as dysfunctional behaviour (Marshall and Roland 2017; Roland and Guthrie 2016;

---

[8] Poor design meant the QOF cost considerably more than the government had expected. It overshot by £1.76 billion, mainly because the thresholds were set too low and were thus easily attained by most GPs.

Doran et. al. 2014). The QOF appeared to contain perverse incentives because it was financially advantageous to focus on people with milder disease, rather than those with the greatest capacity to benefit (Walker et al. 2010). Finally it proved easier for practices to achieve the targets in less deprived areas because in these areas patients were more likely to present for those treatments which were the subject of targets. As a result, the QOF increased health inequalities.[9]

However, research also revealed beneficial effects of the QOF. The incentives in the QOF induced providers to improve targeted quality and to make investments in quality that extended beyond the scheme (Sutton et al. 2010). Moreover, the resulting improvements in measuring the quality of health and social care encouraged the idea that if pay can be tied to quality it could be a mechanism for improving quality (Gravelle et al. 2010).

PBR systems have shortcomings which are of particular significance to health care. It has long been recognized that this form of payment system provides powerful incentives for 'over-provision' (more provision than a fully informed purchaser would buy). This feature of PBR is particularly important in health care because of the asymmetries of knowledge between patient and doctor throughout large areas of health care. There is evidence that such over-provision has occurred in the private health care sector. The revelation of breast surgery reportedly needlessly undertaken within a private sector hospital appears to be an example.[10] The research literature also provides evidence of the potentially harmful effects of over-treatment by dentists paid under fee-for-service (Birch 1988; Chalkley and Listl 2018).

The QOF revealed that GP principals respond to financial incentives, and other research has revealed that dental practitioners do so too (Sutton et. al. 2010; Gravelle et al. 2010; Brockenhurst et. al. 2013). This may be explained by the particular circumstances of these two occupations, which are very different to those of the vast majority of workers in health and adult social care. GP principals and dental practitioners are self-employed, owner-managers of small businesses, who contract their services to the NHS, and their income is a share of the difference between practice income and costs. The commercial orientation of these small businesses should be unsurprising.

However, research into PBR in other countries has revealed that hospital doctors will also respond to financial incentives and change what they do in response

---

[9] As the weaknesses of the scheme became better known, the target conditions were steadily reduced in number and in some areas of England the scheme was substantially modified, while in Scotland it was abandoned. A recent evaluation of the overall cost-effectiveness of the QOF concluded that continuing the QOF was not cost-effective, and recommended that to improve population health efficiently, the UK should redesign the QOF or pursue alternative interventions (Pandya et al. 2018). A comprehensive review conducted by NHS England concluded there was a need to refresh the scheme 'to support a wider view of high quality care and to align better with professional values' (NHS England 2018).

[10] See https://www.theguardian.com/uk-news/2017/may/31/breast-surgeon-ian-paterson-sentenced-for-carrying-out-needless-operations

to changing rewards. It has shown that doctors have altered treatment patterns in response to changes in the relative price of different treatments (Lee et al. 2020). It has also shown that doctors who were paid for the time they worked rather than a fee for each item of treatment ran fewer tests, undertook fewer procedures per patient, held longer consultations, and provided more preventative care (Godsen et al. 1999). The research was conducted in the USA into the behaviour of doctors practising in the USA.

We should be careful about reading across from the different cultural and social context and the different institutional arrangements for providing health care that exist in the USA. Around a quarter of hospital health care providers in the US are for-profit organizations and fee for service is a prominent feature of payment systems for doctors in the USA. The health care system in the US is more commercially oriented than in the UK (Commonwealth Fund 2020). The greater orientation of US physicians toward financial goals is embedded before they enter medical school. The private costs of investment in health care human capital in the USA are several multiples those in the UK and graduates from US medical schools emerge with levels of debt several orders of magnitude greater than in the UK. The financial imperative to pay off that debt and to secure a return on the investment is much stronger in the US than the UK. It is therefore not surprising that US doctors respond more overtly to financial incentives than might doctors in the UK.

Finally, an important reason why payment-by-results systems might not be appropriate for much of frontline care is the motivation of many, or most, people attracted to this work. If people are, as we discussed in Section 2.3, attracted to this work by some intrinsic motivation, this will reduce their responsiveness to financial incentives. In which case, a PBR system will prove much less effective and a time rate payment system will be more appropriate. How pay should be structured under such a system is discussed in the next section.

6.4 The Role of Incremental Scales

Time rate of payment systems define contribution in terms of time spent at work and tie pay to the units in which time is measured: hours, weeks, months, or years. In some areas of adult social care, payment is per hour or week, while in much of health care, payment is specified as an annual salary, and the amount that a worker receives depends on the proportion of the year they work. Most people paid annual salaries will be paid on a salary scale which contains a number of steps, or increments, each offering a higher salary. For this reason, these salary scales are also called incremental scales. Higher steps are usually accessed by either years of service or assessed performance. Most salary scales are uprated, all points on the scale are increased, annually.

The underlying economic rationale for a salary scale where an increment is awarded at the end of each of the initial years of service is that workers' performance increases during these early years. Performance increases because workers learn through experience, acquiring new skills and competences as they undertake a variety of different tasks and are exposed to different work settings. This type of learning is seldom recognized by the award of qualifications and so remains undocumented, it constitutes a type of informal training.

An additional reason for paying frontline health and social care workers on incremental scales is that they can be structured to encourage continuity of service. Continuity of service is a necessary condition for continuity of care, which is judged to be of particular importance in some health, and particularly social care, settings. The elderly and vulnerable, in both residential and domiciliary settings, are reported to place great value on attendance by the same care worker, by a 'familiar face'. Salary scales can be structured to reward long service through the addition of salary points at the top of the scale, which can only be accessed by long service.

The award of annual increments produces a time profile of pay like the stepped profile in Figure 6.1. The stepped profile shows pay increasing through the award of a pay increase at the end of each year, an annual increment, as reward for improved productivity and proficiency. This profile of pay growth contrasts with the actual profile of productivity and proficiency growth, indicated by the broken line; both are likely to increase much more continuously during the first few years of service. The award of the annual increment constitutes recognition of improved performance during the previous year. Job evaluation techniques can be used to distinguish the years during which performance increases and therefore the number of 'steps', the number of annual increments, on the pay scale.

Incentives to improved performance can be incorporated within salary scales by making incremental progression within a scale conditional on assessed

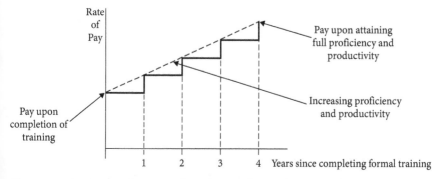

Figure 6.1 Pay Progression upon Completion of Formal Training (＿＿ indicates pay progression)

performance. Superior performance can be rewarded by accelerated progression up the scale and unsatisfactory performance penalized by withholding progression. Who undertakes the assessment of performance is important. If it is undertaken by co-workers or superiors it can lead to issues related to favouritism and bias. The transparency of the assessment process is central to worker confidence in such schemes.

Incremental payment systems can also be structured to offer incentives for improved performance by splitting them into a number of separate scales and making access to the higher scales conditional on promotion. If improved current performance increases the prospect of promotion in the future, it incentivizes current performance. How much it incentivizes improved performance depends on the size of the rewards from promotion. Promotion rewards relative performance: the promoted person has performed better than other people.

Rewarding relative performance is something that happens in a tournament, where the prize goes to the person who has performed better than all other competitors. It is for this reason that we can think of incremental payment systems which offer opportunities for promotion as tournaments (Lazear and Rosen 1981). These systems do not require measuring performance in fine detail, and thus promotion is a way of motivating performance when it is difficult to measure the detail of performance, promotion requires only that the better performing workers are identified. Because of the complexity of the jobs that most frontline workers do, incremental payment systems which incorporate promotion are particularly appropriate in health and social care.

6.5 The Importance of Geographical Pay Variation

The theory of net advantages reveals that the geographical area in which the job is located is an important driver of pay. Geographical variations in the pay of the different health and social care occupations should be built into incremental payment systems. Frontline health and social care workers are to be found working in every geographical labour market in the UK and the conditions in these labour markets differ between areas. Conditions differ because of factors on both the demand and supply side of the labour market. On the demand side people in different areas have different health and social care needs, and so the provision of health and social care services and the demand for the occupations which provide these services differs between areas. On the supply side people find working in some areas more attractive than working in others because there are differences in the amenities and the cost of living in different areas. We would expect these differences in supply and demand to result in different rates of pay in different areas.

In the UK, the differences between areas in the demand for health and social care occupations reflects in part differences in the funding allocated to meet health and social care needs. NHS activity is supported by funding allocated through formulae by the four UK administrations. The formulae allocate funds to Care Commissioners in England and Northern Ireland and Health Boards in Scotland and Wales. The formulae are intended to reflect differences in population need for health care, which are predicted using the age and gender composition of the populations and indicators of life circumstances, such as deprivation. In England, the formulae also take account of differences in the costs of providing health care services. Commissioning Groups and Health Boards then allocate the resources delivered through the formula to meet local priorities. The health care services which are funded result in differences between areas in both the level and composition of labour demand.

On the supply side of the labour market there are differences in the attractiveness of the areas in which frontline workers work. Areas differ in the attractiveness of the physical environment and in the employment opportunities they afford the partners of frontline workers, in their facilities for schooling children, in recreational and cultural amenities, and in their remoteness and rurality. Moreover, the attractiveness of an area as a place to work is determined by the characteristics of both the area and those surrounding it from which people can travel to work. Travelling to and from work, commuting, from one area to another involves time and expense and people take this into account when deciding whether to live in the area in which they work or commute over a longer distance. If they avoid living in an unattractive area by commuting, this will involve more time and greater expense.

On the supply side there are also cost of living differences. The cost of living is higher in some areas of the UK than it is in others, and because what matters to workers is the goods and services that they can buy with their pay—their real not their nominal pay—they will judge high-cost areas less attractive than low-cost areas because in high-cost areas their pay will buy fewer goods and services. One of the major drivers of differences in the cost of living is the price of accommodation. House prices are a proxy for this, but a poor proxy, because they reflect both the price of accommodation and the price of housing as an investment. A house is both a consumption good, it provides accommodation, and an investment good, an asset which people buy for investment purposes. In consequence, house prices in different areas of the country reflect differences in the attractiveness of housing as an investment good. Moreover, housing provides consumption services additional to accommodation, such as access to high-quality schooling where school places are allocated to those resident within a school's local area. For all these reasons, house price differences are far from an exact measure of cost-of-living differences.

Nonetheless, there are substantial differences in the cost of living between different areas of the UK, and when workers in an occupation are paid the same regardless of the area of the country in which they work, labour supply will be higher in lower cost areas and lower in high-cost areas. It will also be higher in areas judged attractive and lower in those judged less attractive. This means employers will need to pay more if they are to attract people to work in the less attractive, higher cost areas, and for this reason we should expect nominal rates of pay to vary geographically.[11]

Figure 6.2 provides a stylized illustration of a geographic profile of nominal rates of pay which compensate for differences in the cost of living and attractiveness of different areas. Rates of pay are lowest in the lowest cost, most attractive areas of the country and highest in the least attractive, highest cost areas. In the UK the lowest cost, most attractive areas are likely to be rural areas, while the highest cost, least attractive are the inner boroughs of some of our major cities. The actual shape of the schedule is of course an empirical matter, and will be discussed later in Chapter 7.

Where pay is set in competitive labour markets competition for workers and jobs would be expected to give rise to a geographical profile of nominal pay similar to that in Figure 6.2. However, where pay is set through an administrative process, the geographical profile can look very different. This is because there appears to be much less agreement among pay setters that real pay differences caused by geographical variations in the cost of living, still less those warranted by differences in the attractiveness of different areas, should result in differences in nominal pay. This contrasts with widespread recognition on the part of pay setters that pay

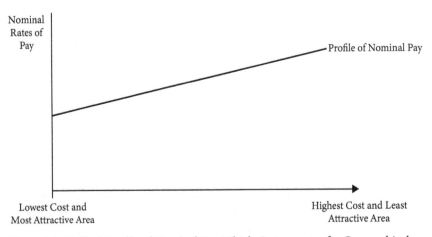

Figure 6.2 Stylized Profile of Nominal Pay Which Compensates for Geographical Differences in the Cost of Living and Amenity of Different Areas

---

[11] This does not ignore the fact that some people will be attracted to dangerous, 'edgy' urban environments with poor amenities and that people vary in their taste for different amenities. However, if the numbers with the taste are insufficient to meet the demand for people to work in the areas with the characteristics then additional compensation will need to be offered to induce a sufficient number of people to work in these areas.

should be adjusted annually, often with the declared intention of offsetting all or some part of the rate of inflation, and therefore that, at least in this context, real pay matters. In health care, the objection to geographical pay differences appears to reflect the preferences of those who negotiate on behalf of health care workers who believe that there should be a 'rate for the job' regardless of the differences in real rates of pay that result. The consequence is substantial differences between areas in real rates of pay for occupations in health and adult social care and substantial differences in vacancy and turnover rates between areas, as we shall see in section 6.8.

6.6 Measuring Departures from Equilibrium

In Section 4.2 we discussed the concept of an equilibrium rate of pay. We saw that it is central to the economics of the labour market and should sit in the minds of all involved in setting pay. In Section 4.3 we identified the forces that are set in motion if we depart from equilibrium. There we saw that the magnitude of any labour shortage (or surplus) will depend upon how far pay was from the equilibrium rate. The magnitude of any labour shortage is measured by the difference between labour demand and labour supply and where demand exceeds supply results in job vacancies.

The relationship between the level of pay and vacancies is illustrated in Figure 6.3. At P_1, in Figure 6.3 pay is below the equilibrium rate and there is a labour shortage, employers are unable to hire all the labour they want. The magnitude of the shortage is given by the difference between the labour that is demanded at pay level P_1, as indicated by N_2, and the number of people that are willing to supply labour at this rate of pay as indicated by N_1 and the magnitude of the shortage is therefore N_2-N_1. The labour shortage will mean that advertised vacancies remain unfilled even after employers have hired all the labour that wants to work at pay level P_1.

It can also be seen that there is a labour shortage at the higher rate of pay P_2, though here the magnitude of the shortage is less than at P_1. This shows that the magnitude of the shortage depends on how far pay is from the equilibrium rate, the rate at which the labour supply and demand schedules intersect. Evidently, P_2 is closer to the equilibrium rate than P_1 and the magnitude of the shortage is accordingly smaller.

At P_1 vacancies are above the equilibrium, or natural vacancy rate—recall that the natural vacancy rate is the vacancy rate associated with a normal rate of labour turnover and equilibrium in the labour market. This means that at the point at which the labour supply and demand schedules intersect, equilibrium, there will be some vacancies, but these are vacancies which employers are able to

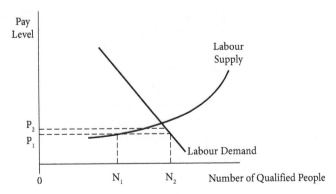

Figure 6.3 Measuring the Shortage

fill. It follows that N_2-N_1, represents a measure of excess or, what we might call hard-to-fill, vacancies.

As should be evident from Figure 6.3 a simple count of vacancies, N_2-N_1, will not reveal the seriousness of the labour shortage. The seriousness of the shortage is only revealed once we take into account the size of an organizations workforce; the seriousness is revealed once we express the number of vacancies as a proportion of either the current or the intended level of employment. In Figure 6.3, N_2-N_1 could be expressed either as a proportion of N_1, the current level of employment, giving N_2-N_1/N_1 or as a proportion of N_2 the intended level of employment, giving N_2-N_1/N_2. In both cases, the number of vacancies has been standardized by taking account of the size of the organization's current workforce. Once vacancy rates have been computed they can be compared to the natural vacancy rate or to the rates in other occupations and areas. Many areas of the public sector such as education and public administration and defence, and all industries and services calculate the vacancy rate as:

$$\frac{Number\ of\ Vacancies}{Current\ Employment} \times 100$$

However, the NHS and adult social care calculate their vacancy rates as:

$$\frac{Number\ of\ Vacancies}{Total\ Intended\ Workforce} \times 100$$

where the total intended workforce is the current level of employment plus the number of vacancies. The vacancy rate is clearly going to be lower, for any given number of vacancies, if the vacancy rate is calculated in the way the NHS calculates vacancy rates because the denominator includes the number of vacancies and is therefore larger. It is reasonable to argue that the way the NHS calculates its vacancy rates understates the seriousness of its labour shortages.

At this juncture a number of points need to be made. First, as we saw in Figure 6.3, the vacancy rate falls as pay increases. This is because two things are happening—first, employers are only willing to employ the more productive workers at these higher rates of pay and so as pay rises we move back up the labour demand schedule and labour demand falls. Second, the higher rates of pay mean that people who will only work for higher pay are once again looking for work, and so we also move up the labour supply schedule. As we move up the labour demand schedule, N_2 is no longer the target level of employment, and as we move up the labour supply schedule, N_1 is no longer the quantity of labour that is supplied. For both these reasons, the number of vacancies and the vacancy rate in excess of the natural rate are falling as pay increases.

How much the vacancy rate falls as pay rises will depend upon the slopes of the labour supply and demand schedules. If labour supply is particularly unresponsive to wage change, if labour supply is inelastic, the vacancy rate will fall slowly as pay rises. Again, if the additional labour that could be employed adds little of value, if the labour demand schedule is steeply sloped, is inelastic, the vacancy rate will fall slowly as pay rises. Where either or both schedules are steeply sloped, the vacancy rate will remain stubbornly high in the face of rising pay.

A further point to remember is that pay represents the rate of return on human capital investment. If pay is below its equilibrium level, the rate of return on human capital is below its equilibrium level. Thus, a vacancy rate above the natural rate also signals that the rate of return on human capital investment is below its equilibrium level and the incentives to invest in human capital are weaker, and thus it portends future labour shortages.

A final point to bear in mind is that our focus has been on the average vacancy rate of an occupation and there may be quite substantial variations around the average. The vacancy rate may differ at different points on the salary scale, indicating that the competitiveness of pay differs at different points along the scale. For example, the pay scale may offer attractive rewards for new entrants but fail to offer sufficient reward to experienced workers, with the consequence that while the organization has little trouble attracting people to work for it, it cannot retain experienced workers. Thus, even though the vacancy rate for the occupation might be at its natural level, the organization is losing experienced workers. A way to reveal this is to calculate vacancy rates for cohorts of workers with different experience.[12]

---

[12] A cohort is a group of workers with a shared characteristic such as age or the year of joining the organization.

6.7 Vacancy Rates in Frontline Care

What, then, was the position in frontline health and social care prior to the onset of the pandemic? In this section we provide an overview of the situation in the four countries of the UK in 2019. The procedures for recording and reporting vacancies differ between the four countries of the UK and they have undergone several changes in recent years, as different authorities have taken on responsibility for recording vacancies. As a result, it is impossible to build up a picture of how vacancies have evolved through time, to detail the vacancy rates for each of the main frontline occupations in the four countries, or to reveal how they differ between primary, secondary, and social care sectors in the four countries. The data to enable this, if it is collected, are not in the public domain.

The average vacancy rates for the three largest occupational groups in the NHS in England, Northern Ireland, and Scotland at end of 2019 are shown in Table 6.1.[13] The Table reveals that the rates vary substantially both between occupations and countries. The vacancy rate for qualified nurses stood at 11.1 per cent in both England and Northern Ireland in 2019, which is the highest of any occupation in the three countries. In both countries the rate for qualified nurses was much higher than that for doctors; higher by nearly four percentage points in England and by 7.5 percentage points in Northern Ireland. In Scotland, the rate for qualified nurses was half that in England and Northern Ireland and, at 5.6 per cent, was lower than that for doctors in Scotland. There also appeared to be variation between the vacancy rate for AHPs in the three countries,[14] with the rates highest in Northern Ireland. What is striking about the rates reported in Table 6.1 is just how high they were in 2019, the year immediately prior to the onset of the pandemic. More than one in every nine nursing posts was vacant in England and Northern Ireland and one in every thirteen doctors posts was vacant in England and Scotland.

We can see just how different these rates were from those in the rest of the economy at that time by comparing them to both the rates in the rest of the public sector and those in the private sector. The Office for National Statistics monitors trends in vacancies in England across the public and private sectors. The data for 2019 reveal that the vacancy rate was 1.9 per cent in Education, 1.6 per cent in Public Administration and Defence, and across all industries it was 2.8 per cent (ONS 2019a and 2022).

---

[13] In 2012, the Welsh government said it would no longer publish the biannual statistics on doctor and nurse vacancies following a public consultation. The Royal College of Nursing, Wales (2019, p7) report that 'the Welsh Government and/or NHS Wales fail to publish national figures for nursing vacancies in the NHS using an agreed definition of what constitutes a vacancy'. Commenting that 'this is a critical indicator of the pressure specific Health Boards or disciplines are under', 'which is published in the other countries of the UK'.

[14] Scotland reports vacancy rates for AHPs while England reports those for other workers, many of whom will be AHPs, and Northern Ireland reports those for professional and technical staff, the vast majority of whom are AHPs, but which also includes scientists and technical officers.

Table 6.1 Vacancy Rates in the NHS in England, Northern Ireland, and Scotland in 2019

	England	Scotland	Northern Ireland
	2019 4th Quarter	2019 December	2019
Nurses (and midwives in Scotland)	11.1	5.6	11.1
Doctors* (consultants only in Scotland)	7.2	8.2	3.6
Other Staff (AHPs in Scotland)	6.8	5.7	8.4**
Total Workforce	8.1	N/A	8.2

Note: *In Scotland and Norther Ireland, includes a very small number of hospital dental consultant vacancies. **Includes scientists, scientist support, medical technical officer and assistant technical officer
Source: England, NHS Vacancy Statistics, NHS Improvement Vacancy Statistics 2020; Northern Ireland health and social care (HSC) workforce vacancies, December 2021, Department of Health; NHS Education for Scotland, TURAS Data, Workforce, Vacancy Data, 1 March 2022. Data for Wales are unavailable. See Footnote 13

In England, NHS Digital now have responsibility for reporting vacancy rates for doctors and qualified nurses. Data on a consistent basis, a new Experimental Series, are available only from 2017/18 onwards. The data reveal little change in the annual vacancy rates for doctors and qualified nurses in 2017/18 and 2018/19, the two years immediately prior to the pandemic. A longer run view of trends in vacancy rates is available for Scotland.[15] Data from 2011 for doctors and AHPs and from 2015 for nurses and midwives show that vacancy rates have been rising for some time. In March 2015, the nursing and midwifery vacancy rate was 3.5 per cent, but this had risen to 5.6 per cent at the end of 2019. In December 2011, the consultant's vacancy rate was 2.7 per cent but had risen to 8.2 per cent by the end of 2019, while the AHPs vacancy rate was around 1.8 per cent in 2011 but had risen to 5.7 per cent by the end of 2019.

Nursing vacancy rates in Scotland increased by more than two percentage points over the four years to 2019, while vacancy rates for AHPs trebled and those for consultants more than doubled over the longer period from 2011. Scotland therefore entered the pandemic with vacancy rates much higher than previously. In England, vacancy rates for qualified nurses were also very high in the years immediately prior to the pandemic and indeed they were much higher than in Scotland.

---

[15] Source: NHS Education for Scotland, TURAS Data, Workforce, Vacancy Data, 1 March 2022. See: https://turasdata.nes.nhs.scot/data-and-reports/official-workforce-statistics/all-official-statistics-publications/01-march-2022-workforce/dashboards/nhsscotland-workforce/?pageid=6429

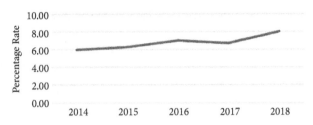

Figure 6.4 Vacancy Rates in Adult Social Care in England: 2013–2018

Source: ONS Adult social care vacancy rate, England, financial year ending 2013 to financial year ending 2018

ONS have also reported the vacancy rates in adult social care in England from 2014. Over the years between 2014 and 2018 the vacancy rate in adult social care climbed steadily from 6 to 8 per cent, as shown in Figure 6.4. The high vacancy rates in adult social care have been reported as due to the perceived low status of the work, low pay, poor training, poor levels of in-work support, and few opportunities for career progression (Health Foundation 2019).

It is important to set these vacancy rates in context. The 'all industries and services' vacancy rate at the end of 2019 was, at 2.8 per cent, close to what has historically been judged the natural rate of vacancies.[16] There is no compelling reason to believe that the natural rates in adult social care and in frontline health care occupations in the NHS are much different; they too are likely around 3 per cent. It is therefore clear that, prior to the onset of the pandemic, vacancy rates in adult social care in England and for frontline workers in the NHS in England, Scotland, and Northern Ireland were above their natural rates, in some cases very substantially so. These vacancy rates signal that the level of pay for these occupations was too low to attract the required numbers.

Apart from the ONS data for England there is little systematic collection of data on vacancies in social care, so we do not know how vacancy rates in social care differ between the nations of the UK. Moreover, there is no systematic collection of vacancy data for health care occupations outwith the NHS.

6.8 Geographical Differences in Vacancy Rates

The average vacancy rates for doctors and nurses reported in the previous section mask very substantial differences in the rates in different areas. Vacancy rates for

---

[16] The natural vacancy rate in the UK was judged to be around 3 per cent in the years prior to the pandemic. Post-pandemic, the rate may have risen; at the time of writing, the labour market appears to be exhibiting greater churn, or higher rates of labour turnover than in the period up to 2019.

doctors and nurses in different areas of England and Scotland[17] are reported in Tables 6.2 and 6.3 respectively. The data for England are compiled by NHS Digital, which reports vacancy rates for the two main groups of NHS workers, nurses, and doctors in seven regions of England. The Scottish data is richer, reporting vacancy data for three groups of workers by Health Board. Though both sets of data are far from sufficient to reveal the true extent of area differences in vacancy rates, they provide enough evidence to suggest that they are likely to be substantial.

Table 6.2 shows the regions with the highest and lowest vacancy rates for registered nurses and doctors in England in 2018/19. The highest rate for nurses was in London, while the highest rate for doctors was in the East of England. The lowest rate for nurses was in the North East and Yorkshire while the lowest rate for doctors was in the South West. The difference in rates between the highest and lowest regions was substantial. Among doctors, the rate in the highest vacancy region was more than double that in the lowest region, while among nurses, the rate in the highest region was almost double that of the lowest region and more than six percentage points above the lowest region.

The geographical variation in vacancy rates in Scotland is revealed in data reported by Health Boards. Most Health Board areas are much smaller than English regions and some have very small populations; those of Orkney and Shetland are each a little over 22,000. Table 6.3 reveals very substantial variations in the vacancy rates among Health Boards. The highest vacancy rate among consultants was 40.4 per cent in Shetland and the lowest just 3.6 per cent in Lothian, the Board which serves Edinburgh. The two Health Boards are of course of very different size, and the number of consultants employed by Lothian far exceeds the number employed by Shetland. The vacancy rate in Shetland amounted to just over seven full-time equivalent posts, while the rate in Lothian equaled thirty-four posts.

Table 6.2   Vacancy Rates in the NHS Regions of England (2018/19 Q4)

	Average All Regions	Region with Lowest Rate	Region with Highest Rate
Registered Nurses	11.1	7.8 North East and Yorkshire	14.1 London
Doctors	7.2	4.1 South West	9.2 East of England

Source: NHS Digital, NHS Vacancy Statistics, April 2015, December 2021 Experimental Statistics, Excel Tables. Publication date 3 March 2022

[17] Northern Ireland does not publish a breakdown of vacancies by occupation and region or area.

Table 6.3 NHS Nurse, Consultant, and AHP Vacancy Rates in the Health Boards of Scotland, December 2019

	Average All Regions	Region with Lowest Rate	Region with Highest Rate
Nurses and Midwives	5.6	0.5 Ayrshire and Arran	8.7 Highland
Consultants	8.2	3.6 Lothian	40.4 Shetland
AHPs	5.7	1.5 Ayrshire and Arran	10.9 Borders

Source: NHS Education for Scotland, TURAS Data, Workforce, Vacancy Data, 1 March 2022

Amongst nurses and midwives, the region with the highest rate was Highland at 8.7 per cent, and the region with the lowest was Ayrshire and Arran at 0.5 per cent. Ayrshire and Arran was again the Health Board reporting the lowest vacancy rate for AHPs at 1.5 per cent, while Borders was the Health Board with the highest rate of 10.9 per cent. In both Scotland and England, there is evidently very substantial geographical variation in vacancy rates for nurses and doctors.

The regions reported in Tables 6.2 and 6.3 are in general far too large to reveal the true extent of the geographical variation in vacancy rates, and they do not remotely, save perhaps in the case of nurses in the two Scottish Islands, conform to the labour markets from which the hospitals and other health care providers recruit their labour. The detailed data we require to allow us to dig deeper and reveal the full extent of differences in vacancy rates between areas are not in the public domain.

However there is research which looked in depth at this issue. This research reported average vacancy rates in the NHS for doctors and nurses over the period 2003 to 2006 at the detailed level of 230 local authority districts in England. It revealed substantial geographical variation during a period when both nursing and doctor vacancy rates were much lower than in 2019 (Elliott et al. 2010). The average vacancy rate for nurses at that time was 2.5 per cent, but around this average there was a standard deviation of 2.8 per cent and one local authority district reported a rate of 16.9 per cent. For doctors, the average vacancy rate at the time was higher than that for nurses at 4.6 per cent. Around this average, the standard deviation was 4.8 per cent and the rate in the highest vacancy area was 22.1 per cent. Though this was a period of generally low vacancy rates, it is clear that hospitals in some areas of England were finding it extremely difficult to recruit doctors and nurses. These area differences in vacancy rates provided evidence of substantial geographic differences in the competitiveness of frontline workers' pay, and we shall return to this issue in Section 7.5.

6.9 Summary and Conclusions

This chapter has detailed the theory which should inform the inquiries and deliberations of those tasked with setting the pay of frontline health and social care workers. It has identified the payment systems most appropriate for frontline workers, discussed how labour shortage should be measured, and identified the magnitude of these shortages in frontline labour markets in the years to 2019. The key points to take away from this chapter are outlined below.

The theory of net advantages developed by Adam Smith nearly 250 years ago provides the framework required to understand what frontline workers believe their jobs should pay. It states that it is the characteristics of their jobs that affect their beliefs and which therefore affect their labour market behaviour. It directs our attention to the advantages and disadvantages of frontline jobs and it is central to understanding the dynamics of health and social care labour markets.

The theory identifies five sets of characteristics which will enable us to distinguish the key features of frontline jobs. The first is the level of human capital investment required to do these jobs. Pay represents the rate of return on human capital investment, and differences in the scale of the investment workers have made is the principal explanation for differences in rates of pay between occupations in health and social care. Human capital theory explains why doctors are paid more than nurses and AHPs, and why they in turn are paid more than adult social care workers.

The second is the type of work done by frontline health and social care workers, which is very different from that done by workers in other jobs. Frontline work involves intimate contact between the carer and the people cared for or treated, people who are encountered at some of the most challenging and distressing stages of their lives. It was proposed that this could account for the high levels of stress reported to be experienced by frontline workers and the higher rates of suicide among nursing and medical workers than among workers in other jobs. The recent Covid-19 pandemic revealed that the work done by residential and domiciliary care workers also generates high levels of stress.

The third set of characteristics is the working environment, and this is a more important consideration for frontline workers than for many other workers. Frontline work has to be undertaken at the designated place of work because, in all but a few special cases, care has to be delivered personally. For this reason, the characteristics of the designated place of work matter to health and social care workers. The environment in which frontline workers work can expose them to health risk, as happened during the early months of the Covid-19 pandemic. Jobs outwith frontline care offer opportunities for working from home, something not available to frontline workers.

The fourth characteristic is the geographical area in which a person works. Pay must reflect conditions in the area in which the workplace is located. If the workplace is located in a high-cost area of the country, people will require higher nominal pay to compensate for the higher cost of living. If the workplace is located in an unattractive, perhaps unsafe, locality, people will need to be paid more to attract them to work there. Nominal rates of pay must vary to take account of differences in the cost of living and amenity, of different areas. Though there are practical difficulties finely calibrating nominal rates to fully reflect local variations in the cost of living and amenity, failure to do so will result in differences in vacancy rates between areas of the UK.

The final characteristic is the status of the job. The status of a job is associated with the ranking of a job in the pay hierarchy. The status of a job determines the appeal of a job and therefore affects the supply of labour to a job. The ranking of an occupation also matters because ranking determined access to scarce goods. In the past, doctors were at or near the top of the pay ranking, but this appears to have changed, as we shall see in the next chapter. Status may be an important consideration with respect to the labour supply to some health care occupations, doctors and perhaps nurses, but it has been little studied.

The theory of net advantages represented the conceptual framework required to determine what frontline workers should be paid. A further consideration was how they should be paid: under PBR or a time rate payment system? There were several reasons why it was inappropriate to pay frontline workers under PBR. The first was because of the difficulty of distinguishing with any accuracy the magnitude of individual contribution in many areas of work; improved health and social care are frequently the result of teamwork. The second was because PBR can provide powerful incentives for 'over-provision', which is of particular concern in health care because of asymmetries of knowledge between health care providers and patients. The third was because PBR can distort activity by providing incentives to narrow the focus of care to the neglect of other aspects of care. The fourth was because PBR can produce perverse incentives to focus on those patients who are easiest to treat rather than those with the greatest capacity to benefit. Additionally there was the argument that if workers are intrinsically motivated to choose frontline work, this reduces their responsiveness to financial incentives. To pay frontline workers by results appeared inappropriate for all these reasons.

The alternative to PBR was a time rate payment system. This type of payment system can be designed to reward experience and, through opportunities for promotion, can incentivize performance. The length of the incremental scale for an occupation should correlate with the period over which worker productivity improves through experience. The payment system should include higher salary scales accessed through promotion. Like tournaments, this will incentivize individual performance where it is difficult to accurately measure a person's performance.

Identifying and setting the equilibrium rate of pay should be the principal objective of wage setters, as failure to set this rate will result in either shortages or surpluses of labour. If it is the former, health or social care services that people value are not being produced. If it is the latter, people who will likely have invested substantial resource in health care human capital will find their investment goes unrewarded, and this acts as a deterrent to others to undertake similar investment. If pay setters fail to identify and establish an equilibrium rate of pay, forces will be set in motion which will destabilize the labour market as workers respond to labour market imbalance.

The concept of equilibrium implies balance, in the context of the labour market, balance between the aspirations of workers as to the rewards they expect to earn from the work they do, and the expectations of their employers about the value they will produce relative to what they are paid. The quality of the information that pay setters have at their disposal to enable them to identify and adjust toward the equilibrium rates is of vital importance.

High-quality vacancy data are key to understanding the balance between supply and demand in occupational labour markets. Vacancy data provide the essential measure of labour market imbalance. The quality of vacancy data in health and social care leaves a great deal to be desired. If vacancy data are to perform the task required, there must be clear and straightforward criteria setting out what constitutes a vacancy and they must be recorded at a level of detail sufficient to interpret the position in each labour market.

Vacancy data measure labour market balance and are therefore central to the pay-setting process. There is balance when vacancy rates are at their natural rates. The concept of the natural vacancy rate informs us that the goal of pay setting can never be zero vacancies, that there will always be labour market churn, and that the natural rate therefore lies above zero. However, the average vacancy rates for doctors and nurses in England and Scotland in 2019, prior to the onset of the pandemic, were above their natural rates, in some cases substantially so. They provided prima facia evidence that in 2019 average pay rates for these occupations were below their competitive levels, and in some cases very seriously below. Vacancy rates in 2019 also revealed substantial geographical variation. They revealed that in many areas of Scotland and England frontline workers' pay was uncompetitive, and in some areas again seriously so. In the next chapter, we will look at the data on the pay of frontline workers and detail how the pay of these workers has changed in recent decades.

7

Setting the Pay of Frontline Care Workers in Practice

In previous chapters we have looked at the economic theories which explain why people want to work in frontline health and social care, and how organizations delivering health and social care decide how many workers to employ. We have explored the concept of labour market equilibrium and, to the extent that vacancy data would allow, detailed how the labour markets for the three largest health and social care occupations were, in the period immediately prior to the onset of the Covid-19 pandemic, very far from achieving balance. We detailed the substantial geographic variation in vacancy rates and how foreign-born, and largely foreign-trained, workers contributed to labour supply in both health and social care but were too few to balance the market. Now we turn to consider the reasons for this imbalance in the years prior to the pandemic; we detail what happened to the pay of frontline workers over this period.

Pay plays a pivotal role in labour markets. Pay compensates workers for the advantages and disadvantages of the jobs they do and provides a return on their prior investment in human capital. The competitiveness of their pay now and in the recent past will affect their morale and their current labour market decisions. It will also affect human capital investment decisions taken today and therefore future labour supply. It is therefore of critical importance that we understand what has happened to the relative pay of frontline health and social care workers in recent years.

In the previous chapter we outlined the economic theories which should inform pay setting for health and social care workers and distinguished the payment systems appropriate for these workers. What remains is to examine the extent to which these principles are being realized in practice. In this chapter we look at the existing pay setting arrangements in more detail and at their outcomes. We discuss the strengths and weaknesses of the available pay data and that used by those involved in setting the pay of health care workers. We chart what has happened to the pay of the largest frontline health occupations relative to that of other workers over the past fifty years (we cannot go back any further) and we compare the lifetime returns to investment in health care human capital to the lifetime returns to other types of human capital investment. First we describe how the pay of health and social care workers is set today.

The Economics of the UK Health and Social Care Labour Market. Robert Elliott, Oxford University Press.
© Robert Elliott (2024). DOI: 10.1093/oso/9780198883142.003.0007

7.1 Administrative Pay Setting in Frontline Care in the UK

Frontline health care workers in the NHS are paid on UK-wide, national, pay scales. Nurses and AHPs across the UK working in the NHS are paid under a UK-wide pay and grading structure. Called Agenda for Change, it was introduced in 2004 and covers all NHS frontline workers with the exception of doctors and dentists. Within this structure, jobs are allocated to pay bands, incremental pay scales, as a result of job evaluation. Each pay scale contains a small number of different salary levels and, conditional on delivering satisfactory performance, which is decided through an annual appraisal, workers advance up the scale with each additional year of service until they reach the scale maximum. In most years these scales are uprated through the implementation of an annual pay award.

The basic pay for a grade or occupation is approximately the same across all Trusts and Health Boards in the four nations of the UK.[1] NHS nurses and AHPs are paid a basic salary which is related to the hours they work each week, and nurses and most AHPs (all those in Grades 1–7) receive additional pay for working overtime and bank holidays and shift pay for working nights. Those working in Greater London and the counties immediately surrounding London (called the fringe zone) receive supplements to pay which are designed to compensate for the higher cost of living in these areas. In Inner London, the supplement amounts to an additional 20 per cent of basic pay.

NHS hospital doctors are paid a basic salary under UK-wide salary scales with customized scales for doctors in training, specialty and associate (SAS) doctors, and consultants. Under each of these scales, salary progression is related to years of service. Doctors in training receive a number of supplements. They receive additional pay for any hours over forty per week and they are also paid a substantial enhancement for working nights (37 per cent in 2019) an allowance for working at weekends and an availability allowance if they are required to be available on call. Consultants can apply for local and national Clinical Excellence Awards[2] which are intended to reward work over and above the basic job requirements. Consultants are also paid more if they take on extra management or education responsibilities, and they can supplement their salary by working in private practice. All doctors working for a London NHS Trust are paid a London Allowance providing an additional 5 per cent to basic salary.

Some of the additions to the basic pay of nurses, AHPs, doctors in training, and consultants offer scope for differentiating pay between hospitals and geographic

---

[1] In recent years the devolved governments of Scotland, Northern Ireland, and Wales have on occasion awarded higher pay increases than England. This has resulted in a small divergence in rates of pay on the national salary scales.

[2] Since 2022, called Clinical Impact Awards. Their counterpart, Distinction Awards, were frozen in Scotland in 2010, since when no new awards have been made.

areas, but the scope for doing this is restricted by national guidelines. Geographical variations in what NHS workers are paid is modest.

In England and Wales, major changes to terms and conditions of service, such as new or revised salary scales, are negotiated between the trade unions representing NHS workers and NHS Employers (England) and NHS Wales Employers. In Scotland and Northern Ireland, direct negotiations between the trade unions and government do the same thing. The three largest trade unions representing front-line workers in the UK are the Royal College of Nursing, representing qualified nurses and midwives, the British Medical Association, representing doctors, and Unison, representing some qualified nurses and midwives, health visitors, health care assistants, and social care workers. Unison represents about 500,000 frontline workers, the RCN about 460,000, and the BMA about 160,000.

In all four nations, the annual uprating of the national pay scales is decided by the governments, and in each country this decision is informed by the rec-ommendations of two review bodies, the Review Body on Doctors' and Dentists' Remuneration (DDRB) and the NHS Pay Review Body (NHSPRB). The former covers doctors and dentists; the latter all NHS workers, except these two and the most senior NHS managers. In all nations, employers and trade unions sub-mit evidence for the scrutiny of the two review bodies. The Review Bodies were established to undertake independent scrutiny of all the available evidence and to make recommendations for pay increases based upon this scrutiny. In practice, this scrutiny appears to have placed little weight on labour market imbalance, and though it was expected that this independent and arm's-length approach to uprat-ing pay would result in the recommendations being implemented in full, this often did not happen. As a result, the usefulness and independence of this process has been increasingly questioned by the trade unions.

In addition to those employed in the NHS there are doctors, nurses, and AHPs employed in the community and the private health care sector. These employers are not tied to pay under national pay scales, though they are likely to follow the uprating of pay for comparable workers in the NHS. In some other health care occupations, the majority are self-employed, this is the case with physiotherapists, podiatrists, chiropodists, osteopaths, dental practitioners, and opticians. Most are paid on a fee-for-service basis, mixing NHS with private work, and an increasing number are paid through private health insurance schemes.

GP principals are also self-employed; they are independent contractors to the NHS who run their own practices, operating these as a business either as a sole proprietor or in partnerships. The principal's income is a share of the surplus of practice income over costs, a share of the profits of the practice. In England, GP services are commissioned by NHS England and practices paid through a mixture of capitation payments within the framework of the QOF. In Wales, payments are made within a framework which is a development of the QOF called the QAIF (quality assurance and improvement framework). In Scotland, GPs are paid under a GP Workload Formula with payment based on the number of consultations per patient weighted by the patients' age, sex, and deprivation to reflect differences in the workload of GPs associated with these characteristics. A simplified version of this formula pays GPs in Northern Ireland. In recent years an increasing number of GPs have become salaried. There is no pay scale for salaried GPs, just a minimum and maximum pay range. It is for the employer, typically a GP practice, in discussion with the salaried GP, to determine the level of pay and how it should vary over time.

Adult social care workers are employed by charities, local authorities, and private organizations. Where there is a union recognized for this purpose, negotiations between employers and trade unions set rates of pay. Adult social care workers employed by local authorities have their pay set in this way, but elsewhere pay negotiations are fragmentary or non-existent in which case employers will set pay.

In the short run, the forces of competition in the labour markets for health care workers are far from sufficient to establish a market rate of pay and so they leave much scope for negotiation. The outcome of any negotiations will depend upon the relative power of the parties to the negotiation. In health care, the power of employers results from the dominance of the NHS on the demand side of the labour markets while the power of health care workers results, ultimately, from the robustness of the demand for health care and the degree to which the NHS and other health care providers are able to meet this demand without them. At the level of a single health care occupation workers power also results from the extent to which employers can replace their contribution with that of either another occupation or capital. In Section 3.8, we discussed the factors which determine the complementarity and substitutability of occupations. Complementarity strengthens the power of workers, substitutability weakens it. It is therefore easy to understand why the representatives of workers might seek to reduce opportunities for labour substitution and view with concern any that are beyond their control.

Pay setting in UK health care in recent years has failed, in what should be its principal objective, to balance labour supply and demand. The serious and persistent shortages of both nurses and doctors for several years prior to the onset of the Covid-19 pandemic, provide evidence that the rates of pay for these workers were below competitive levels. This suggests an imbalance in bargaining power in the health care sector, that union bargaining power is relatively weak, and that the scrutiny of the review bodies has done nothing to offset this. In the adult care sector, where competition would be expected to play a more prominent role, turnover and vacancy rates are extremely high—this again suggests that pay is below the equilibrium level. Yet here, bargaining plays a more modest role in setting rates of pay, and so the question is: why are employers in social care either reluctant or unable to raise pay closer to equilibrium levels and hire the workers they need? We shall explore these issues in the rest of this chapter.

7.2 The Data Required for Pay Setting

Administrative pay setting requires high-quality data to inform the deliberations of the parties involved. Where rates are being set for a workforce with the occupational diversity and geographical coverage of the NHS, high-quality data is essential. Identifying the appropriate rate of pay for an occupation within each geographical area in which people work can be challenging. High-quality pay and vacancy data are required.

The most useful pay data is survey data. The two most widely used and comprehensive sources of pay data in the UK are produced by the Office for National Statistics. They are the Annual Survey of Hours and Earnings (ASHE)[3] and the Quarterly Labour Force Survey (QLFS). ASHE extracts data from employers payroll records, while the QLFS is a household survey of the working age population; each survey has its strengths and weaknesses. The QLFS has been conducted since 1992,[4] while ASHE and its predecessor the New Earnings Survey (NES) have run since 1970. The strength of ASHE is that because the data comes from employers' payroll records, it is extremely accurate. The weakness of ASHE is that because it is supplied by employers it has no data on the self-employed. The strength of the QLFS is that because it is a survey of the working age population there is data for both employees and the self-employed. The weakness of the QLFS is that because the pay data is self-reported, it is prone to reporting errors. ASHE and the QLFS are compiled for research and policy purposes, and aggregate data from both surveys is in the public domain, but access to the detailed individual level data can only be obtained by approved researchers. Both surveys detail pay by occupation,

[3] The Annual Survey of Hours and Earnings (ASHE), known as the New Earnings Survey until 1996, is a 1 per cent sample of all employees in the UK. It is conducted in the same week in April each year and has been running in essentially the same form since 1970, though in the years to 1996 it covered only GB. A pilot with a smaller sample size was conducted in 1968, and results from this are also available. Since 1970, it has reported earnings by gender, age, occupation, industry, and region. The reporting of earnings by occupation is of most interest to those involved in pay setting for health and adult social care workers. The system of classifying occupations changed in 1990 with the introduction of the Standard Occupational Classification (SOC). Prior to 1990, the New Earnings Survey (NES), as it was then, used a bespoke system for classifying occupations. The SOC distinguished many more non-manual occupations than the previous system. Moreover, as the share of employment accounted for by non-manual jobs has grown, the SOC has been refined to distinguish the increasing number of non-manual occupations. It was only with the introduction of the SOC in 1990 that occupations in adult social care were distinguished.
    ASHE provides the most accurate reporting of what employees are paid. The data comes from employers' payroll records and therefore does not suffer from the reporting errors (confusing pre- and post-tax earnings, misreporting hours worked) that plague earnings surveys that rely on self-reported data. ASHE reports a number of measures of what employees earn. Among these, the average gross weekly earnings of those employees whose pay was not affected by absence has been consistently reported since the inception of the survey. We use that measure in this chapter.
[4] The Labour Force Survey has been run as a quarterly survey in Great Britain since 1992 (1994/95 for Northern Ireland). Until spring 2006, the quarterly surveys were run on a seasonal basis, while from May 2006 they were moved, due to a requirement under EU regulation, to calendar quarters.

industry, and area and can be used to establish average rates of pay both within and across these three dimensions in health and social care and other sectors of the economy.

Commercial organizations also undertake pay surveys which vary greatly in detail and sophistication. They are the property of the commercial companies and thus generally not in the public domain. They are typically commissioned by an organization seeking to identify what other employers are paying. They identify 'comparator' occupations and use these to benchmark pay levels in the same or similar occupations employed by the commissioning organization. The surveys are sometimes extended to compare other aspects of the remuneration package such as pension benefits and premium payments for working either beyond normal hours or unsocial hours. The DDRB uses pay surveys to compare the pay of doctors and dentists to that of a selected group of comparator occupations: actuaries, legal professions, tax and accounting, pharmaceutical roles, vets, and higher education roles (DDRB 2019, para 4.15). This enables them to map how the pay of doctors has changed relative to these comparator groups over the years.

These pay surveys have their weaknesses. Comparators are often chosen because they have the same professional status, but this makes little economic sense. As we have seen in earlier chapters, pay constitutes both a return on prior human capital investment and reflects the advantages and disadvantages of jobs. There are many differences between the net advantages of the jobs done by health care workers and those done by professionals in the private sector, and there is a considerable difference in the level of human capital investment required in these jobs. This is evidently a weaknesses of the surveys used by the DDRB. It would make more sense if comparators were chosen because they have the same length of training, even though differences in the net advantages of the different jobs would remain.

Data on the pay of NHS workers in England is also available from the Electronic Staff Record (ESR) and is made publicly available at the level of NHS staff group by NHS Digital. This dataset takes payroll data and reports the pay of full-time and part-time workers by staff group, reporting basic pay and the principal additions to basic pay such as shift pay, overtime, on-call payments etc[5]. However while a very useful source of pay data for NHS workers, it excludes GPs, workers in GP practices, other primary care providers such as dentists and the whole of social care. Moreover, because the ESR does not use the Standard Occupational Classification system, it cannot be used to compare the pay of NHS staff groups to that of occupations in other sectors of the economy.

---

[5] The ESR will present an incomplete picture of the total pay of some NHS employees, those who also work outside the NHS such as nurses who do part-time agency work, and doctors who work part-time for other employers.

Alongside pay data, administrative pay setters also need data on the state of each occupational labour market. Vacancy and turnover data are available for this purpose. In the previous chapter we used the vacancy data that were in the public domain to report levels of vacancies in the period to 2019 in the main frontline occupations. From this, it was evident that this data left much to be desired.

Vacancy data that are detailed, accurate, and timely are central to informed and accurate pay setting. These data are essential for establishing directly whether existing rates of pay are equilibrium rates. Where detailed and accurate vacancy data exist they eliminate the need for pay comparisons because they provide direct evidence of the appropriateness of current rates of pay. The data must allow comparison of the current vacancy rate with the 'normal' rate in each occupation and each geographical labour market.[6] Where the current rate is above the normal rate it indicates that pay is uncompetitive.

If vacancy data are to enable this analysis, there must be clear criteria for what constitutes a vacancy. The vacancy data for some frontline occupations, those in social care, understate the true level of vacancies because the count of vacancies is done by counting job advertisements and the job adverts can be for several posts. Recorded vacancy rates can also understate the true level of vacancies when vacant posts are not advertised because the organization has previously tried and failed to fill the vacant posts. When this happens, the available data provide a less than accurate picture of the true position, though they are frequently the only data that are available.

7.3 The Pay of Frontline Care Workers

So what has been happening to the pay of health and social care workers in recent years, and how does recent experience compare with that of earlier periods? Many of those working today will have made their human capital investment decisions many years ago, some decades ago. How do the returns to investment in health care human capital that existed when they made their investment decisions compare to the returns they earn today?

The returns to investment in health care human capital cannot be viewed in isolation; they must be compared to the returns to other types of human capital investment. The decision to invest in health care human capital is typically a career choice and it has been made after evaluating the attractiveness of several different careers. To distinguish the attractiveness of frontline pay the pay of frontline health and social care workers must therefore be compared to that of other workers.

In this section we report how the relative pay of frontline workers has changed over the long run, using data that allows us to look back over a period of nearly

---

[6] The normal rate can be established by analysis of past vacancy data over the period of an economic cycle, removing the peaks and troughs in the data and identifying the underlying trend rate.

fifty years. We report how the average pay of the very largest frontline health and social care occupations has changed relative to the average of all employees in the UK over the period since 1970.[7]

We use data from ASHE and its predecessor the NES to distinguish the average levels of pay for each of the largest occupations in health care over the period from 1970. This is the only dataset which enables us to analyse the relative pay of the largest health and social care occupations over a period of almost fifty years. Since the introduction of the NES in 1970, the surveys have reported the average earnings of Medical Practitioners, Qualified Nurses, and Midwives and Nursing Auxiliaries, and from 1990 onwards they have reported the average earnings of adult social care workers. Because ASHE and the NES cover only employees, the self-employed are not included and therefore the medical practitioners in the survey are those working predominately in NHS hospitals and, toward the end of the period, some who are working as salaried GPs in primary care. The earnings of GP principals and dental practitioners, who are self-employed, are not reported in this data.

The surveys report gross weekly earnings, a measure of total pay before tax, which includes both basic salary and any additional payments on top of this. For many in these occupations these additional payments could be substantial. During the period analysed, the earnings of many consultants exceeded their basic rates of pay because they received Clinical Excellence and Distinction Awards. Doctors in training received the several additions to basic rates of pay detailed in Section 7.1. The basic pay of nurses, and nursing auxiliaries was supplemented by shift allowances, which were paid to over three-quarters of nurses, and geographical allowances, which were paid to around one-fifth of nurses. Nurses and nursing auxiliaries were also paid overtime and they received some other small supplementary payments which Trusts awarded following national guidelines. The earnings of some adult social care workers were supplemented by a range of allowances, though some who worked in domiciliary care did not have a basic rate and were paid according to the number of visits they made in a week.

ASHE reports the average gross weekly earnings of those in the survey in one representative week in April each year.[8] ASHE reports average earnings, both the

---

[7] This approach can be contrasted to one which compares changes in the pay of each frontline occupation to changes in the pay of those occupations which these frontline workers consider as alternatives. For such comparisons to produce meaningful results highly detailed data is required. Ideally they should distinguish and control for changes in the net advantages of the two occupations being compared. The data for such analysis do not exist. Where the comparator group is all employees two countervailing features will be at work. The net advantages of the jobs done by some occupations within the comparator group will have improved while the net advantages of other jobs will have deteriorated. The implicit assumption when selecting all employees as the comparator group is that on average, save for generalised improvements in working conditions which have been enjoyed by all employees, the two features will cancel out.

[8] ASHE records pay per job, not pay per employee, because it does not aggregate the pay data across all the jobs where the person works, as an employee. As a result, where a person holds more than one job, ASHE will under-report this person's total earnings from employment. Whether this means

mean and median,[9] by occupation in one of its tabulations, but unless otherwise stated it is the mean pay data for each occupation that we report. In what follows we use only pay data which is in the public domain, and which the interested reader can therefore check for themselves.[10]

We use this data to track pay over the years from 1970 to 2019, almost half a century, with the end point the last year of data unaffected by the pandemic.[11] Over this period, average earnings across the whole economy increased very substantially. In 1970, the average pay of full-time employees was just £26 a week, by 2019 it had reached £702.8 a week, a twenty-seven-fold increase. It is not surprising therefore to discover that the nominal pay of health care workers has also risen very substantially over these years. The data reveal that the average pay of full-time doctors (medical practitioners) increased twenty-four-fold between 1970 and 2019, that the pay of auxiliary nurses increased thirty-fold, and that of qualified nurses increased forty-one-fold. Over the shorter period between 1990 and

the total earnings of health and social care workers are under-recorded more than are the earnings of other employers is impossible to say. Some doctors work as employees in other jobs, as teachers and researchers in universities, and some nurses work for the NHS and for nursing agencies. Social care workers also often hold other jobs, for example working for more than one care provider. How this compares to multiple job-holding by employees in other occupations we do not know.

[9] The median is an alternative measure of average pay. It measures the level of pay at the centre of the pay distribution and therefore is less influenced by outliers at the top end of the pay distribution—very high, and perhaps, 'unrepresentative' levels of pay—which will tend to drag the mean upwards. Using the median made no difference to the picture reported here. Though the median for full-time staff was always higher than the mean, by about ten percentage points, it displayed exactly the same pattern of changes in relative pay as the mean.

[10] It should be noted that the average level of pay of any group of workers is likely to be affected by the composition of the group. For example, the average for a group which contains young and old workers will be affected by the proportions of these two. Because the young will be recently qualified, and recently qualified workers typically earn less than the average for an occupation, a high proportion of young workers will reduce the average while a smaller proportion (a higher proportion of old workers) will push up the average. Where the group covers both men and women, or full-time and part-time workers, then changes in the gender composition of the group or in the proportion of part-time workers will also have an impact on average pay. In many occupations, women still earn less than men and part-timers earn less than full-timers, even after adjusting for hours worked. These differences can be important in comparisons of health and adult social care workers' pay, and we therefore need to remain alert to them.

There are other ways in which changes in the composition of the group surveyed can affect average earnings. Consider for example doctors. If the proportion of hospital doctors who become consultants increases we should expect the average earnings of hospital doctors to increase, because consultants are paid more than other hospital doctors. On the other hand, if there were years in which there was a significant increase in the number of newly qualified doctors starting work, the average earnings of doctors might fall because an increased proportion of doctors would be junior doctors who are paid less than the average for all doctors.

Similar observations can be made with regard to nurses. The average gross weekly earnings reported here are for nurses and midwives. There have always been several different grades of nurses in the NHS, they now range from 'newly qualified' to 'consultant', and each one of these is covered by at least one pay band. A significant increase in the proportion of nurses who become nursing consultants will increase nurses and midwives average pay. A recruitment drive which resulted in many more entering as newly qualified nurses would be expected to reduce average pay. We need to bear the possibility of such compositional changes in mind as we analyse the pay data.

[11] The ASHE data for April 2020 and 2021 will have been affected by the pandemic.

2019, when inflation was much lower and nominal rates of pay increased much less rapidly, the pay of adult social care workers increased almost three-fold.

These substantial increases in average levels of pay do not of course mean that doctors in 2019 were twenty-four times better off, auxiliary nurses thirty times better off, and nurses over forty times better off than their predecessors back in 1970. To distinguish how much better paid these occupations were in 2019 than in 1970 we need to distinguish increases in real pay—we need to adjust the nominal increase in pay for price inflation over the period.

Over the period 1970 to 2019, inflation as measured by the Retail Price Index increased almost sixteen–fold.[12] However, the period splits into two rather different regimes; an initial one of high inflation and a second when inflation was much more subdued. The 1970s and early 80s was the period of very high inflation; in 1975 the annual rate of inflation peaked at 24 per cent, and it was above 5 per cent each year between 1970 and 1982 and again in several of the years through to 1990. Though the period 1990 to 2019 contained some years when inflation ran at over 5 per cent per annum, there were other years when it dipped below 1 per cent and the RPI ran at an annual rate of less than 2.5 per cent for the majority of this period. Between 1970 and 1990 the RPI increased seven-fold. Over the subsequent and longer period, from 1990 to 2019 the RPI increased less than three-fold.

Over the period as a whole, the rise in prices was much less than the increase in the nominal pay of doctors, nurses and midwives, and nursing auxiliaries, thus the real pay of these health care workers advanced very substantially over these forty-nine years. Unsurprisingly, the advance was far from smooth. In the early years of very high inflation there were years during which prices advanced more rapidly than pay. This was in large part due to the incomes policies which were introduced by governments to limit the size of pay awards (Fallick and Elliott 1981). Pay restraint returned in the second decade of the twentieth century. In this period of 'austerity', ceilings on public sector pay awards resulted in inflation again outstripping pay increases. As a result, the last decade of our period saw substantial reductions in the real pay of most health care workers and some social care workers.

The increase in the real pay of the three health care occupations that can be tracked over the years between 1970 and 2019 is significant. Over this period, the real pay of doctors increased one and a half times, that of qualified nurses and midwives by over two and a half times, and that of auxiliary nurses nearly doubled.

---

[12] The Consumer Price Index (CPI) is the inflation measure used in the Government's target for inflation. This was first published in 1997 as the Harmonised Index of Consumer Prices (HICP) and first used as an official measure of inflation in 2003. The CPI cannot be used to deflate pay increases from 1970. For this reason, the much older Retail Price Index (RPI), which was introduced in 1947 and has been in existence throughout the period of interest to us here, is used. The RPI generally produces a higher inflation rate than the CPI and for this reason deflating nominal pay growth by the RPI will produce smaller real pay growth.

Over the shorter period from 1990 to 2019 social care workers also saw their real pay increase. Over this period their pay increased almost three-fold against a rise in prices of less than two and a half times. As far as can be established with the available data, the real pay of other frontline health and social care occupations also saw sometimes substantial advances over this period.

Over the period 1970 to 2019, real pay also increased in the rest of the UK economy. To understand what happened to the competitiveness of frontline workers' pay we need to compare the pay increase of workers in frontline occupations to those of workers in other jobs; we need to establish what happened to their relative pay. If the pay of the health and social care occupations we identify in the data increased more rapidly than that of workers in other parts of the economy then the relative attractiveness of working in health and social care is likely to have increased. If, on the other hand, the pay of the health and social care occupations increased less rapidly than pay elsewhere, then the relative attractiveness of these jobs is likely to have decreased.

Table 7.1 reports what has happened to relative pay over the period from 1970 to 2019, it compares the average pay of full-time employees in each of the four health and social care occupations to the average pay of all full-time employees in the UK. Table 7.1 reports average gross weekly earnings in each of the four health and social care occupations as a proportion of the average gross weekly earnings of all employees.

Table 7.1 shows that the relative pay of three occupations increased. The pay of nurses and midwives advanced from 68 per cent of the average in 1970 to 103 per cent in 2019. The pay of full-time auxiliary nurses advanced, much more modestly, from 54 per cent of the average in 1970 to 63 per cent in 2019, and the pay of care assistants and attendants (adult social care workers) advanced, modestly, over the shorter period from 1990, from 57 per cent of the average in 1990 to 60 per

Table 7.1 The Pay of Health and Adult Social Care Workers Relative to Pay of All Employees, 1970–2019

	1970	1990	2000	2005	2010	2019
			Mean Earnings			
Full-Time Men and Women*						
Doctors (Medical Practitioners)	2.25	2.12	2.28	2.60	2.45	1.95
Qualified Nurses and Midwives	0.68	0.94	0.98	0.99	1.03	1.03
Auxiliary Nurses	0.54	0.60	0.58	0.59	0.61	0.63
Care Assistants and Attendants	N/A	0.57	0.51	0.58	0.59	0.60

Note: *Average gross weekly earnings of all full-time workers in each of the health and social care occupations compared to the average gross weekly earnings of all full-time employees
Source: New Earnings Survey and Annual Survey of Hours and Earnings

cent in 2019. In contrast the relative pay of doctors deteriorated over the period. It stood at 225 per cent of the all employees average in 1970 but had fallen to 195 per cent of the average by 2019.

The Table also reveals that the timing of these changes in relative pay differed between occupations. Between 1970 and 1990, there was substantial improvement in the relative pay of qualified nurses and midwives, while auxiliary nurses saw only modest improvement and that of doctors deteriorated. In contrast, between 1990 and 2005, there was a steep rise in the relative pay of doctors, while that of qualified nurses and midwives advanced only modestly and that of nursing auxiliaries stood still. In the subsequent period from 2005 to 2019, the relative pay of care assistants changed very little, while that of auxiliary nurses and qualified nurses and midwives again advanced modestly. Most striking of all is the deterioration in the relative pay of doctors over this last period. Having improved dramatically between 2000 and 2005, doctors' relative pay fell back sharply over the subsequent years to 2019. By 2019, doctors' relative pay had fallen to a level lower than it had been in 1970.

The Table suggests that over this (almost) half century, qualified nurses and midwives have become much better paid, nursing auxiliaries a little better paid, and doctors much less well paid,[13] and that over the shorter thirty-year period from 1990, the relative pay of adult social care workers has not changed very much. The Table also shows that in 2019, the pay of auxiliary nurses and care assistants, the two lowest paid occupations, was still well below the national average. In 2019, the pay of a significant proportion of both these groups was still affected by the National Minimum Wage (NMW). The Low Pay Commission estimated that in 2019, 13.6 per cent of all those aged 25 and over working in adult social care in the UK were on the National Living Wage. In April 2019, the NLW was £8.21 an hour (Low Pay Commission 2019).

The period 1970 to 2019 saw some fairly major changes in the UK labour market. There was a considerable expansion in the employment opportunities open to women and a substantial improvement in their pay. The Equal Pay Act of 1970 which came into force at the end of 1975 was the first piece of UK legislation to enshrine the right to pay equality between women and men. Over the first three decades of the period from 1970, women's pay advanced more rapidly than that of men and the gender pay gap narrowed (Harkness 1996; Prefect 2011). This advance in women's pay relative to that of men meant that, while over the period 1970 and 1990 the pay of qualified nurses and midwives increased faster than the average for men and women taken as a whole, when it is compared to that of only non-manual women workers in the rest of the economy, it just kept pace with

[13] Table 7.1 also tells us that the relative cost of employing nurses and doctors changed over this period, it became relatively more expensive to employ nurses. This may be one reason why, as recorded in section 1.2, the number of doctors has increased more rapidly than the number of nurses.

the increases they received. Full-time qualified nurses and midwives were paid at the average for women in full-time non-manual jobs in 1970, and this had not substantially changed by either 1990, 2000, or indeed by 2019.

Why did the pay of qualified nurses and midwives advance in line with that of non-manual women in the economy as a whole? The answer lies in the dramatic changes in the labour market for women that occurred over this period. In 1970, nursing was one of the few careers open to more highly educated women while the following period saw job opportunities expand most rapidly for these women. More highly educated women whose choices had previously been constrained to a narrow range of occupations now had a much wider range of jobs open to them. This undoubtedly changed labour supply to nursing over this period. We can depict this as shifting the labour supply schedule to nursing to the left, for example shifting LS_2 to LS_1 in Figure 4.1. Such a shift will have exerted pressure on the NHS and the other employers of qualified nurses and midwives to improve their pay.

It is interesting to note that while qualified nurses and midwives benefited from these developments, less skilled labour, nursing auxiliaries, did not. There appears to have been no similar opening up of employment opportunities for women who were doing less skilled jobs. There appears to have been no leftward shift in the labour supply schedule for auxiliary nurses, or if there was, this must have been offset by a leftward shift in the labour demand schedule for these nurses.

The NHS responded to the changing labour market for more highly educated women in a number of ways. In 1983, a Nursing Review Body was established for the purpose of making independent recommendations to government on nursing pay. In 1989, a new grading structure was introduced to offer additional recognition and reward for those in clinical roles, and in 2004, Agenda for Change was introduced. Agenda for Change introduced a new pay and grading structure for all NHS workers except doctors, dentists, and senior managers. Job evaluation was introduced, and its application allocated qualified nurses to an extended range of pay bands. Prior to 2004, nurses, and the other workers covered by Agenda for Change, had been paid within the 'Whitley System', which had been designed to structure the pay of civil servants. By the start of this century, the Whitley System was judged too centralized and inflexible and unable to deal with issues of equal value as required under equal pay legislation. Agenda for Change recognized and rewarded the greater range of activities that qualified nurses were performing. In the years since 2004, there have been further modest changes to nurses' pay and grading structures within the framework of Agenda for Change, though the rate at which nurses' pay in general has advanced has been constrained by public sector wage restraint following the financial crisis in 2008.

Nurses' pay had to increase relative to the average for all full-time men and women if nursing was to retain its attractions as a career, but that it advanced no faster than the average for non-manual women is perhaps surprising. Over the period analysed here, the costs of investing in nurse training have risen; nursing has become a graduate career, entry standards have increased, and government subsidies to nurse training have reduced. A rise in the costs to individuals of investing in human capital without a compensating increase in the returns to that investment is a prescription for reduced human capital investment. It is not therefore surprising that we have found that attrition during and following training and nursing vacancy rates have increased over the latter part of this period.

The changes in the relative pay of doctors over the period since 2000 also merit further discussion. The first five years of this period saw doctors' relative pay increase from 2.28 average weekly earnings in 2000 to 2.6 times in 2005. Consultants received a 27 per cent pay rise over the three years to 2005–2006 as result of a new consultants contract introduced in 2003.[14] In the previous year, a new junior doctors' contract had been introduced, and the pay of junior doctors was further improved by the enhanced payments they received as a result of the arrangements made to meet the European Working Time Directive, which came into effect throughout most of the UK in 2004. However, over the five years from 2005 to 2010, as Table 7.1 shows, doctors' relative pay began to deteriorate, and over the nine years between 2010 and 2019, it declined from 2.45 times average earnings in to 1.95.[15]

It might be argued that a comparison of doctors' pay to average pay understates the real deterioration in doctors' pay after 2005. Part of this period was characterized by growing pay inequality (OECD 2011), which meant that the pay of many high-paying occupations with whom it might be more appropriate to compare doctors was increasing more rapidly than average rates of pay. Both the BMA and the DDRB have argued that doctors' pay should be compared to that of other highly paid occupations, and the DDRB compares the basic pay of full-time consultants with five years' experience (the fifth point on the consultants pay scale) to the ninetieth percentile of the distribution of average earnings. The DDRB report that 'the consultants' pay lead has fallen every year since 1999, except in 2003 when the new consultant contract was introduced, from 82 per cent in 1999 to 45 per

---

[14] A further consequence of the new contract was a reduction in the hours consultants were recorded as working for the NHS in the years after 2005. The new consultants contract aimed to ensure that consultants NHS pay was more closely aligned to the hours they worked for the NHS. It broke the consultants working week up into three or four hour blocks of activities known as 'programmed activities' and tied their NHS pay to the number of these activities they supplied to the NHS. The reduction in the average number of hours that consultants reported they worked for the NHS was 1.4 hours a week, from 51.6 to 50.2 hours (National Audit Office 2007). However, this is unlikely to provide a significant part of the explanation for the decline in the relative pay of hospital doctors because consultants account for a minority of this group.

[15] It should also be noted that over the same period the pay of part-time doctors declined relative to the pay of part-timers in the rest of the economy. It declined from 3.97 in 2010 to 3.28 times average pay for part-timers in 2019. These ratios reveal that part-time doctors' relative pay is a lot higher than is full-time doctors' relative pay. This should come as no surprise because, there are a lot of very low-paid part-time workers in the rest of the economy. The gap between the pay of full-time and part-time doctors is less than it is between full-time and part-time workers in the rest of the whole economy.

cent in 2018' (DDRB 2019: para 4.12). However, a comparison of average earnings with basic pay is not a like-for-like comparison; average earnings include payments on top of basic pay, while basic pay, self-evidently, does not.

A comparison of the average gross weekly earnings of all full-time doctors to the average gross weekly earnings of full-time employees at the ninetieth percentile of the earnings distribution, as reported in ASHE, reveals a sharper deterioration in doctors' pay from 2005 onwards than reported by the DDRB. Table 7.2 reports that the relative pay of doctors declined from 1.58 times pay at the ninetieth percentile in 2005 to 1.19 times in 2019. The substantial decline in doctors' pay relative to the mean and ninetieth percentile of the earnings distribution in the period since 2005 can be very clearly seen in Figure 7.1.

The DDRB also compares the pay of doctors in training (Foundation years 1 and 2 and specialty registrars) and specialty doctors in England to a number of comparator professions: actuaries, legal professions, tax and accounting, pharmaceutical roles, vets, and higher education roles. For doctors in training, they conclude that 'overall, despite a continued period of pay restraint, the pay levels of those in our remit group were not out of line with the comparator groups' (DDRB 2019: para 4.42).

All pay comparisons raise questions about the relevant comparator group and making comparisons between specific occupations requires considerable care. We should expect the pay of doctors to be the same as that of those in the DDRB comparator group only if they require the same levels of investment in human capital and the other pecuniary and non-pecuniary advantages and disadvantages of the jobs they do are the same. The private investment costs incurred by doctors in training and specialty doctors are, however, typically greater than those of the comparator professions chosen by the DDRB. It would nonetheless be reasonable to compare changes in doctors' pay to changes in the pay of this group if it could be

Table 7.2 Doctors' Pay Relative to Pay of Other Highly Paid Employees 2000–2019

Year	Doctors' pay Relative to Pay at ninetieth percentile
2000	141.7
2005	157.9
2010	148.6
2019	119.1

Source: Annual Survey of Hours and Earnings Table 1.1a
Note: Weekly Earnings of doctors relative to pay at the ninetieth percentile of the 'all employees' weekly earnings distribution for full-time employees

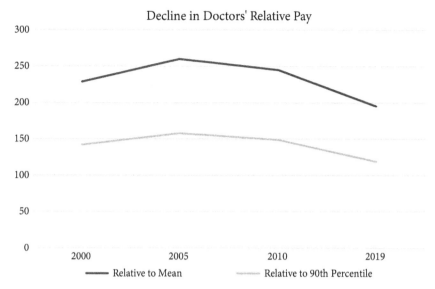

Figure 7.1 Doctors' Pay Relative to all Employee Average and 90th Percentile of Earnings Distribution, 2000–2019

Source: Annual Survey of Hours and Earnings 2000–2019

assumed that there had been no change in the difference between the net advantages of the jobs in the comparator group and those of doctors.[16] However, this appears unlikely to have been the case. Over the last few years, the job of a doctor has become more arduous as the pressures from understaffing have increased, which suggests that the relative pay of doctors should have improved rather than remained 'in line' with the comparator group.

One explanation for the decline in doctors' relative pay might be compositional effects. The gender composition of the medical workforce has changed over the period and so therefore has that of the ASHE sample. In 2000, women accounted for 27 per cent of the ASHE sample, but by 2019 this had increased to 42 per cent. The ASHE data also reveal that women doctors earn less than male doctors: the pay of full-time women doctors was 82 per cent of that of full-time male doctors in 2000 and 79 per cent in 2019.

Several, familiar, explanations have been offered for the persistence of a gender pay gap among doctors. Caring responsibilities are divided unequally, with women doctors more likely to take time out to care for others, and so more women are

---

[16] Economists and statisticians describe this as taking 'differences in differences'. Thus, even though the initial level of investment in human capital was very different for doctors and actuaries, if this difference has not changed, we can then compare the changes, the differences, in those things that have. So if it is reasonable to assume all of the differences in the advantages and disadvantages of the jobs done by doctors and actuaries have remained the same over the period being compared, it would then be reasonable to compare changes in the pay of doctors and actuaries.

likely to have once worked part time, As a result more women are to be found in the lower paid roles and clinical specialties because the higher paid roles and specialties are reported to require greater time commitment. A further reason why men were more likely to be found in the higher paid roles and specialties was that the men tended to be older than the women and to have been in practice longer. As a result, men were disproportionately represented amongst the highest paid positions of consultants and associate specialists, and this in turn meant that more men received Clinical Excellence Awards (Dacre 2020).[17]

However, this compositional effect provides only a small part of the explanation for the overall decline in doctors' relative pay, as we can see from Figure 7.2. In this Figure, we distinguish between men and women doctors and chart what has been happening to doctors' pay relative to that of the same gender in other occupations. We are able to do this only for the period from 2010 onwards, but we find that the patterns of relative decline for male and female doctors are very similar. Whichever way we look at it, the returns that male and female doctors have been earning on their investment in human capital have been declining since 2010 and that investment is therefore becoming much less attractive.

Pay comparisons also raise questions about the time period over which comparisons should be made. Going back to 1970 reveals long run changes in relative pay. It might be thought that developments over such an extended period are merely of historical interest and will have little impact on current behaviour. However, because of the time it takes to train to become a consultant, it is the relativities

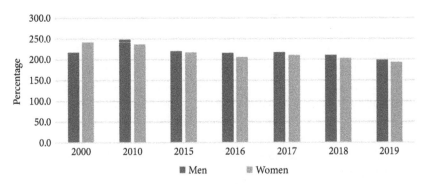

Figure 7.2 Relative Pay of Full-Time Male and Female Medical Practitioners, 2000–2019 (Pay Relative to Pay of All Employees of Same Gender)

Source: Annual Survey of Hours and Earnings, 2000, 2010, 2015 - 2019

[17] No similarly detailed study has been conducted into gender pay inequality among nurses, though it appears that here, in an occupation heavily dominated by women, there is also a gender pay gap. Research into the gender composition of each of the nursing pay bands under Agenda for Change has revealed that men are over-represented, compared to their overall proportion in the UK nursing population, amongst the highest bands (Punshon et al. 2019).

of well over a decade ago that informed the investment decisions of recently appointed consultants and the relativities of some considerable time before that which informed the decisions of the rest of this workforce. Expectations about relative pay are strongly linked to expectations about relative lifestyle, and expectations about relative pay and relative lifestyle which have not been realized would be expected to affect current labour market behaviour.

The decline in the relative pay of doctors and the stagnation in the relative pay of nurses and midwives, and of auxiliary nurses and social care workers, is not what we might have expected considering what has been happening on the demand side of these labour markets. The UK demand for these workers has been stronger than labour demand in the economy as a whole. In Table 1.6 we saw that the share of the total working population accounted for by frontline health and social care workers increased sharply between 1951 and 2011. This means that the demand for frontline workers has outstripped that for other occupations, and so we might have expected their pay to have outstripped pay growth in general. That it did not is revealing, suggesting forces were at work through the wage setting system, suppressing the rates of pay increase and the advance in relative rates of pay that would otherwise have occurred.

The pay data we have used up to this point do not, however, reveal the full picture because they do not include pay from self-employment. The ASHE data does not include the self-employed, and though many among the comparator occupations used by the DDRB are self-employed, their pay is not included in the comparisons they make. This means the DDRB miss the pay that some doctors receive from private practice as well as the pay of many in the comparator groups.[18] Information on the pay of the self-employed is extremely difficult to obtain and the required data can only be accessed by those approved researchers who have access to anonymized tax records.

Information on the pay that some doctors receive from private practice is not in the public domain. The only detailed study was several years ago and used data from the financial year 2003/4. The study revealed that many NHS consultants received substantial additional earnings from private practice. In that year, average consultant income from NHS work was £76,628 and income from private work added an additional 44.6 per cent, £34,144, to the average earnings of consultants, resulting in average total income of £110,773 in 2003/4. Incomes varied by age, type of contract, specialty, and the region in which they worked. Average private income varied across specialties, ranging from £5144 for paediatric neurology to £142,723 for plastic surgery. Plastic surgery was the specialty with the highest ratio of private income to NHS income, at 1.90, and paediatric neurology the specialty

---

[18] The only UK pay data which attempts to gather data on the earnings of the self-employed is the QLFS. But this data is plagued with reporting errors and omissions due to the self-selection of those reporting, and is not therefore a remotely accurate measure of earnings from self-employment.

with the lowest ratio of private income to NHS income, 1.07. Private income was highest for those working in Essex, at £56,221, and lowest for those working in South Yorkshire at £20,178 (Morris et al. 2008).

It is evidently important to include pay from self-employment in any analysis of doctors' pay. Data taken from surveys of employees earnings, such as the ASHE, clearly understate the average level of doctors' pay. However, if we are to make meaningful comparisons with other occupations, we also need to include their self-employed pay. Moreover, it is unlikely that the inclusion of self-employed pay would change the broad picture presented here, which is of a steep decline in hospital doctors' relative pay after 2005. Doctors in many specialties and areas of the UK as well as those in non-consultant grades may have little or no self-employed pay, and it would require a steep increase in pay from private practice to arrest the recorded decline in NHS pay.

Data on pay from private practice is important for another reason—it would improve understanding of doctors choice of specialty and geographic location. Some doctors will be drawn to geographic areas in which there are greater opportunities for private practice, and opportunities for private practice may influence specialty choice. We know nothing about how opportunities for private practice influence both these choices in the UK, though we do know from research in other countries that it is important (Gagné and Léger 2005; Sivey et al. 2012). If we understood better what attracts doctors in training in the UK toward certain specialties and areas of the country, we would be better placed to address the acute shortage of doctors in some specialties and geographic areas.

The analysis in this section reveals the difficulties that confront the researcher or the pay setter seeking to obtain an accurate picture of what has been happening to the relative pay of frontline health and social care workers in the UK. Nonetheless, it seems clear that the relative pay of doctors has deteriorated and that of nurses and social care workers has at best marked time. These developments would be expected to affect the ability of the NHS and other employers of frontline care workers to recruit and retain the workers they require. Pay is the instrument that employers use to balance labour supply and labour demand. and when pay is set at the wrong level. imbalances will result. In the previous chapter we saw evidence that there were serious imbalances, serious shortages in each of the three most important frontline occupations. The vacancy data suggested that the rates of pay for these occupations were seriously misaligned.[19]

---

[19] Vacancy data can also be used to identify the pay relativity required to restore equilibrium. The vacancy rates for doctors, for example, can be used to identify a time when the average vacancy rate for doctors and their comparator group were both at their natural rates. The pay of doctors relative to that of the comparator group at this time would then provide a benchmark against which the current level of relative pay should be judged. A comparison of current vacancy rates against natural rates for both doctors and their comparators would then tell us how the relative pay of doctors needs to be adjusted from the benchmark level. If the vacancy rate for doctors is above its natural level and rising relative

One final observation on pay data before we leave the subject. There has been little detailed research into pay differences between workers of different ethnicities in health and adult social care because there are no large datasets recording ethnicity, occupation. and pay in sufficient detail for this workforce. The only results we have originate in research which was confined to the NHS in England where the ESR pay data records self-identified ethnicity. There appear to be no data or research for Scotland, Northern Ireland, and Wales.

Researchers found that in England. there was no significant ethnic pay gap for most grades of doctor, though one existed among consultants. The median basic pay of white consultants was found to be 4.9 per cent higher than for Black and Black British consultants (Appleby 2018). Research into the pay differences among NHS workers in England paid under Agenda for Change (all workers except for doctors and senior managers) found that there was no significant pay gap between white workers and ethnic minority workers across the NHS workforce taken as a whole. However, the picture changed when comparisons were drawn between white workers and specific ethnic groups. The researchers found pay gaps ranging from 6 per cent in favour of white workers when compared to mixed heritage workers, to over 15 per cent in favour of Chinese workers. When researchers looked in more detail at nurses and health visitors, they found pay gaps which favoured white workers. One of the reasons for this was the distribution of ethnic groups across the different pay bands (Appleby et. al. 2021). Other research found that in NHS Trusts and Care Commissioning Groups in England in 2018 the higher the pay band, the lower the proportion of Black and ethnic minority nurses. The research found there were only eight (3.5 per cent) Black and ethnic minority chief nurses that year (NHS Improvement England 2019).

7.4 The Returns to Investment in Health Care Human Capital in the UK

The sum of the pay received each year during a person's working life gives their lifetime pay, and their lifetime pay relative to that of other occupations represents the most complete measure of the returns to the human capital investment they have made. It is important to compare the lifetime pay of those who invested in training to become nurses and doctors to the lifetime pay of those who chose other forms of human capital investment. Until recently this was not possible but a recent programme of research conducted by the Institute for Fiscal Studies and commissioned by the Department for Education (DfE) now enables us to do this.[20]

---

to the vacancy rate of the comparator occupation then the relative pay of doctors needs to rise further above the benchmark value, and vice versa.

[20] The research reported the returns to undergraduate (Belfield et al. 2018) and postgraduate degrees (Britton et al. 2020b) awarded by an institute of higher education in the UK. It simulated how the

The research employed a unique dataset—the Longitudinal Education Outcomes (LEO) dataset—which was developed by the IFS in collaboration with the DfE. The LEO tracked students through school, university, and into the labour market, linking school records from the National Pupil Database (NPD), higher education records from the Higher Education Statistics Agency (HESA),[21] earnings, tax and employment records from Her Majesty's Revenue and Customs (HMRC), and benefits data from the Work and Pensions Longitudinal Study (WPLS).

A strength of the dataset is that it records pay from both employment and self-employment, which is important because a large number of people who work in some of the highest paid jobs in the UK are self-employed.[22] The researchers estimated the returns to studying different subjects at an HE institute by calculating the lifetime pay of those qualifying in the different subjects. The lifetime pay of those who studied medicine will therefore include those who now work in health care management or higher education, or indeed those who pursued a completely different career after graduation, not just those who currently work as frontline doctors in the UK.

We should note two important methodological points at the outset. First, in order to calculate the addition to lifetime pay from successfully completing higher education, the researchers had to estimate what the people who completed their studies would have been paid if they had not gone on to higher education (in our earlier discussion of human capital we represented this by the line SZ in Figure 2.3). They judged that even if they had not attended higher education graduates would have earned more than the average because they were likely to be more able and more highly motivated than the average non-attendee. They therefore took the pay of a comparator group which comprised individuals with similar background characteristics and prior educational attainment to those who

---

earnings of those graduating in the UK evolved over the course of the graduates' working lives. Most importantly for our purposes the research also reported the additional lifetime pay of English domiciled graduates who had studied different subjects in the UK (Britton et al. 2020a). This last study therefore enables us to distinguish the private monetary returns to human capital investment in health care qualifications.

[21] One noteworthy feature of the HESA records is that medical degrees are classified as undergraduate degrees even though the vast majority of those studying medicine complete the full five or six years of a medical degree; thus in duration at least medical degrees are comparable to completing a Masters degree in other subjects. Only a very small proportion of those studying medicine as an undergraduate degree, just 3 per cent, go on to complete either a Masters or a PhD. In contrast, the proportion taking an undergraduate degree which can be identified as leading to a career as an Allied Health Professional who went on to take a Masters degree was 8.2 per cent, while 3.3 per cent went on to take a PhD (the percentage of those taking a nursing qualification who took either a Masters or PhD is not recorded due to small sample size). Because the vast majority of health care workers terminate their degree studies at the undergraduate stage it is appropriate to focus on the returns to this degree.

[22] The dataset therefore gives a much more accurate picture of the true returns from work than do those studies which are based on either pay from employment only, as recorded in ASHE, or which attempt to include self-employment income, as recorded in the LFS. One deficiency of the LEO data set however is that it cannot reveal the intensity with which people work to achieve their earnings. High pay is often associated with longer hours of work and therefore the LEO likely overstates the real earnings differences that result from equivalent hours of work.

completed higher education. Second, only some of the costs of attaining the higher education qualification were deducted, but they were the two most important: tuition fees and subsistence covered by student loans.[23]

The estimates of lifetime pay were based on the pay of people who were born in the mid-1980s and went to university in the mid-2000s. These were the oldest people for whom the researchers had detailed education records, but this meant that the oldest cohort for whom they had pay data were aged 29–40. To overcome this limitation, the researchers simulated pay over the remainder of these people's working lives using data from the LFS, which involved the assumption that earnings profiles in the future would look like those today.[24] They simulated the pay and employment trajectories of each person up to retirement age, and then adjusted their pay to express it in today's pay levels. They then applied the current tax and student loan system to calculate lifetime pay net of tax payments and repayments to the student loan system (Britton et al. 2020a).

In section 2.4 we reported the economic proposition that pay in the future is valued less than pay today and that future pay should therefore be discounted. The researchers report all lifetime figures in discounted present value terms and argue they should be interpreted as the equivalent of cash at the point of entering university. As there is no universal consensus on the appropriate discount rate, they report results using alternative discount rates whenever practicable. They used a real discount rate of 3.5 per cent for the first thirty years and 3.0 per cent after that, as recommended by the Treasury's Green Book. Discounting makes a big difference.

The researchers found that the average discounted addition to lifetime pay from an undergraduate degree was £430,000 for men and £260,000 for women (Britton et al. 2020a). Once they had accounted for differences in characteristics between those who did and those who did not attend HE, they obtained a discounted lifetime increase in gross pay of £240,000 for men and £140,000 for women as a result of attending HE.

Of specific interest to us here is the additional lifetime pay for the three health care subjects identified in the study. The values are shown net of taxes and repayments of student loans and at different rates of discount in Table 7.3. It is quite evident that when earnings are taken over a lifetime, the rate at which future pay

---

[23] This might appear to understate the costs of attaining a medical degree. Medical degrees require more years of study and each year of study is more intensive than in many other degrees, since there are more compulsory hours of attendance at university. In turn, this means that medical students have fewer opportunities for part-time work while studying, which is a way many students now seek to reduce debt. However, the understatement is likely to be small because the final year of study for many medical students is supported by a bursary.

[24] It is important to recognize that the estimates or future earnings are subject to several sources of uncertainty. The researchers cannot know either what retirement patterns will look like in fifty years' time, or whether the earnings trajectories of future graduates will be similar to those of past graduates. The researchers note that this uncertainty is particularly acute for women, who have experienced many more significant changes to their education choices and their earnings patterns in recent years than have men.

Table 7.3 Average Net Lifetime Returns by Subject Studied

Subject Studied	Women			Men		
	0% discount rate	0.7% discount rate	HM Treasury rate of discount	0% discount rate	0.7% discount rate	HM Treasury rate of discount
Medicine	827	670	340	1350	1072	505
Nursing	224	189	110	81	64	28
Allied to Medicine	222	183	100	240	185	78
Russell Group	268	219	115	635	506	238
Pre-1992 Universities	203	165	87	370	293	133

Source: Table 9 Britton et al. 2020a
Note: Returns are in £000s, are net of taxes and repayments of student loans, and shown at different discount rates

is discounted can make a big difference. This is of course the power or perhaps we should say the impact of compounding; taken over such a long period even small rates of discount can cumulate to have very big impact. Which rate is the right rate cannot be known, rates will differ between individuals—how little or how much they value future earnings will depend on how in general they view the future. It is therefore up to the reader which column they choose.

There is a striking difference between the value of additional lifetime pay for men and women studying medicine. At zero rate of discount, the additional lifetime pay of men is over 60 per cent higher in medicine and 8 per cent higher in subjects allied to medicine. The reverse is, however, the case in nursing, here the value of additional lifetime pay, at zero rate of discount, is nearly three times higher for women than for men. In medicine, the predominance of men, and in nursing, the predominance of women among the most senior and therefore highly paid in these occupations provides the explanation.

Also of great interest is how these returns compare to the average returns to a university education. Table 7.3 records the returns to two different types of university education, what might be thought of as the 'top' universities, the Russell Group, and the returns to the more technical degrees, those awarded by pre-1992 universities. It is noteworthy that the lifetime returns to men who studied Medicine exceed the average returns to those studying at a Russell Group university by between £715,000 and £267,000, depending on discount rate, and the lifetime returns to women studying medicine exceed the average returns to women studying at Russell Group universities by between £559,000 and £225,000.

In contrast, the lifetime pay of women who study nursing is lower than the average for those studying at Russell Group universities, while those for men who study nursing is very substantially lower. However, the study also shows that nurse training offered women a return that was a little higher than the average to subjects taken at pre-1992 universities, and until recently it was these universities that dominated nurse training. We should recall that, toward the end of this period, the costs of nurse training rose, and a larger part of them was shifted back onto the trainee. Nurse training is therefore now likely to prove a less good investment than suggested here, a development which threatens the future supply of this key frontline occupation.

The researchers simulated pay growth through to retirement using data on past pay growth. Whether the pay growth of women in the past provides a good guide to women's future pay growth is, as a general proposition, debatable, though in nursing this might be a reasonable assumption. This is because in nursing, women are already represented in senior roles and so there may be less scope for transformation in the career opportunities for women than there is in other parts of the economy. However, the same cannot be said for those studying medicine for as we have noted in the previous section there is a significant gender pay gap among hospital doctors. We would expect this to be addressed in the future.

The research reveals that investing in the human capital required to become a doctor has been a good investment. On average, the returns to both men and women were higher than those to any other degree. However, the research does not tell us what the returns are to working as a doctor in the NHS. We do not know how many of those graduating with a medical degree are working solely as doctors in the NHS, how many are in receipt of private earnings, and how many have gone on to other careers. The study reveals that investing in a medical degree offers a good return, but it does not reveal the size of that return when employed as doctor in the NHS.

Nor does the research reveal the very high returns enjoyed by some who took other degrees. The data reveal that investing in training to become a doctor offers the prospect of a good average return on the investment, though there may be little prospect of the really high returns that some graduates in subjects such as law and finance might enjoy. These really high returns emerged during the period we have analysed in this chapter, and it is against this background that the deterioration in the relative pay of doctors must be judged.

7.5 Geographical Variations in the Competitiveness of Pay

In Section 6.8, we saw that there was substantial geographical variation in the vacancy rates of frontline occupations in the UK. This was evidence that the attractiveness of frontline work varied between different areas of the UK because the competitiveness of frontline workers' pay differed between areas. The pay of frontline doctors, nurses, and AHPs employed by the NHS exhibits very little geographic variation, because they are paid under UK-wide national salary scales, in contrast to the pay of those working in the private sector of the economy which exhibits substantial geographical variation because it reflects conditions in local labour markets. In the private sector, pay compensates for differences in the cost of living and amenity of different areas, and as a result, nominal rates of pay very geographically. They generate a profile of area pay differences like that depicted in Figure 6.2 and discussed in Section 6.5.

The profile of area pay differences in the NHS looks very different to that in Figure 6.2 because the NHS pays the same rates throughout the UK, except in London and the surrounding areas where a premium over the national rate is paid. Administrative pay setting in health care in the UK has resulted in UK-wide, national, pay agreements (Buchan et. al. 2014) and national rates of pay which exhibit very little regional variation. The profile of area pay differences in the NHS that results from the system of pay setting is depicted in Figure 7.3 below.

These two different systems of pay setting affect the competitiveness of frontline workers' pay in different areas and this can be illustrated by superimposing Figure 6.2 onto 7.3. The resulting Figure 7.4, reveals how the competitiveness of the pay of frontline workers in the NHS, varies geographically. Figure 7.4 shows that there are areas of the country in which NHS pay is below that in the private sector of the economy and areas in which it is above. It shows that this variation in the competitiveness of NHS pay is because NHS pay does not vary from area to area in the same way as it does in the private sector.

The relationship between NHS and private sector pay in each of the different areas of the UK depicted in Figure 7.4 will differ between occupations. If it were drawn for NHS nurses, it would map NHS rates of pay for nurses against the pay that nurses could earn in those occupations in the private sector which they considered alternatives to working in the NHS. The smoothly rising line would plot average pay in the alternative occupations in each area of the country, and the line with steps, the average pay of nurses in those areas. The competitiveness of NHS nurses' pay in each geographical area would then be measured on the vertical axis by the size of the gap between the two lines. In some areas, NHS nurses' pay

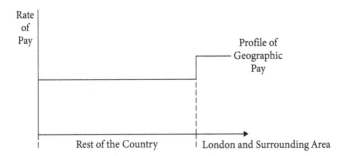

Figure 7.3 Geographical Pay Variation in the NHS

exceeds pay in those private sector jobs they consider alternatives, and in others it falls short.

These differences in the competitiveness of nurses' pay have consequences for nursing vacancy rates, as also indicated in Figure 7.4. In areas where the gap in pay is positive, where nurses are paid more for working in the NHS than they would earn in private sector jobs, we should expect the vacancy rates in hospitals in these areas to be at their natural rates and hospitals might even have waiting list for nursing jobs. In contrast, in those areas where the gap is negative, where nurses are paid less for working in the NHS than they could earn in other jobs, we would expect the vacancy rates in NHS hospitals in these areas to be above the natural rate, and in some areas substantially above.[25]

The relationship between the competitiveness of nurses' pay and nursing vacancy rates depicted in Figure 7.4 has been established in research. One study calculated the competitiveness of nurses' pay, as measured by the size of the gap depicted in Figure 7.4, in each of 230 small geographical areas of England and then investigated the extent to which the size of the gap was associated with the nursing vacancy rate in the area. The researchers found that vacancy rates for nurses were higher the more negative the gap and lower the more positive (Elliott et al. 2007 and 2010).[26]

A second study took a different approach. Instead of measuring the competitiveness of nurses' pay, it looked at the association between nursing vacancy rates

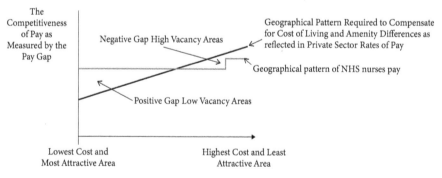

Figure 7.4 Geographical Differences in Competitiveness and Vacancy Rates

[25] Exactly how these lines look in practice has of course to be determined by reference to data and that data is not readily available. Data on NHS and comparator group pay by occupation and local labour market area has only been available in appropriate form in ASHE. ASHE contains sufficient detail and sample numbers to allow these two schedule to be plotted for a small number of NHS occupations. Where the two lines can be plotted the magnitude of the gap between them can be calculated.

[26] The research was undertaken for nurses because this is the largest occupational group employed by the NHS. This meant that both pay and vacancy rates could be identified with confidence in quite small geographical areas, which approximated local labour markets. It was also possible to identify the jobs in which qualified nurses who no longer worked in the NHS were working and the rates of pay in these jobs.

and the cost of living in different areas of England. The study found that, despite attempts by NHS Trusts in England to increase the attractiveness of nurses' pay in high-cost areas, by offering extra hours of work, bank work, and faster promotion, Trusts were unable to fully compensate for cost of living differences. As a result, the researchers found increased turnover and leaving rates in NHS Acute Trusts in higher cost-of-living areas (Propper et al. 2021). The key result of both these studies, is that nurses pay must compensate them for differences in the cost of living and amenity of the different areas of the country in which they work.

We might expect doctors to hold similar views and to move from hospitals in high-cost areas to hospitals in low-cost areas, resulting in vacancy rates that are highest in the former areas and lowest in the latter. However, researchers found this was not the case; they found that vacancy rates for doctors were lowest in some high-cost areas. In particular, they found that though doctors' relative pay was lower in London, the NHS had little difficulty attracting and retaining doctors to work in London hospitals (Elliott et al. 2007 and 2010). There are several possible explanations for this finding.

First, doctors may be less concerned than nurses with the competitiveness of their current pay because their focus is on lifetime pay, and what they are currently paid is a poor indicator of what they expect to be paid over their lifetime. London is attractive because it offers doctors greater opportunities to increase lifetime pay than other parts of the UK. In London there appear to be more opportunities for promotion than other parts of England due to the greater concentration of teaching hospitals in London; teaching hospitals offer doctors opportunities to undertake research and research increases the prospects of promotion.

Second London may be more attractive because it offers some senior doctors greater opportunities for private practice. A third reason that London may be more attractive could be that, although both nurses and doctors attach value to the social and cultural amenities that London offers, doctors are better placed to take advantage of these opportunities; the higher pay of doctors affords them greater access to these amenities. Finally London may be more attractive to doctors because the London labour market is a better match for the work and career ambitions of other members of the household, a better match because of both its sheer size and its more diverse employment structure.

The reverse of the above also holds, rural and remote parts of the country are disadvantaged when seeking to attract doctors. They offer fewer cultural and social amenities, fewer job opportunities for other household members, and fewer opportunities to increase lifetime pay. Attracting health care workers, and particularly doctors and GPs, to work in these areas has been a persistent problem in the UK and has led the Medical Practices Committee to discourage GPs from practising in areas the Committee designated as already well served. Moreover, this problem is not unique to the UK. Many countries experience difficulties attracting doctors and other health care workers to rural and remote areas. Internationally, the use of financial incentives to influence the recruitment and retention of GPs to underserved areas has become more widespread (McIssac 2019) and though Scotland has long paid an 'island allowance' to attract health workers to the remote islands, the UK employs only very modest financial incentives for this purpose.

The conclusion from this research into geographical differences in the competitiveness of frontline workers pay is that the UK should dispense with UK-wide national rates of pay. The pay of frontline workers will need to differ between different geographical areas of the UK if the NHS is to offer competitive rates of pay and set vacancy rates at their natural rates. This entails acknowledging that the high vacancy rates that the current system generates in some areas impose substantial costs on patients, as well as staff, as evidenced in the next section.

7.6 The Impact of Labour Market Disequilibrium: Agency Staff and Temporary Workers

Hospitals with high vacancy rates hire temporary workers, agency and bank nurses, and locum doctors. In England, agency nurses often work across a number of NHS hospitals, and placements are almost entirely short term. Researchers have reported differences in the quality of patient care between high and low vacancy areas. Poorer patient care in high vacancy areas has been attributed to the lack of continuity in key roles, which results in unfamiliarity with ward procedures, policies, equipment, and poorer communication with colleagues and patients (Runge 2017). Research has also revealed that patients' experience of care was poorer where larger numbers of agency workers were employed (Sizmur and Raleigh 2018). A further study reported that, in geographical areas in which there was a higher incidence of temporary, agency, workers, there were higher mortality rates in some clinical procedures (Propper and Van Reenen 2010).

The high levels of vacancies in the NHS in the years prior to the pandemic resulted in considerable use of agency and bank nurses and temporary doctors. Agency and bank nursing placements are short term, while those for medical locums are typically longer, filling gaps created by lengthy recruitment processes as well as filling vacancies in medical specialties.[27] The bank represents a reserve of NHS workers who are paid NHS rates of pay and are deployed to fill vacant posts. Bank workers can be NHS workers working beyond normal hours or a pool employed by an NHS Trust who have agreed to work flexible shifts. Bank workers generally work within a single Trust, and thus offer the prospect that a patient will be treated by the same health care worker throughout their care.

---

[27] In Scotland, medical locums are hired through private agencies. Expenditure on medical locums peaked at £110 million in 2016/17 but had fallen to £98 million in 2018/19.

It is very different with agency workers. They are contracted to work for the NHS by commercial agencies who either employ the workers themselves or act as the agents for the self-employed. Many have previously been employed by the NHS but have quit because they either wish to work more flexibly than full-time NHS employment will allow, or they are attracted by higher rates of pay. Agency workers are paid more than comparable NHS workers, and because the agencies who supply these workers also receive a payment, the total cost to the NHS is considerably higher than employing permanent staff.

Agency workers have accounted for a significant share of workforce costs in England.[28] Expenditure on agency workers increased from 3.4 per cent of total workforce costs in 2011–2012 to 7 per cent or £3.3 billion, in 2014–2015 (NHS Improvement 2019b). In 2016, in an attempt to reduce the attractiveness of this form of working, which was drawing in increasing numbers of NHS workers, NHS England capped pay for agency workers at 155 per cent of basic NHS hourly rates. In Scotland, while agency workers comprise a very small proportion of the overall NHS workforce, 0.4 per cent of FTE hours in 2016, expenditure on agency workers rose in the period prior to the pandemic to total £26.2 million in 2018/19.

In England, Hospital Trusts can afford to employ agency nurses to fill nursing vacancies because the formula that deliver funding to Trusts allocates additional funding to Trusts in areas with high nursing vacancy rates. This component of the funding formula, known as the Staff Market Forces Factor (SMFF), distributes substantial additional funding to high vacancy areas (Elliott et al. 2010). We might expect Trusts to use the additional funding to improve the pay of their permanent staff, because if they did this they would reduce their dependence on agency workers and improve patient outcomes. However, they appear to prefer to pay their workers within the framework of UK-wide national agreements and continue to hire agency workers despite the evident shortcomings of this approach. It is puzzling that Trusts neither exert pressure to change national agreements nor have explored alternative arrangements.

7.7 Summary and Conclusions

In this chapter we have looked at the pay of frontline health and adult social care workers. We have detailed the way that pay is set and revealed how these arrangements have produced rates of pay for frontline workers which are uncompetitive and which, as a result, fail to clear the market. In the previous chapter we saw that the labour markets for key frontline occupations were in a state of serious

---

[28] In 2018, the NHS in England spent £2.4 billion on agency nurses, though this was down from £3.6 billion in 2016. However, over this same period, spending on bank workers—workers who can be allocated at very short notice to fill critical vacancies—has increased steadily. Spending on bank workers was predicted to be £3.3 billion in 2018 (NHS England Shared Business Services 2019).

imbalance, and the detail of what has happened to frontline workers' pay explains why. The key points to take away from this chapter are outlined below.

While market forces might play a role in setting the pay of adult social care workers, they have little impact on the pay of health care workers. This is because the pay of health care workers is set through an administrative process, involving direct negotiations between employers and trade unions, in which labour market imbalance has had little impact on the outcome of these negotiations. Though the degree of imbalance differs between different geographical areas, the pay setting arrangements for health care workers take very little account of this.

In recent years, this disregard has become more pronounced, even though the administrations in the four nations of the UK have assumed a more prominent role in pay setting. There has been little change in the pay structures for doctors and nurses in recent years, where the focus has been on uprating the pay scales. Uprating, through an annual pay award, is intended to be informed by the recommendations of two review bodies, the DDRB and NHSPRB. These bodies were established to undertake independent scrutiny of the available evidence and make recommendations for pay increases based upon their interpretation of that evidence.

It was expected that an independent and arm's-length approach to uprating pay would balance the competing interests of the parties to the negotiations and produce recommendations that would be implemented in full. It might further have been expected that they would recommend rates of pay which balance supply and demand. In practice' neither has happened, governments have often decided what the uprating should be, and arm's-length scrutiny has placed little weight on labour market imbalance. The pay setting arrangements in health care have as a result produced persistent labour shortages. It is not unreasonable to question the usefulness of the Review Bodies in health care.

The challenge facing those involved in pay setting is to understand exactly what the state of the labour market is. If they are to do this, they must be able to detail the balance between supply and demand in each occupation and then calculate the changes in pay that are required to affect this balance. Essential to the wage setting process is high-quality data on both pay and vacancies. Those involved in pay setting make extensive use of the NHS ESR and ASHE when looking at pay. Both datasets provide high-quality payroll data that can be accessed at the individual level by approved researchers. However, neither provide sufficient detail nor any detail on pay from self-employment. Thus, we have an incomplete understanding of how the attractiveness of some frontline jobs has changed in recent years.

These substantial weaknesses notwithstanding, ASHE enables us to distinguish some important long-run changes in the relative pay of the two largest occupations in the health service, doctors and nurses, and to distinguish more recent changes in the relative pay of adult social care workers. These changes in relative pay reveal the changing appeal of frontline jobs over the period. The picture that emerged was very mixed. When the average pay of full-time frontline workers was compared to the average pay of all full-time workers in the UK over the long period from 1970 to 2019, the relative pay of qualified nurses and midwives appeared to have advanced substantially, the pay of auxiliary nurses to have advanced modestly, and that of NHS doctors to have deteriorated. Over the shorter period from 1990, the relative pay of care assistants and adult social care workers also advanced modestly. These results were not undermined by the shortcomings of the data, but certainly require further investigation.

It was found that the advance in qualified nurses and midwives pay 'merely' mirrored the general advance in women's pay over this period. In 1970, nursing was one of the few careers open to women and so the NHS faced little competition when encouraging women to become nurses. Over the subsequent decades, career opportunities for women expanded dramatically and competition among employers intensified, with the result that women's pay in general rose much faster than that of men. The response of health care, though not of adult social care, was enhanced professionalization of nursing and the increasing recognition and reward of the different roles that qualified nurses performed.

Women account for a very substantial majority of the nursing workforce, and the roles that have been assumed by the nursing workforce over this period have increased in complexity and responsibility. These new roles and responsibilities were recognized in Agenda for Change. Yet despite this, the pay of qualified nurses just kept pace with the general advance in women's pay over the period since 1970, no more. This general picture was confirmed in a study conducted by the IFS, which distinguished the lifetime returns to investment in nurse training. It revealed that the returns to women training as a nurse were little better than the average for subjects taken at pre-1992 universities, and the returns to male nurses were much worse.

We would have expected nurses' pay to have outstripped the general advance in women's pay over this period if nursing was to retain its attractions as a career. Over the period from 1970, the demand for nurses has increased at a faster rate than has labour demand in the UK in general, while the costs to individuals of investing in nurse training have increased. Over the period, nursing became a graduate career, entry standards to training increased, and government subsidies to nurse training reduced. This rise in the costs to individuals of investing in nursing human capital without any compensating increase in the returns to that investment is a prescription for reduced human capital investment. It is not, therefore, surprising that in earlier chapters we found that attrition during and following training and nursing vacancy rates had increased substantially over the latter part of the period. The decline in the returns to investing in nurse training threaten the future supply of this key frontline occupation.

Over the period from 1970 to 2019, the relative pay of doctors working in the NHS deteriorated. In 1970, it stood at 2.25 times the pay of all employees, but by 2019 had fallen to 1.95 times. In the interval it had peaked at 2.6 times average weekly earnings in 2005, shortly after the introduction of the new contract for consultants and changes to the pay structure for junior doctors. The sharp deterioration in relative pay between 2005 and 2019 should be a cause for concern. NHS doctors' pay also declined relative to that of other high-earning employees. The pay data revealed that the relative pay of doctors declined from 1.58 times pay at the ninetieth decile in 2005 to 1.19 times in 2019. It appeared there had been a very serious deterioration in the attractiveness of the career of doctor, which would be expected to reduce the number of applicants to train as doctors in future.

However, some doctors employed by the NHS receive self-employed income, as do many in the occupations to which doctors are usually compared, and so a complete picture of doctors' pay can only be achieved once this is included. Research revealed that, in 2003/4, self-employed income added substantially to the average pay of a consultant, though it also revealed the size of this addition varied greatly according to the specialty and area of the country in which the consultant worked. Opportunities for NHS doctors to work in private practice have been open to them for a long time and it is highly unlikely they increased sufficiently to offset the relative decline in their NHS pay.

Income from self-employment was included in the study of the returns to investment in different forms of university education conducted by the IFS. The research revealed that investing in the human capital required to become a doctor had been a good investment. On average, the returns to both men and women who trained as doctors were higher than those to any other degree. The study revealed that investing in training to become a doctor offered the prospect of a good average return but perhaps little prospect of a really high return, as might, for example, be enjoyed by some graduates in subjects such as law and finance. Pay from self-employment may have cushioned the effects of the declining relative pay from NHS work for some doctors and it may go part way to explaining why there has been less discontent than might have been expected to accompany such a dramatic decline. However, while additional pay from other work may mean that training to become a doctor remains an attractive investment, it does not mean that working in the NHS remains attractive and so does not resolve the shortage of doctors working in the NHS. On the contrary, it encourages doctors to substitute out of NHS work and into these other activities.

The pay data also revealed that the pay of adult care workers and auxiliary nurses fell well below the national average. In 1990, the pay of both occupations was around 60 per cent of the national average, and in 2019, it was 63 per cent. Other data revealed that around 14 per cent of all those aged 25 and over working in adult social care in the UK were on the National Living Wage. At these low levels of pay it was unsurprising to find vacancy rate and turnover rates in adult social care which were both well above their natural rates.

Given the evidence on the relative pay of frontline workers, it is unsurprising to find that 2019 vacancy data revealed a serious shortage of workers in key health and social care occupations. The data reported in the Chapter 6 revealed that, prior to the onset of the pandemic, the vacancy rates for doctors, nurses, AHPs, and adult social care workers were all substantially above their natural rates. Average vacancy rates at these levels provided strong evidence that average pay rates for all these occupations were below their competitive levels, and in some cases very seriously below.

The previous chapter also reported that there was substantial geographical variation around these average vacancy rates, and though the data were not sufficiently granular to reveal the precise detail, it was clear that recruiting care workers, nurses, and doctors to some areas of the UK was extremely difficult. London appeared the least attractive to nurses, and remote and rural areas of Scotland the least attractive to doctors. The geographical variations in vacancy rates were evidence of geographical variations in the competitiveness of doctors' and nurses' pay and that the geographical structure of their pay was therefore seriously misaligned. The vacancy rates for nurses and doctors revealed that both average rates of pay and the geographical structure of pay needed substantial revision.

High vacancy rates have consequences for the quality of care. We reported that the serious shortage of nurses in London had led to the widespread use of agency nurses and that the use of agency nurses had been found to be associated with poorer patient care, poorer patient experience of care, and poorer health outcomes. Poorer patient care and experience of care was attributed to the lack of continuity in key roles. Moreover, the greater use of agency workers had been shown to be associated with higher mortality rates in some clinical procedures. Yet in England, the funding that is used by hospitals to employ agency workers is provided through a formula, the Staff Market Forces Factor, which allocates additional funding to NHS Trusts in areas in which nursing vacancy rates are highest. Trusts have the resources to move rates of pay toward competitive levels in high vacancy rate areas but do not do so.

There is another dimension to pay relativities about which we know surprisingly little. We have reported the ethnic diversity of the health and social care workforce and that women occupy four out of every five jobs in the NHS. Despite this, there is evidence of both gender and ethnic pay gaps. On average, female doctors earn less than male doctors. One reason for this is that more women work part time, but even after adjusting for differences in hours worked, a gender pay gap remains. Further, men are disproportionately represented amongst the highest paid positions of consultants, associate specialists, and this in turn has meant that more men received Clinical Excellence Awards.

Asian and Asian British doctors account for almost 30 per cent of the medical workforce and Black and Black British nurses account for 8 per cent of the nursing, midwifery, and ambulance workforces. Health care is an important source of employment and pay for those of Asian and Black ethnicity. However, the median basic pay of full-time white consultants is 4.9 per cent higher than for Black or Black British consultants, and the median basic pay of white nurses nearly 9 per cent greater than that for Black or Black British nurses. One of the reasons for these pay differences among nurses was the distribution of ethnic groups across the different nursing pay bands. Research revealed that Black and ethnic minority nurses were poorly represented in the higher pay bands.

Research into pay differences between workers with different ethnic backgrounds is hampered by the absence of large datasets recording ethnicity, occupation, and pay in detail in health and social care jobs outside the NHS. We do not know what is happening in community or social care. Moreover, the research that has been undertaken has been for NHS England only, and there appears to be no similar research for Scotland, Northern Ireland, and Wales. It is important to fill this gap.

8

The Economics of Workforce Policy

In this book we have explored five economic theories central to understanding the behaviour of labour markets. They are the theories of net advantages, human capital, the production function, the labour demand schedule, and labour market equilibrium. Together they provide the theoretical framework we need to understand the labour markets for frontline workers in health and social care. Two of these theories, those of net advantages and human capital, are required to understand the principal influences on the supply side of the market, while the theories of the production function and labour demand schedule are required for the demand side of the market.

In a perfectly competitive labour market the behaviour of workers who supply labour and organizations who demand labour would be expected to produce balance, equilibrium in the market. Moreover, if the market were subject to an exogenous shock, as labour markets often are, their reactions would set in train forces which would seek to re-establish equilibrium. The concept of equilibrium in the labour market is central to understanding how labour markets work and the forces which seek to restore balance if it is disturbed. These forces are at work even in labour markets which are far from perfectly competitive; they reveal themselves in the aspirations and behaviour of workers and so should not be ignored. The evidence has shown that the labour markets for health care and adult social care workers are far from equilibrium. Thus, it falls to policymakers to introduce policies which will balance labour supply and demand in these labour markets. In this chapter we suggest what some of these polices might be.

8.1 Restoring Pay Relativities to Resolve Labour Shortages

The theory of net advantages makes clear that the pay of any one occupation must be judged relative to that of other occupations, because workers compare the costs and benefits of different jobs and can move between different jobs. Doctors, nurses, and indeed all health and social care occupations are no different from other workers, in this respect. They compare what they are paid, the costs they incurred during training, and the net advantages of the jobs they do to those in other occupations. What they discover from such comparisons determines the attractiveness of frontline jobs and their willingness to do these jobs.

The Economics of the UK Health and Social Care Labour Market. Robert Elliott, Oxford University Press.
© Robert Elliott (2024). DOI: 10.1093/oso/9780198883142.003.0008

Chapter 7 revealed that the relative pay of the three largest health and social care occupations had in recent years either deteriorated or marked time. Moreover, over the same period the costs to individuals of investing in the training required for frontline jobs have risen as many trainees have assumed responsibility for tuition fees. It also seems likely that the conditions of work for frontline workers have deteriorated relative to those of other workers, as a result in large part of the persistent shortages of frontline workers. More recently, the pandemic has added an additional layer of challenge to the jobs they do. It is thus not surprising that the current pay of the three largest frontline occupations appears insufficient to attract and retain the required numbers, and that there are severe labour shortages of these workers in most areas of the UK. Pay relativities need serious scrutiny and a reset. The specific position of each of these three occupations is described in more detail below. We follow this with a set of policy proposals to address the problems identified.

Adult Social Care Workers

Chapter 7 reported that in 2019 the pay of adult care workers was significantly below the national average level of pay for all employees. In that year, pay was 63 per cent of the national average, which was little changed from the position in 1990. The data also revealed that prior to the onset of the pandemic around 14 per cent of all those aged twenty-five and over working in adult social care in the independent sector were on the National Living Wage. In Chapter 6 we saw that, immediately prior to the onset of the pandemic, the average vacancy rate for adult social care workers was 8.2 per cent and the average annual turnover rate was 31 per cent. Vacancy rates for adult social care workers at that time also revealed substantial geographical variation, ranging from 5.5 per cent in the North East of England to 9.5 per cent in London.

Rates of pay for adult social care workers are set in a competitive labour market, and we would therefore expect them to be set at levels which clear the market. The question is: why did this not happen? How were care home owners able to resist the pressures to increase pay which were exerted by high turnover and the associated high transaction costs? For some reason, employers in social care were reluctant, or unable, to increase pay to market-clearing levels. Perhaps they traded off the high transaction costs, associated with high turnover, against a higher pay bill and identified the former as the least cost solution. However, this implies that they had little regard for their residents' preferences because it is widely recognized that high turnover reduces continuity of care and that in adult social care this is highly valued by the recipients of care. Care home residents and those receiving domiciliary care have strong preferences for building relationships with their carers.

The failure to pay competitive rates also suggests that the recipients of care, or their agents, who are most likely relatives, are unable or unwilling to translate residents' preferences for greater continuity of care into the payment of higher fees, and through this, into higher pay for domiciliary and residential care workers. Perhaps they have little confidence that higher fees will translate into higher pay for care workers. There appear to be factors on the demand side of this labour market which are working to suppress pay, though it is unclear precisely what they are.

Brexit may have exacerbated the shortage of applicants for jobs in adult social care, though prior to the pandemic, only 7 per cent of the adult social care workforce were non-British EC citizens. An (as yet unknown) number of these workers has left following Brexit, but whether this will have any impact on pay levels in this sector appears open to question. It is not clear why employers should prove any more amenable to these pressures than they were to the pressures exerted by the pre-pandemic labour shortages. The nature of the imperfections preventing market-clearing require more detailed enquiry.

Qualified Nurses

In Chapter 7 we saw that the labour market for qualified nurses in England in particular was distinguished by severe shortages. Prior to the onset of the pandemic, vacancy rates for nurses stood at 11 per cent in England and at 5 per cent in Scotland. Both rates were above the natural rates, that in England substantially so. Indeed, in England immediately prior to the pandemic the vacancy rate for nurses was higher than that for adult social care workers. Part of the reason for these high vacancy rates was the high attrition rates during nurse training and upon completion of training. Around 25 per cent of those who started nurse training never completed, and many of those who completed did not go on to work as nurses. It appeared the numbers fell away as they began to understand what nursing entailed and what other labour market opportunities existed.

Unlike adult care workers, the relative pay of qualified nurses and midwives improved between 1970 and 2019, from around 70 per cent of the national average for men and women in 1970 to slightly above the national average in 2019. However, this advance meant that nurses pay just kept pace with the general improvement in women's pay which occurred over the same period and which resulted from a profound change in the UK labour market. In 1970, almost 80 per cent of all women who were working worked in either an office or a manual job, and nursing was one of the few professional careers open to women. Over the subsequent five decades, job opportunities for women expanded dramatically. Competition among employers for women intensified and women's pay increased more rapidly than men's, with the result that the gender pay gap narrowed.

This expansion in women's job opportunities occurred at a time when there was also a substantial increase in the demand for qualified nurses. In 1970, around 4 per cent of working women, less than one in every twenty, worked as a qualified nurse, but by 2019 over 6 per cent of working women, or one in every seventeen, was working as a qualified nurse. It was evident that over these fifty years, the demand for qualified nurses expanded more rapidly than job opportunities for women in general. Nurses' pay would therefore have been expected to outstrip the general rise in women's pay if the increased demand was to be satisfied. That it did not is one explanation for the recorded shortage of nurses.

A second reason was the increased costs of investing in the human capital required to become a nurse. Research into the lifetime returns from nurse training, reported in Chapter 7, revealed that, at the end of the period examined in this book, these were little better than the average for subjects taken at pre-1992 universities. During the period analysed here, nursing became a graduate profession and the requirements for entry to nurse training rose accordingly. Moreover, in most of the UK the costs of investing in nurse training were shifted from the government to trainees. Taken together, these changes substantially increased the costs of investing in nurse training. Confronted by stagnant returns and higher costs, it is hardly surprising that many who once might have considered a career as a nurse have been looking elsewhere.

The data also revealed that there was substantial geographical variation in the competitiveness of nurses' pay. The UK-wide scales under which nurses were paid produced very little geographical variation, while pay in the jobs which were alternatives to nursing revealed substantial geographical variation. The result was that vacancy rates for nurses across the regions of England ranged from a high of over 14 per cent to a low of just under 8 per cent and across the Health Boards of Scotland from 9 per cent to under 1 per cent.

The serious shortage of nurses in London resulted in the widespread use of agency nurses. Chapter 7 reported research which had shown that the use of agency nurses was associated with poorer patient care, poorer patient experience of care, and poorer health outcomes, and that the poorer patient care and experience of care was due to the lack of continuity in key roles. The greater use of agency workers had also been shown to be associated with higher mortality rates for some clinical procedures.

In England, the resources required to employ agency workers are provided through the formula that delivers funding to NHS Trusts. This formula allocates additional funding to those areas in which nursing vacancy rates are highest. This component of the funding formula, known as the Staff Market Forces Factor, distributes substantial additional resource to high vacancy rate areas. Trusts have the resources to increase rates of pay toward competitive levels in high vacancy rate areas.

Doctors

Chapter 7 detailed a substantial decline in the relative pay of doctors. The data revealed that the pay of doctors, the vast majority of whom were working in NHS hospitals, had deteriorated from a level 2.25 times the national average in 1970 to 1.95 in 2019. In the interval it had peaked at 2.6 times in 2005, shortly after the introduction of a new contract for consultants and increased payments to junior doctor. Doctors' pay also declined relative to that of other high-paid employees; between 2005 and 2019 it declined from 1.58 times pay at the ninetieth decile of the distribution of weekly earnings to 1.19 times. The data pointed to a very serious deterioration in the attractiveness of the career of an NHS doctor over the period after 2005.

In Chapter 7 we examined the possibility that the decline in the pay of doctors from NHS work might have been arrested by increased pay from other work. We reported the results of a study which revealed the substantial levels of pay that some doctors could earn in private practice. Though the data used in the study was over two decades old, it gave an indication of the levels of pay that could be generated from other work. We also reported the results of very recent research by the Institute for Fiscal Studies which revealed that the lifetime returns from studying medicine were substantial. The study included income from both employment and self-employment and thus captured the total pay in different jobs. The research revealed that training as a doctor produced the highest returns of any subject studied in higher education. This would explain the appeal of medical training, though the steady decline in the relative pay of doctors working in the NHS from 2005 onwards may well have reduced this.

It is unlikely that income from private practice arrested the reported decline in NHS doctors' relative pay. Opportunities for private practice were open to doctors well before 2005 and are unlikely to have expanded sufficiently to make up for the deterioration in relative pay from NHS work. Moreover, while additional pay from private practice may mean that training to become a doctor remains an attractive investment, it does not mean that working in the NHS remains attractive and so does nothing to resolve the shortage of doctors working in the NHS. On the contrary, the availability of private work alongside the decline in relative pay from hospital work encourage doctors to substitute out of NHS work and into other activities.

The decline in relative pay is likely to be a significant part of the explanation for the serious shortage of doctors in the NHS. Prior to the onset of the pandemic, the vacancy rates for doctors ranged from nearly 13 per cent to just under 6 per cent across the regions of England and from 18 per cent to 6 per cent across the health boards on the Scottish mainland. The sharp deterioration in doctors' relative pay from NHS work should be a cause for concern. As the relative attractions of a career as an NHS doctor decline, it would be expected that the quality of applicants to work in the NHS will also decline. A severe decline in the relative pay of an occupation so central to health care delivery has severe consequences for the quality of health care services delivered by the NHS in the future.

The context in which the shortage of nurses and doctors needs to be judged was reported in Chapter 4.6, and was that of a workforce which had in the period prior to the pandemic, achieved a high rate of productivity growth. Over the decade from 2005/6 to 2015/16, labour productivity growth in the NHS outstripped that in rest of the UK economy. The pay data revealed that real pay growth in the NHS over the decade to 2015/16 had been less than labour productivity growth in the NHS, and so the wage bill associated with providing the same level of care in 2015/16 as in 2005/6 had reduced.

Policy Actions

It is evident that the relative pay of key health and social care occupations is not at the level required to eliminate the severe labour shortages we have recorded. Action needs to be taken to adjust pay relativities to their equilibrium levels, and though it is not possible to identify what these levels should be from the publicly available data, the methodology that should be employed is clear. It involves the following two steps:

1) **Identify the Equilibrium Pay Relativity.** To do this, trace the vacancy rates for each health care occupation and its comparator group back in time to find a year when the vacancy rates for both were at their natural, or equilibrium, rates. The pay of the health care occupation relative to that of the comparator group in that year then constitutes the benchmark against which the current relativity should be judged. The comparator group comprises those occupations outside the health service which the occupation views as alternatives to working in the health service. The purpose of pay setting is then to restore this pay relativity, unless it is judged it needs to be adjusted to take account of structural changes in the underlying labour markets. Therefore it is necessary to;

2) **Identify and Evidence any Structural Changes in Labour Markets That Should Modify the Relativity.** This means identifying any substantial changes in the relative attractiveness of NHS work and in the demand for the health care occupation. Where substantial change is identified, the equilibrium relativity, identified at 1) above, will need to be adjusted.

A number of points should be made at this stage. First, if no equilibrium can be identified from historical data, it must be concluded that structural features of the labour market have prevented it from clearing, and action should be directed toward removing the impediments to clearing. Second, the time at which vacancy rates were at their natural, or equilibrium, rates and thus the dating of the equilibrium pay relativity will differ between occupations. Third, there will be geographical variations in vacancy rates around the equilibrium rate, and the pattern of these variations will differ between occupations, which means that the exercise must be conducted at the local labour market level for each occupation.

This task should be undertaken by an independent body, a Commission. The Commission should be charged with: first, identifying the equilibrium pay relativities and the geographical variations in these, for each of the shortage health care occupations; second, identifying any structural changes in labour markets that may require the identified relativities to be modified; third, reporting the required relativities to the government who then decide over what period they will restore the pay relativities required to eliminate the shortages; fourth and finally, handing back responsibility to the Independent Commission to identify the pathway to realizing the appropriate pay relativities. This is analogous to the task that has been set the Low Pay Commission, namely, to identify the pathway to achieving the government goal of a National Living Wage equal to two-thirds of median earnings by 2024. Undertaking such an exercise and implementing the recommendations of such a review would offer a major step forward to solving the labour shortages.

It may not be possible to conduct the same exercise for social care workers, because the government does not set the pay of these workers. However, a priority for action is increasing the general level of pay of these workers and restructuring their salary scales to recognize geographical variations in the attractiveness of working in different areas of the UK. The resulting pay structures must also reward experience and encourage longer tenure to improve continuity of care in this sector. How this should be done is for care home owners and the representatives of workers to agree.

8.2 Health Improvement–Based Recruitment

Restoring relative pay levels to their equilibrium values will attract more people to train in frontline occupations. However alongside this action on the supply side, changes need to be made on the demand side of the labour market. Just as the National Institute for Health and Care Excellence (NICE) engages in a cost–benefit analysis of new drugs and procedures to determine whether they should be adopted by the NHS, so cost–benefit analysis should be undertaken of any proposal to expand NHS employment. The NHS needs to develop a method which will enable it to identify the monetary value of the improvement in health that will result from increasing employment in any area of activity so that it can be compared to the costs of increasing employment in that area of activity. Health care organizations need to develop a mechanism which will enable them to identify the optimal level of employment for each of the different procedures and interventions they deliver.

At present, the demand for labour in frontline care is determined by the size of the budget that a non-commercial health care organization or a workforce team in the NHS has at their disposal. The size of the budget that a commercial organization has at its disposal to spend on labour also affects its' demand for labour. However, the way in which this budget originates and the drivers of the demand for labour in each of the different activities the commercial organization undertakes are completely different to those of the non-commercial health care organization. In the commercial sector, the demand for labour is driven by a direct measure of the value that it produces, and that measure is the market price. The non-commercial health care provider has no such direct measure of the value it produces.

How much labour the commercial organization demands is determined by equating the additional value that is produced by employing more labour to the cost of employing the extra labour. When the two are equal, employment and output are at their optimum level; taking employment beyond this level means paying labour to produce output which the public does not value as highly as it costs to produce, while keeping employment below this level means that output which the public values more highly than it costs to produce is not being produced. The strength of the commercial approach is that it requires an organization to address the following question: will I be paying the additional labour that I propose to hire more or less than the additional value it will produce? This question is as relevant to the non-commercial health or social care organization as it is to the commercial organization.

The value that the commercial organization produces is judged by the consumers of its products. The value that a non-commercial health care provider, such as the NHS, produces could be judged in a similar manner by its patients. Identifying the labour demand schedules for each procedure and intervention the NHS produces would enable it to identify the optimal level of employment and output for each procedure.

The starting point to achieving this is to recognize that all NHS activity, all of the procedures and interventions the NHS delivers, aim ultimately to produce the same output, which is improvement in the health of the UK population. What we often judge to be the outputs of the health service, the number of procedures delivered, for example the number of hip replacements delivered, is not final output, but an intermediate output, an input to the production of the final output of the health service, which is improvement in population health.

Robust methods now exist with which to measure the extent of improvement in health delivered by different procedures and interventions. Quality Adjusted Life Years (QALYs) constitute a generic measure of improvement in health and are now widely used and internationally recognized. The improvement in health produced by each procedure can be specified in terms of the number of QALYs produced.

Moreover, QALYs can be assigned a monetary value. They are employed by NICE to judge the cost-effectiveness of different drugs, clinical procedures, and other interventions proposed for use by the UK public health service. The framework they employ could be adapted to offer a way forward. The objective would be to develop a methodology which a clinical team, or at the higher level a health care organization, could employ when making employment decisions. The method should provide a simple way of quantifying the change in health improvement that resulted from the change in the quantity of a health procedure delivered as a result of a change in workforce, calculating the monetary value of that change in health improvement and comparing it to the change in workforce costs. As we saw in Chapter 3, this amounts to identifying the labour demand schedule for the health procedure and deciding on the optimal level of employment by identifying the point on the labour demand schedule at which the value of the additional output produced equaled the pay of the labour which produced it. This would ensure that the resources of the NHS were employed in their most efficient use, that the contribution of each clinical team to health improvement was equal at the margin at which they were operating.

Policy Actions

The development of a system for measuring and valuing the change in health that results from a change in the production of each procedure and intervention the NHS delivers - QALYs appear to represent the most appropriate unit of measurement available. In parallel devising a system for assigning a unique monetary value to a QALY and a system for weighting QALYs to take account of specific circumstances that society judged merited special treatment.

Once this has been achieved, the NHS would then proceed as follows. When recruitment was being undertaken it would compare the monetary value of the (weighted) units of health improvement that would be produced by the additional workers to the costs of employing these additional workers. It would initially apply this 'benefit–cost calculus' to those areas of NHS activity where it is proposed to increase the workforce, and which are therefore judged priorities for recruitment. Eventually the method should be applied to the margins of all other activities to distinguish those areas where the greatest health improvement relative to cost could be achieved through workforce redeployment.

8.3 Researching Workforce Diversity

Migration, together with the increased recruitment of those from an ethnic minority background who are resident in the UK, has produced an ethnically diverse health and social care workforce in the UK. However, there is evidence that the diversity of the workforce in general is not matched by diversity in senior roles. Black and Black British nurses are underrepresented in the highest nursing pay bands, while among consultants working in the NHS in England, Asian and Asian British doctors on average receive lower pay than white doctors.

It is important that the reasons for these differences be understood, and their causes addressed if workforce performance and motivation are not to be adversely affected. Research similar to that undertaken to inform the inquiry into gender inequality in the medical workforce should be commissioned. Behaviours within health care and social care institutions and the wider social circumstances that discourage and prevent some ethnic groups from realizing opportunities for promotion and advance need to be identified and addressed.

In order to better understand the issues in workforce diversity, there needs to be more detailed and systematic recording of workforce characteristics in workforce data collected by the four nations of the UK. We know much less about differences in opportunities for advancement of health care workers from minority ethnic backgrounds in Scotland, Wales, and Northern Ireland than we do in England.

Policy Action

Research into workforce diversity, ethnic pay gaps, and promotion inequalities should be commissioned. Research should aim to identify the behaviours within health care institutions and wider society, and the social circumstances of people from different ethnic groups and backgrounds that have discouraged and prevented some from realizing opportunities for promotion and advance in health and social care. To enable research, there needs to be more detailed and systematic recording of workforce characteristics in workforce data collected in the four nations of the UK.

8.4 Improving Data

Our understanding of health and adult social care workforce labour markets is significantly impaired by poor data. There is no UK-wide dataset in either health care or adult social care recording the numbers and pay of every frontline occupation. Each country in the UK is responsible for its own data collection, which means there are discrepancies in the ways that data are collected and reported. The most detailed data available on pay and the size and composition of the workforce is only for the NHS workforce. There is no similar data for either community health or adult social care.

NHS workforce data is insufficient to inform either workforce strategy or administrative pay setting. For both these purposes, data on the wider labour markets in which health and social care operate is required. This can only be obtained from external datasets, compiled from surveys conducted by ONS. However, this data is incompatible with that produced by the NHS. The ONS and NHS employ different occupational coding systems and thus occupational titles, they record hours worked and pay in different ways, and they use different administrative areas. ONS data enable choice of geographic area, so that data on employment and pay can be mapped to areas which better match occupational labour markets. Common methods of collecting data and common definitions need to be employed if a detailed understanding of health and social care labour markets, and how they relate to the wider external labour markets, is to be achieved.

This could easily be achieved. Those ONS surveys which collect the data most appropriate to inform NHS workforce strategy and administrative pay setting should be identified. The samples within these datasets for the occupations of interest to health and adult social care should be boosted to generate a sample size which is sufficiently large to enable detailed analyses. The resource required for ONS to achieve this should be transferred from health and social services, from NHS Digital and Skills for Care, among others, to ONS and the data-collecting activities of these organizations scaled back accordingly.

High-quality vacancy data are of central importance for administrative pay setting and are key to understanding the balance between supply and demand in occupational labour markets. The quality of health and social care vacancy data leaves a great deal to be desired. If vacancy data are to perform the task required, there must be clear and straightforward criteria setting out what constitutes a vacancy. Accurate data are essential if we are to distinguish true vacancy rates and identify how these differ from natural vacancy rates.

Policy Action

Those ONS surveys which collect the pay and employment data required to inform NHS workforce strategy and administrative pay setting should be identified. The samples within these datasets for the occupations of interest to health and adult social care should be boosted to generate a sample size which is sufficiently large to enable detailed analyses. The resources required to fund this expansion of ONS activity should be transferred to ONS from NHS Digital, Skills for Care, and other agencies currently collecting this data. The data-collecting activities of these organizations should be scaled back accordingly. Robust criteria for identifying a vacancy must be introduced and detailed vacancy data collected on a consistent and regular basis, at a level of detail which identifies the rates in the different geographical labour markets for health and social care workers and at the frequency required to inform pay and employment policy. The data should allow for robust comparisons across the four nations of the UK and this work should be undertaken as a matter of urgency.

8.5 Workforce Planning

Current workforce planning models are deficient in several respects. They assume no funding constraint and that forecast health care needs will be met—that health care need translates into effective health care demand. We know that this often does not happen, that funding constraints restrict treatment numbers. We also know that health care needs may not translate into effective demand for health care even though funding has been provided to meet those needs because some people, particularly those in low-income and deprived communities, may fail to present for treatment.

Current workforce planning models take no account of the concept of optimality, the idea that at a given cost of labour there will be an optimal level of employment and output for each procedure and intervention, yet this is central to efficient resource allocation. They make no attempt to calculate the value of the improvement in population health which will result from expanding the workforce and to balance this against the costs of this expansion. They make no attempt to assess the costs and benefits of expanding the health care workforce.

Workforce planning models make no use of key labour market data; the pay of different occupations which reveal the costs of different workforce configurations; the relative pay of different health care occupations which determine the extent to which recruitment targets will be realised; vacancy rates which reveal how far health care labour markets are from equilibrium; and the returns to human capital investment in key health care occupations which determine long term labour supply. Vacancy rates are required to inform the initial starting point for the forecasts, and relative pay is required to estimate the likely supply response of key occupations and therefore the likelihood of realizing the workforce projections and the efficiency of the different workforce configurations.

Policy Action

The forecasts produced by workforce planning models must recognize the existence of expenditure constraints and modelling should take account of different funding regimes. The models should make use of key labour market data, data such as vacancy rates, and relative pay rates because these affect the likelihood that the forecasts will be realized. They should also seek to quantify the value of the improvements in population health which the workforce projections are expected to produce in order to balance these against the costs of employing that workforce.

8.6 The Post-Covid-19 Labour Market

At the time of writing the impact of the pandemic on the UK labour market in general and health and social care labour markets in particular is still emerging. Labour markets are in a state of transition, unemployment is low, job vacancies high, and activity rates below their pre-pandemic levels. Inflation is also high, living standards are being squeezed, but the full impact of the policies designed to reduce inflation have yet to be felt. These are conditions that many in the labour market have not previously experienced, and so their responses are difficult to predict.

NHS employment increased during the pandemic. By the end of 2021 the nursing workforce was 8 per cent larger than in September 2019[1] and the number of doctors was 9 per cent higher than at the end of 2019.[2] There were over twenty thousand more nurses and ten thousand more doctors (FTE) working in the NHS and GP settings in England at the end of 2021 than there were at the end of 2019. The increase in numbers reflected the increase in NHS labour demand during the pandemic; the effective demand for labour by the NHS increased as a result of the sharp increase in health care spending. At the same time labour supply to the NHS increased as job opportunities in the rest of the economy and abroad contracted.[3] Because job opportunities expanded in the NHS but reduced elsewhere, NHS leaving rates fell. Nurses and doctors who might otherwise have retired now stayed on, and those who might have looked to work outside the NHS no longer did so. The attrition rates of nurses completing training fell because job opportunities, locally and internationally, fell. Yet it appears that this increase in the number of doctors and nurses has failed to address the persistent shortage of these occupations.

The tighter UK labour market which emerged at the end of the pandemic will have intensified competition in many of the occupational markets in which health and social care providers hire workers. Tighter labour markets will increase pay in jobs considered to be alternatives by nurses and social care workers and may tip the balance between the costs and benefits of investing in health and social care

---

[1] Department of Health and Social Care (DHSC) (2022) 50,000 Nurses Programme: Delivery update. Policy paper, 7 March.

[2] NHS Digital (2022) NHS Workforce Statistics—November 2021 (Including selected provisional statistics for December 2021), 3 March.

[3] ONS Vacancies and jobs in the UK: February 2022.

human capital further against these investments. In addition, they will increase attrition rates from nurse training and reduce NHS retention rates for nurses.

The pandemic has changed perceptions of the attractiveness of frontline work. It has changed perceptions of the safety of the working environment for frontline workers and made more evident the stress associated with working on the front line. In light of the challenges they have faced, some NHS workers will have reassessed their lifestyle choices and will now retire earlier, while still others may decide that a career in the NHS is no longer for them.

An important consequence of the pandemic is a change in the pattern of working in some occupations that are alternatives to working in health and social care. The pandemic resulted in increased working from home for workers in many occupations outwith health and social care, and consequently fewer journeys to the designated place of work for these workers. As a result, they now have both less exposure to any disadvantages of the workplace and, because they commute less and are therefore willing to commute over longer distances, they now have a greater choice over residential location.

None of these advantages of home working are open to frontline workers. They are less able to avoid workplace costs through working from home, continue to commute to work, and have a restricted choice of residential location compared to many other workers. A distinguishing characteristic of frontline jobs is that they have to be undertaken at the designated place of work, in a hospital, GP practice, or care home—except in a few exceptional cases care cannot be delivered remotely. The pandemic has increased the disadvantages of frontline work.

Increased home working will have a big impact on the attractiveness of frontline jobs. The precise impact of these developments on labour supply to frontline occupations and on the equilibrium rates of pay for these occupations will take time to emerge, but it is likely to be profound. At present, the impact of these changes on the appeal of frontline jobs is little recognized and poorly understood, though because, on balance, jobs on the frontline have become less attractive, it means action on pay is of even greater importance.

One thing the pandemic did was to reveal a substantial advantage of the structure of health care provision in the UK. The dominance of the NHS has several negative features, which have been spelt out in this book, but Covid revealed an advantage which should not be forgotten. The NHS is what economists would describe as a vertically integrated organization, which means that a large number of the activities which contribute to the final output it produces are conducted in-house, they are not contracted out to separate companies. The NHS is not completely vertically integrated: some activities which used to be conducted in-house forty years ago have been outsourced (cleaning is an example), but there has been far less contracting out than in many other industries.

Vertically integrated companies offer the advantage of labour flexibility. During the pandemic, the number of workers in frontline and key supporting roles were boosted by switching workers engaged in other activities into these jobs. In many university and hospital trusts, those with medical training who, in pre-pandemic days, were engaged in teaching and administration were switched to frontline work. It will be important to retain labour flexibility, and therefore the NHS must resist the pressures to contract out jobs and functions, pressures which will certainly intensify over the next few years.

Moreover, the NHS can learn from this experience. It should research cases of role-switching to distinguish the ease with which workers were able to change roles and undertake new tasks. The research would help the NHS identify the barriers to and the facilitators of role reassignment. The exercise could identify new training requirements and new possibilities for workforce deployment, and it might also reveal the extent to which current training has produced a workforce which is too specialized. The research would also reveal which nursing and medical specialists proved most adaptable and which least so.

A vertically integrated organization also offers other workforce advantages. It offers workers a greater number of entry points to the internal occupation and grade structure, and therefore it offers workers greater opportunities for career progression than organizations which have contracted out many activities. One example is that the NHS offers opportunities for those hired as auxiliary nurses to progress to qualified nurses and more senior nursing roles. These advantages of the NHS structure need to be recognized and retained.

Policy Action

Commission research into the impact of increased homeworking on the attractiveness of frontline work and explore its implications for the recruitment and retention of frontline workers. Commission a study into the experience of workers who changed roles during the pandemic in order to identify barriers to and facilitators of increased flexibility. Evaluate the longer-term consequences of this for future workforce deployment, training requirements, and workforce planning.

8.7 Workforce Policy under Expenditure Constraints

Health spending rose sharply during the pandemic. Preliminary estimates by the OECD for 2020 (OECD 2021) suggest that the share of GDP allocated to health and social care in the UK rose from 10.2 per cent of GDP in 2019 to 12.8 per cent in 2020. This was a result of both the extra health spending needed to combat Covid-19 and sharp reductions in GDP caused by the restrictions on economic activity. The share will fall back as pandemic-related spending ends and as GDP recovers. While increasing the share of national income that the UK spends on these activities is essential if the UK is to reduce workforce shortage in the longer term, at the time of writing, the appetite of politicians for increasing public spending on health and social care appears limited. If this remains the case, other ways to improve the volume and quality of health care need to be identified. There are three main ways of containing labour costs, which may also leave scope for increasing pay.

1. Improving the efficiency of the existing workforce

The methods by which this can be achieved have already been discussed at 8.2 above. They require calculating the value of the health improvement produced at the current margins of activity and redeploying labour from those activities producing the least improvement relative to cost to those producing the greatest improvement relative to cost. This should be done up to the point at which the ratio of the value of the health improvement to the cost of the labour which produced that improvement is equalized across all frontline activities.

2. Reviewing the prominence of consultants in service delivery

As the NHS data in Chapter 1 make clear, the NHS has become a consultant-led service. Since its creation, the rate of growth in consultant numbers has outstripped that of other doctors and nurses. Between 1949 and 2018, the number of consultants working in NHS hospitals in England and Wales increased three times faster than the number of nurses. Indeed, once we adjusted for hours worked, this understated the relative growth in the number of consultants. A consultant-led workforce is a more specialized and less flexible workforce, and it responds less quickly to changing patterns of demand for health care because it takes much longer to train consultants than other frontline workers. The prominence of consultants in the delivery of hospital procedures should be reviewed and new workforce configurations developed and evaluated. New workforce configurations will require other frontline workers to undertake some of the tasks done by doctors, and so a necessary corollary of such a policy is increased task substitution.

3. Increased task substitution

The skill sets of different occupations often overlap, the skill sets of senior house officers, registrars, and consultants can overlap, those of physician associates (PAs) and some doctors grades overlap as do those of advanced nurse practitioners, ANPs, and qualified nurses, and qualified nurses and nursing assistants. In UK health care, the task substitution made possible by these overlapping skill sets has proceeded cautiously and the reasons for this need to be explored. Overlapping has been engineered through the development of new occupations, ANPs, and PAs, but as yet their numbers are small. Task substitution offers opportunities to contain health care costs (substituting less expensive labour) and to enhance workers' contribution by allowing occupations to extend their roles. It is also an effective mechanism for addressing doctor shortages within a relatively short time frame. Increased task substitution can be achieved by extending the scope of practice of existing roles and encouraging greater numbers to train in the new occupations.

8.8 Final Thoughts

The detail of all the above policy recommendations need further work. They are proposed to stimulate discussion about frontline labour market policy; discussion about what tools we need to develop to decide how many frontline workers we need to employ, the way we should pay them and how well we should pay them. They are presented on the understanding that the labour markets for some other occupations have a profound effect on frontline labour markets and have changed as a result of the pandemic.

Any discussion of the UKs frontline workforce, concerning its size, composition, and pay, must have at its core a sound theoretical framework to integrate these different dimensions into a coherent whole. Labour economics provides that framework, and its use can bring greater rigour and coherence to policymaking. Without a conceptual framework, the interpretation of data will lack coherence and workforce policy will be piecemeal. Using the conceptual tools of labour economics will reveal the shortcomings of the data currently available to inform policy and the inconsistencies in policy which have resulted from this.

Analysis of frontline labour markets is still something of a rarity within health economics and health services research. It remains a paradox that the largest single item of spend within health and social care in the UK is among the least studied. If this book manages to change that, it will have achieved one of its major aims.

Counting the Frontline Care Workforce: Data Sources

There are three main sources of data on employment and workforce in the UK. The first is the decennial *Census of Population*. The most recent results available at the time of writing were from the 2011 Census of Population. The Census is based on a self-completion questionnaire and enables us to identify in some detail what type of work people did and what they stated the main activity of their business or employer to be. The most recent Censuses classify work using the Standard Occupational Classification (SOC) and activity using the Standard Industrial Classification (SIC). The strengths of the Census are the long runs of data available and the inclusion of both employees and self-employed. The weakness is self-completion, which may result in errors when stating the nature of their main job, their business, or their employers main activity. The results are reported separately for England and Wales, Scotland, and Northern Ireland. Those for England and Wales are reported on the ONS website, which is far from well-organized and thus hard to navigate and interrogate. The sources of the Census data used here are:

For England and Wales see Tables CT0437 and WP605EW which can be located at: https://www.ons.gov.uk/peoplepopulationandcommunity/populationandmigra tion/populationestimates/bulletins/2011censuspopulationestimatesfortheunited kingdom/2012-12-17

For Scotland see Tables C11 and CT0222 at: https://www.scotlandscensus.gov.uk/

For Northern Ireland see KS605NI and CT0458NI at: https://www.nisra.gov.uk/ statistics/census/2011-census

The second source of data is the *Labour Force Survey*, which is a residence-based labour market survey encompassing population, economic activity (employment and unemployment), economic inactivity, and qualifications. It is part of the Annual Population Survey, a quarterly household survey with information gathered by either face-to-face or telephone interviews. The data from the LFS are broken down by gender, age, ethnicity, industry, and occupation and are available at Local Authority level and above. It is updated quarterly.

Industry and occupation are coded differently in the LFS and the Census. In the LFS, 'the data are coded by interviewers using either a computer-assisted system or a manual system assisted by lookups. For the census, automatic coding methods are used, assisted by expert coding using computer-aided technology where necessary. Decision rules on the census are also not always consistent with the ILO definition as it applies on the LFS'. (A comparison of the 2011 Census and the Labour Force Survey (LFS) labour market indicators, ONS 2012).

The third source is health and social care employers data. The NHS, the major employer, reports workforce data for England and Wales at: https://digital.nhs.uk/data-and-information/publications/statistical/nhs-workforce-statistics; for Scotland at: https://www.isdscotland.org/Health-Topics/Workforce/; and for Northern Ireland at: https://www.health-ni.gov.uk/articles/staff-numbers. The data for the other major element of this workforce, the social care workforce, is much less systematically collected. The data reported appear to be on a headcount basis but do not appear to be collected using a common definition. Social care workforce numbers should therefore be treated with care. Sources of these data are as follows. England: *The health care workforce in England*, published by The Health Foundation; and Skills for Care published each year; Scotland: *National health and social care workforce plan: part one*, June 2017; Wales: The Economic Value of the Adult Social Care sector – Wales Final report 5 June 2018; Northern Ireland: *Northern Ireland Health and Social Care Workforce Census March 2018*, https://www. health-ni.gov.uk/sites/default/files/publications/health/hscwc-march-18.pdf. The figures for England, Scotland, and Wales include those working in domiciliary care. Those for Northern Ireland exclude them.

Deriving the Labour Demand Schedule

At the heart of the labour demand schedule is the production function. The production process is detailed in a production function which describes the relationship between inputs and outputs. The production function details the relationship between the inputs that are required to produce a particular type of output and shows how output increases as inputs increase. In health and social care, nurses, doctors, AHPs, and adult social care workers are inputs to the production processes that produce hospital procedures and residential and domiciliary care. Capital, the buildings, theatres, medical equipment, medical devices, and drugs that are used by these workers are other inputs to most procedures. These inputs to production, labour, and capital are called *factors of production*.

Production functions can be detailed for both the long and the short run. The long-run production function allows all inputs to be changed, while the short-run production function details a period in which only one of the inputs, the labour input, can be changed while all of the other inputs are fixed. The short-run production function, for a particular hospital activity or procedure, will therefore describe how the number of procedures delivered changes as the labour input changes.

An example of a short-run production function in health care is the one which produces MRI scans. MRI scans are an intermediate output, a diagnostic tool which constitutes a key input to many clinical procedures. To produce MRI scans, radiologists, the labour input, use MRI scanners, the capital input. In the short-run capital, the number of MRI scanners is fixed and therefore the only way to produce more scans is to employ more radiologists or for those presently employed to work longer hours. This short-run production function can be depicted in Figure 3A.1.[1] The Figure shows how the number of completed scans increases as the number of hours worked by radiologists increases.

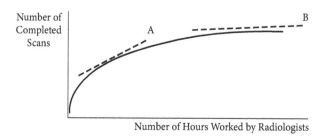

Figure 3A.1 A Health Care Production Function

---

[1] Thus, for a process involving both doctors and nurses working with a particular health technology, the relationship can be written more formally as follows: $Q_{HC} = f(L_N, + L_D + K)$ where Q_{HC} represents the quantity or quality of health care produced, L_N, and L_D represent, respectively, the number of nurses and doctors employed, and K is the quantity of capital with which they work. In each health care setting a different mix of inputs, a different production function will operate and thus in each setting the equation can be given precise form.

The slope of this production function shows the rate at which output is increasing, and the slope changes as the number of hours worked by radiologists increases. In Figure 3A.1 when radiologists are working very few hours, each additional hour they work produces a very large increase in output, as indicated by the increasing slope of the production function. This could be because, as they work more hours, they repeat tasks, and in so doing discover more efficient ways of working, or because, if several radiologists working together work more hours, they are able to achieve a more efficient division of labour between them. However, there will be limits to how much output can increase as hours worked increase because other factors will intervene. Longer hours can lead to exhaustion, while if hours are increasing because the number employed is increasing, beyond some point they are likely to get in each other's way. Eventually, the capacity of the scanner will be reached.

We can see how the slope of the production function is changing by looking at the slopes of the two lines drawn as tangents to the production function at A and B; the slope at A is greater than the slope at B, revealing that output is increasing at a faster rate at A than at B. As we move along the production function, the rate at which output is increasing declines: as radiologists work more hours the rate at which their output increases declines. This is an illustration of the *law of diminishing returns*, which states that if one input to a production process is increased while all other inputs are fixed, the increases in the one input will eventually produce progressively smaller increments to output.[2] The increment to output is called the *marginal product*, and the increment to output which results from employing more labour is called the *marginal product of labour*.

The declining marginal product of labour can be illustrated diagrammatically. The slope of the production function over the region of the production function, where the marginal product of labour declines as the number of hours worked by radiologists increases, is depicted in the *marginal product of labour schedule* drawn in Figure 3A.2. The schedule maps the additions to output, the additional scans, against the increasing amount of the one input, the increasing number of hours worked, which has produced the scans. It depicts how the addition to output declines as more hours are worked. Figure 3A.2 also illustrates a point where the marginal product of labour is zero, this is the point where the marginal product of labour schedule cuts the horizontal axis and it corresponds to the point on the production function where the slope becomes horizontal.

In the short run, every production process will display diminishing returns beyond some level of output,[3] and therefore every process can be depicted by a marginal product of labour schedule like that shown in Figure 3A.2. The marginal product of labour schedule tells an organization how much more output it will get if it employs more labour, and this is the first thing that any organization which employs labour and makes decisions about whether

---

[2] We might have chosen a different example, that of replacement hip operations or some other form of surgery. Surgery provides a good example of the law of diminishing returns. Surgeons become better at performing operations the more they do, up to some point. By repeatedly undertaking the procedure they learn the most efficient way of working and how best to overcome the challenges that different patients present, but there are clearly physical limits to the number of procedures any person can undertake. Replacement hip operations are, however, delivered by a surgical team, and so the production function for this procedure would need to be defined by mapping team input against output. Labour input would be defined in terms of the total hours of the team, perhaps weighting the different inputs according to their contribution (and pay?). This is, evidently, rather more complicated.

[3] What we are less certain about in health care is the point on the production function at which we currently operate. If the funding available to support the delivery of some procedures is so restricted we may be at a point where returns are still increasing. Knowledge of the production function underlying each procedure is essential.

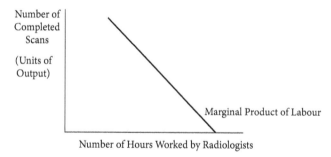

Figure 3A.2 The Marginal Product of Labour Schedule

to employ more or fewer workers needs to know; what changing the number of workers it employs means for its output.

However, organizations need to know more than this before they can decide whether to employ more labour. Commercial organizations need to know what selling the additional output will add to revenue because it is not the quantity of output itself that matters to them but what this means in terms of additional revenue. A non-commercial organization such as the NHS should also want to know whether employing more labour will add to the value of what it produces, but though the principle is the same its realization is different. It is simplest to illustrate how it differs by taking the example of a commercial organization.

The objective of a commercial organization is to maximize profits, and the simplest example of such an organization is one which sells its products in a perfectly competitive market. A perfectly competitive market is one in which the organization can sell all the output it wants to produce, but it must be at a price which is dictated by the market—the organization has no control over price. In order to find out how much additional revenue is generated by selling the additional output the commercial organization simply multiplies the number of additional units of output produced, as mapped in Figure 3A.2 by the market price. The schedule that results is called the *marginal revenue product of labour schedule* and is shown in Figure 3A.3. It looks exactly like the schedule in Figure 3A.2 because we have multiplied each unit produced by a uniform price, but the difference is that Figure 3A.3, records the monetary value of the additional output, rather than units of output on the vertical axis.[4]

Now we have all we need to identify the commercial organization's labour demand schedule. The vertical axis is specified in monetary terms, so we can map both different levels of payment for labour as well as the monetary value of output on the vertical axis. We can map the value of the additional output produced by labour against the cost of that labour.

Now the answer to the question, 'how much labour will this organization want to employ?', is simply found. Because the organization is profit-maximizing, it will want to employ labour up to the point at which the last person employed (or the last hour worked) adds as much to revenue as they add to costs. If employing more workers added more to revenue than to costs it would want to increase employment further because the additional labour is adding to profits. If, however, the last person they were thinking of employing

---

[4] If the firm had market power, if it was not a price-taker but a price-maker, it would only be able to sell additional output if it lowered the price of output. In this case, the sale of the additional output would add less to revenue than in the case of the price-taking firm, and the marginal revenue product of labour schedule would be more steeply sloped.

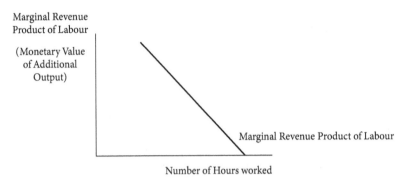

Figure 3A.3 The Marginal Revenue Product of Labour Schedule

would add less to revenue than the firm would have to pay them, then the firm would not take them on, because employing that person would reduce profits.

This is illustrated in Figure 3A.4. If the rate of pay is P_1 the organization will want to hire N_1, and if pay is P_2 the organization will want to hire N_2, and so on because at each of these points the revenue generated is equal to pay. The schedule in Figure 3A.4 maps the unique set of points at which pay is equal to the marginal revenue product of labour, and so it tells us how much labour the profit-maximizing organization will wish to employ at each level of pay. Thus for the profit-maximizing organization, the marginal revenue product of labour schedule is the demand for labour schedule.[5]

The labour demand schedule slopes downwards because it reflects the slope of the marginal product of labour schedule. It slopes downwards not because employers necessarily want to pay people less but because the output produced by each additional hour worked is less than the previous hour. The marginal product of labour, and therefore the marginal revenue product of labour, declines as more labour is employed. When hiring more labour the organization only maximizes profits if what it pays labour is reduced in line with the declining marginal revenue product of labour.

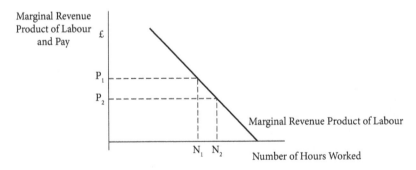

Figure 3A.4 The Labour Demand Schedule

---

[5] A formal derivation of the labour demand function from the production function can be found in most Labour Economics textbooks. See for example Elliott (1990).

The model describes the information that a profit-maximizing organization needs when deciding how much labour to employ and what level of output to produce. Some health and social care organizations, namely private health care providers and some social care providers, are also in business to make profits. These health and social care providers must also consider the relationship between the extra revenue generated by taking on additional workers and what they will have to pay them. As in the model of the profit-maximizing firm, they will want to employ labour up to the point at which the last person hired (or the last hour worked) adds as much to revenue as they add to costs.[6]

It could be argued that this profit-maximizing model is too abstract and that organizations do not make detailed calculations of the marginal revenue that will be generated each time they consider increasing employment. However, though they may not make such explicit calculations, they will form a judgement about whether, if they hire additional workers, they are likely to add more to revenue than they will cost. Profit-maximizing organizations weigh the value that additional workers are expected to produce against the costs of employing the additional workers. They try to judge the benefit to them of expanding employment at the margin, asking: is the extra labour going to generate more value than it will cost?

The strength of the model is that it identifies the very clear criteria that the commercial organization must employ when making employment decisions. The model captures the logic of the decision process of an organization that is in business to make profits. Moreover, the same logic must surely apply to those organizations which are not in business to make profits—they too must surely seek to balance the value that an additional worker contributes against the cost of employing the worker.

Of course in the UK the largest health care provider, the NHS, and many other smaller health care providers are not commercial organizations, and so this model cannot be simply transferred across. However, what the model makes clear is that all organizations, including non-commercial health care organization, need to have a very clear understanding of the value they are producing.

As we have detailed in the main body of this chapter methods exist which will allow the NHS to distinguish the value that it produces. The contribution to health improvement of each additional procedure produced by a non-commercial health care organization could be measured in terms of QALYs. For example, the contribution to health improvement of each additional hip replacement procedure completed could be measured along the production function for hip replacements in terms of QALYs and the increments to health improvement, measured in terms of a count of the number of QALYs, not by a count

---

[6] The markets in which private health care providers operate may not be perfectly competitive and so these organizations may have some discretion over the prices they charge. This might be because they are the only producer in the area and so have something of a local monopoly, or it might be because their customers do not have the information required to make fully informed judgements about what they are producing and so have difficulty comparing the prices which different producers are charging. Where organizations have discretion over the prices they charge, they are not price-takers, and so the relationship between their marginal product of labour and marginal revenue product of labour schedules is not quite as straightforward as that described above. This is because the marginal product of labour is multiplied by a different price at each level of output. Nonetheless, these organizations will still be operating on that part of the production function which is subject to diminishing returns, and they will have a labour demand schedule which is downward sloping. The same reasoning as that employed by the profit-maximizing organisation operating in a perfectly competitive market will inform their decisions. They too will be trying to assess the net benefit to them of expanding employment at the margin, and they will want to employ labour up to the point at which the last person hired (or the last hour worked) adds as much to revenue as they add to costs.

of the number of hip replacements produced. Figure 3A.1, redrawn to represent the production function for hip replacements, would still measure the quantity of the labour input along the horizontal axis but would now record the number of QALYs on the vertical axis.

The production function would exhibit diminishing returns, and the marginal product function would be downward sloping, in the same way as in Figure 3A.2. The vertical axis would record the number of QALYs and the marginal product of labour schedule for hip replacements would be specified in QALYs.

It would also be able to derive a schedule detailing the marginal value of health improvement once it assigned a monetary value to each QALY. Once that were done it would be able to derive the equivalent of the marginal revenue product of labour schedule of the commercial organization; for the non-commercial health care organization this would measure the *marginal monetary value of health improvement (from labour)*.

An example of such a schedule for an NHS procedure is given in Figure 3A.5. Moreover, as was the case with the commercial organization, this schedule would constitute the *NHS Labour Demand Schedule* for that procedure. Just as the marginal revenue product of labour schedule constituted the labour demand schedule of the commercial organization, so the marginal monetary value of health improvement (from labour) schedule would represent the labour demand schedule for this procedure for the NHS. There would be different labour demand schedules for each procedure the NHS delivered, and this would enable it to determine the optimal level of employment for each of these procedures.[7] The optimal level would be where the monetary value of the improvement in health resulting from the delivery of the procedure was equal to the cost of labour which produced the procedure. In Figure 3A.5 the NHS would employ N_1, if pay were P_1, and N_2 if pay were P_2, and so on.

The NHS would proceed in the same way as the commercial organization. In the same way as the commercial organization asks, 'does the addition to revenue that will result from employing more labour exceed the cost of that labour?', so the NHS would ask whether the monetary value of the health improvement from employing more labour exceeded the cost

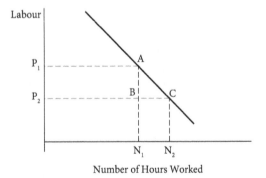

Figure 3A.5 The NHS Labour Demand Schedule
(*A Marginal Monetary Value of Health Improvement (from Labour) Schedule*)

[7] We use the term the rate of pay or just simple pay, as a shorthand for the unit costs of employing labour in the short run. The marginal cost of employing labour includes the rate of pay, and any pension contributions and statutory labour costs, such as employers national insurance contributions, which are related to the level of pay, which employers are required to make.

of the labour that produced the improvement. If employing more people and producing more procedures produced a greater monetary value of improvement in health than was added to costs the NHS should increase employment, but if employing more people added less to the value of improvement in health than it added to costs, it should employ fewer. The NHS hospital, seeking to maximize the value of the improvement in the health of the patients it cared for, would employ health care workers up to the point where their cost was equal to the monetary value of the health improvements they produced. The marginal NHS worker would be the one whose contribution to health improvement was valued equal to their cost.[8]

[8] Alongside the NHS and private for-profit health providers, there are private not-for-profit providers, and the situation is further different for them. They exist in both health and adult social care. They will value the health improvement that workers produce but, because they are also likely to pursue other objectives, including the generation and retention of a surplus (profit) to further their organizational goals, the value of the contribution of the marginal worker may differ from that of the NHS or the government. Yet although they are making a different calculation, these providers will also wish to continue employing health workers up to the point where the weighted value of their contributions (to health and other things) just equals their pay.

The Elasticity and Cross-Price Elasticity
of Labour Demand

The elasticity of labour demand measures the responsiveness of the demand for labour to a change in the price of labour, while the cross-price elasticity of labour demand measures the degree of interdependence between any two labour demand schedules. Thus, the elasticity of demand will reveal the responsiveness of the demand for an occupation to a change in the pay of that occupation, and the cross-price elasticity will reveal the responsiveness of the demand for one occupation to a change in the pay of another occupation; the cross-price elasticity will therefore reveal the degree of interdependence between the demand for any two occupations.

The elasticity of labour demand is calculated by expressing the percentage change in the demand for occupation A over the percentage change in the cost of employing occupation A, or as this cost is usually expressed, the pay of occupation A. Elasticity can be depicted visually by the slope of the labour demand schedules shown in Figures 3A.4 or 3A.5. In general, the shallower the slope of a labour demand schedule, the more elastic the demand for labour, and the steeper the slope, the less elastic is the demand for labour.

The concept of the cross-price elasticity takes this a stage further: it measures the responsiveness of the demand for occupation A to a change in the pay of occupation B. It is calculated by expressing the percentage change in labour demand for occupation A over the percentage change in pay of occupation B. By calculating the cross-price elasticity we can tell if the occupations are substitutes or complements. If the cross-price elasticity is positive, occupations A and B are substitutes because a rise in the pay of occupation A has resulted in an increase in the demand for occupation B. However, if the cross-price elasticity is negative, the two occupations are complements because the rise in the pay of A, which led to a fall in the demand for occupation A, also led to a fall in the demand for occupation B.

The cross-price elasticity of labour demand would be expected to be greater in the long run than in the short run. This is because in the long run, provided there is a substitute occupation, we can always replace more expensive labour with cheaper labour—the long run is, by definition, a time period in which any training the substitute occupation needs can be completed. The cross-price elasticity of labour demand measures the ease with which we can make the substitution. Thus, the more elastic the cross-price elasticity of demand, the easier it is to substitute.

The elasticity of labour demand and the cross-price elasticity of labour demand enable us to distinguish the impact of a pay rise for an occupation on the employment and pay bill for that and other occupations and are therefore important concepts.

In the long run there are four factors which determine the elasticity of demand for an occupation. They are:

1) the ease with which that occupation can be substituted either by another occupation or by capital;
2) the elasticity of supply of any substitute occupations where substitution is possible;
3) the share of the total pay bill that an occupation accounts for; and

4) the degree of resistance to any tax or price increase by those who are paying for the work that is done by the occupation.

Each of these is considered in greater detail in what follows.

The first of these states that the demand for an occupation will be less elastic (demand will fall only slightly as pay rises) the more difficult it is to substitute the occupation by either another occupation or by capital equipment.[1] Many things can inhibit substitution, rules and protocols, and the nature of the technology may mean that only a particular occupation can perform a particular task. Even where technology makes tasks simpler and therefore able to be performed by more occupations in health care, regulations and protocols may prohibit this.

The second states that in those cases where it is easy to substitute one occupation for another or to replace an occupation with capital, the demand for the occupation will be less elastic the more difficult it is to obtain a supply of these substitutes. If it is difficult to recruit the labour which could substitute for the occupation or to obtain the capital which could replace it, this will reduce elasticity. Moreover, if the substitute labour could only be recruited by offering very high wages, this would deter recruitment and reduce elasticity. This amounts to saying the less elastic is the supply of any of the substitute factors, the less elastic is the demand for the occupation in question.

The third factor states that the demand for an occupation will be less elastic the smaller the share in total costs accounted for by the pay bill of the occupation. Suppose that the pay bill for qualified nurses accounts for 5 per cent of total residential care home costs and the pay bill for care workers accounts for 60 per cent of total costs. A 10 per cent increase in the pay of care workers will increase total care home costs by 6 per cent. In contrast, a 10 per cent increase in the pay of qualified nurses will increase total care home costs by 0.5 per cent. The rise in qualified nurses pay has a smaller effect on total care home costs and thus a much smaller impact on care home fees. This matters because an increase in care home fees would be expected to reduce the demand for residential places and this would be to the detriment of the employment of everyone working in care homes.

This has been called 'the importance of being unimportant'. Doctors, qualified nurses, and nursing assistants are all very large occupational groups, and they account for a sizeable share of the NHS pay bill. Therefore, even a modest increase in pay for any of these groups will add substantially to the NHS pay bill. In contrast, a large pay increase for a small AHP occupation or for PAs would have a very modest impact on the pay bill and may be less resisted as a result.[2]

The fourth factor focuses on the resistance to a price rise by those who pay for the services that the workers produce. If, for example, the people who are paying for domiciliary care

---

[1] It is reported that robots are replacing care workers in Japan (World Economic Forum 2021). If this is difficult to do then care workers in Japan need be less concerned that they will lose their jobs if they are awarded a pay rise. If, however, it is easy for employers to substitute robots for care workers then a pay rise for care workers will encourage care homes to substitute robots for care workers. What factors might make demand less elastic; protect care workers' employment if they receive a pay rise? Demand would be less elastic if care workers were considered by residents to be essential to the experience of care. Demand would also be less elastic the more protocols or regulations prohibited anyone other than care workers providing care.

[2] Alfred Marshall, the late nineteenth-century economist, detailed the determinants of the elasticity of factor demand discussed here (Marshall, Alfred, 1920, pp. 241–246). However, the importance of being unimportant was contested by Hicks (Hicks, John. 1932) who showed that when the producer can substitute more easily than the consumer it is important to be important. This is because where the occupation accounts for a large share of total costs it will be difficult and costly to replace it.

are not particularly resistant to an increase in the fees charged for domiciliary care, then a pay rise for care workers will result in a smaller reduction in employment of care workers than would have occurred if those paying for care had resisted the rise in fees. Also, the easier it is for hospitals to pass on higher pay costs to government and taxpayers, the less elastic is labour demand in the hospital sector. If taxpayers are prepared to fund pay increases through paying higher taxes, there need be no reduction in employment. Alternatively, the greater the resistance from government or taxpayers to any attempt to pass on higher pay costs, then the more hospitals will have to cut back employment when they award pay increases.

An understanding of the elasticity of labour demand is important for employers and those trade unions and professional associations who represent health and social care workers when they negotiate over pay. The elasticity of labour demand for the occupations it represents is an important determinant of the strength of a trade unions negotiating positions. One of the main objectives of the trade unions and professional associations who represent health and social care workers is to deliver pay increases without job loss. That objective can be better achieved if unions and professional associations can reduce the elasticity of labour demand, if they can steepen the labour demand schedule they can reduce the employment consequences of any pay rise. The above drivers of the elasticity of labour demand suggest ways to do this.

Bibliography

Allan, S. and Vadean, F. (2017) The impact of workforce composition and characteristics on English care home quality, PSSRU Discussion Paper 2929, Personal Social Services Research Unit, University of Kent, September https://kar.kent.ac.uk/63688/1/DP2929_final.pdf

Allan, S. and Vadean, F. (2021) The association between staff retention and English care home quality, *Journal of Aging and Social Policy*. https://doi.org/10.1080/08959420.2020.1851349

Antonazzo, E., Scott, A., Skatun, D., and Elliott, R. (2002) The labour market for nursing: A review of the labour supply literature. *Health Economics* 12, 465–478. https://doi.org/10.1002/hec.737

Appleby, J., Schlepper, L., and Keeble, E. (2021) The ethnicity pay gap in the English NHS Research report, Nuffield Trust, https://www.nuffieldtrust.org.uk/files/2021-04/1618308266_nuffield-trust-ethnicity-pay-gap-web.pdf

Appleby, J. (2018) What is the ethnicity pay gap among NHS doctors? Nuffield Trust, https://www.nuffieldtrust.org.uk/news-item/what-is-the-ethnicity-pay-gap-among-nhs-doctors

A Vision of Britain through Time. Census Reports. https://www.visionofbritain.org.uk/IV

Bach, S. (2003) International Migration of Health Workers: Labour and Social Issues, Working Paper 209, Geneva: International Labour Office

Bach, S. (2010) Achieving a self-sufficient workforce? The utilisation of migrant labour in healthcare. In Ruhs, M. and Anderson, B. (eds) *Who Needs Migrant Workers? Labour Shortages, Immigration, and Public Policy*, pp. 87–118. Oxford: Oxford University Press

Batson, C.D. (2002) Addressing the altruism question experimentally. In Post, S.G., Underwood, L.G., Schloss, J.P., and Hurlbut, W.B. (eds) *Altruism and Altruistic Love: Science, Philosophy and Religion in Dialogue*, pp. 89–105. New York: Oxford University Press

Bärnighausen, T. and Bloom, D.E. (2011) The global health workforce. In Smith, P.C. and Glied, S. (eds) *The Oxford Handbook of Health Economics*, pp. 486–519. Oxford: Oxford University Press.

Becker, G. (1964) *Human Capital*. New York: National Bureau of Economic Research

Belfield, C., Britton J., Buscha, F. et al. (2018) The impact of undergraduate degrees on early-career earnings, Institute for Fiscal Studies, https://ifs.org.uk/sites/default/files/output_url_files/DFE_returnsHE_exec_summary.pdf

Bevan, G., Karanikolos, M., Exley, J., Nolte, E., Connolly, S., and Mays, N. (2014) The four health systems of the United Kingdom: How do they compare? The Health Foundation and Nuffield Trust. ISBN 978-1-905030-78-1

Birch, S. (1988) The identification of supplier-inducement in a fixed price system of health care provision. The case of dentistry in the United Kingdom, *Journal of Health Economics*, 7, 129–150. https://doi.org/10.1016/0167-6296(88)90012-4

Blau Francine, D. (2016) *Gender, Inequality, and Wages*, edited by Gielen, A.C. and Zimmermann, K.F. Oxford: Oxford University Press

Britton, J., Dearden, J., van der Erve, L., and Waltmann, B. (2020a) The impact of undergraduate degrees on lifetime earnings, Institute for Fiscal Studies. https://ifs.org.uk/publications/impact-undergraduate-degrees-lifetime-earnings

Britton, J., Buscha, F., Dickson, M., van der Erve, L., Vignoles, A., Walker, I., Waltmann, B., Zhu, Y., and van der Erve, L. (2020b) The earnings returns to postgraduate degrees in the UK, Institute for Fiscal Studies. https://ifs.org.uk/publications/earnings-returns-postgraduate-degrees-uk

Brocklehurst, P., Price, J., Glenny, A., Tickle, M., Birch, S., Mertz, E., and Grytten, J. (2013) The effect of different methods of remuneration on the behaviour of primary care dentists. *Cochrane Database of Systematic Reviews*, (11) CD009853, CD009853. https://doi.org/10.1002/14651858.CD009853.pub2

Buchan, J., Parkin, T., and Sochalski, J. (2003) *International Nurse Mobility: Trends and Policy Implications*. Geneva: World Health Organization. https://apps.who.int/iris/handle/10665/68061

Buchan, J., McPake, B. Mensah, K., and Rae, G. (2009) Does a Code Make a Difference—Assessing the English Code of Practice on International Recruitment. *Human Resources for Health*, 3(33). https://doi.org/10.1186/1478-4491-7-33

Buchan, J., Kumar, A., and Schoenstein, M. (2014) Wage-Setting in the Hospital Sector, Health Working Paper No. 77, OECD. https://doi.org/10.1787/18152015

Buchan, J., Dhillon, I.S., and Campbell, J. (eds) (2017) *Health Employment and Economic Growth: An evidence base*, WHO. https://apps.who.int/iris/handle/10665/326411

Buchan, J., Charlesworth, A., Gershlick, B., and Seccombe, I. (2019) A critical moment: NHS staffing trends, retention and attrition. Health Foundation, February. https://www.health.org.uk/sites/default/files/upload/publications/2019/A%20Critical%20Moment_1.pdf

Cairns, J. (2016) Using Cost-Effectiveness Evidence to Inform Decisions as to Which Health Services to Provide. *Health Systems & Reform*, 2(1), 32–38, https://doi.org/10.1080/23288604.2015.1124172

Chalkley, M. and Malcomson, J.M. (1998) Contracting for health services when patient demand does not reflect quality. *Journal of Health Economics*, 17, 1–19 https://doi.org/10.1016/s0167-6296(97)00019-2

Chalkley, M. and Listl, S. (2018) First do no harm—The impact of financial incentives on dental X-rays. *Journal of Health Economics*, 58 (March), 1–9. https://doi.org/10.1016/j.jhealeco.2017.12.005

Charlesworth, A. and Gershlick, B. (2019) Health and social care workforce: Priorities for the next government, Health Foundation, https://www.health.org.uk/sites/default/files/2019-11/GE04-Health%20and%20social%20care%20workforce.pdf

Chilton, S., Jones-Lee, M. et al. (2020) A scoping study on the valuation of risks to life and health: The monetary Value of a Life year (VOLY), Health and Safety Executive, UK government, 28 July 2020. https://www.gov.uk/government/publications/valuation-of-risks-to-life-and-health-monetary-value-of-a-life-year-voly/a-scoping-study-on-the-valuation-of-risks-to-life-and-health-the-monetary-value-of-a-life-year-voly#introduction

Claxton, K., Martin, S., Soares, M., Rice, N., Spackman, E., Hinde, S., Devlin, N., Smith, P.C., and Sculpher, M. (2015) Methods for the estimation of the National Institute for Health and Care Excellence cost-effectiveness threshold. *Health Technology Assessment*, 19(14), 1–503, v–vi. https://doi.org/10.3310/hta19140. PMID: 25692211; PMCID: PMC4781395.

Culyer A.J. and Chalkidou, K. (2019) Economic Evaluation for Health Investments En Route to Universal Health Coverage: Cost-Benefit Analysis or Cost-Effectiveness Analysis? *Value in Health*, 22(1):99–103. https://doi.org/10.1016/j.jval.2018.06.005. Epub 2018 Jul 26. PMID: 30661640; PMCID: PMC6347566

Cometto, G., Scheffler, R., Bruckner, T., Lui, J., Maeda, A., Tomblin-Murphy, G., Hunter, D., and Campbell, J. (2017) Health Workforce needs: Demand and shortages to 2030. In Buchan, J., Dhillon, I.S., and Campbell, J. (eds) *Health Employment and Economic Growth: An evidence base*, pp. 3–26. Geneva. WHO. https://apps.who.int/iris/handle/10665/326411

Commonwealth Fund (2020) International Health Care System Profiles, United States https://www.commonwealthfund.org/international-health-policy-center/countries/united-states

Connell, J., Zurn, P., Stilwell, B., Awases, M., and Braichet, J-M. (2007) Sub-Saharan Africa: Beyond the health worker migration crisis? *Social Science & Medicine*, 64(9) (May), 1876–1891. https://doi.org/10.1016/j.socscimed.2006.12.013

Crosland, M. (2004) The Officiers de Santé of the French Revolution: A case study in the changing language of medicine. *Medical History*, 48(2) (April), 229–244. https://doi.org/10.1017/s0025727300007407

Crossley, M.L. and Mubarik, A. (2002) A comparative investigation of dental and medical student's motivation towards career choice. *British Dental Journal* 193, 471–473. https://doi.org/10.1038/sj.bdj.4801599

Cutler, T. (2010) Performance management in Public Services 'Before' New Public Management: The case of NHS acute hospitals 1948–1962. *Public Policy and Administration*, 26(1), 129–147. https://doi.org/10.1177/0952076710375785

Dacre, J. (2020) Mend the Gap: The Independent Review into Gender Pay Gaps in Medicine in England, Department of Health and Social Care. https://assets.publishing.service.gov.uk/government/uploads/system/uploads/attachment_data/file/944246/Gender_pay_gap_in_medicine_review.pdf

Department of Health (2017) Expansion of Undergraduate Medical Education: a consultation on how to maximise the benefits from the increases in medical student numbers, March. https://assets.publishing.service.gov.uk/government/uploads/system/uploads/attachment_data/file/600835/Medical_expansion_rev_A.pdf

DDRB (2019) Review Body on Doctors' and Dentists' Remuneration, Forty-Seventh Report CP148, July. https://assets.publishing.service.gov.uk/government/uploads/system/uploads/attachment_data/file/819453/DDRB_2019_report_Web_Accessible.pdf

Di Tommaso, M.L., Strøm, S., and Saether, E.M. (2009a) Nurses wanted: Is the job too harsh or is the wage too low? *Journal of Health Economics* 28(3), S. 748–757. https://doi.org/10.1016/j.jhealeco.2009.01.003.

Dolea, C., Stormont, L., and Braichet, J-M. (2010). Evaluated strategies to increase attraction and retention of health workers in remote and rural areas. *Bulletin of the World Health Organization*, 88(5), 379–385. https://doi.org/10.2471/BLT.09.070607

Doran, T., Kontopantelis, E., Reeves, D., Sutton, S., and Ryan, A.M. (2014) Setting performance targets in pay for performance programmes: What can we learn from QOF? *British Medical Journal*, (4 March), 348. https://doi.org/10.1136/bmj.g1595

Drummond, M.F., Sculpher, M.J., Claxton, K., Stoddart, G.L., and Torrance, G.W. (2015) *Methods for the Economic Evaluation of Health Care Programmes*, Fourth Edition. Oxford: Oxford University Press

Eberth, B., Elliott, R.F., and Skatun, D. (2015) Pay or conditions? The role of workplace characteristics in nurses' labour supply. *European Journal of Health Economics*, 17, 771–785, https://doi.org/10.1007/s10198-015-0733-6

Economic Survey (2020/21) Government of India, Ministry of Finance. https://www.indiabudget.gov.in/economicsurvey/

Elliott R.F. (1990) *Labor Economics: a comparative text.* London: McGraw-Hill Publishing Co

Elliott, R.F., Lucifora, C., and Meurs, D. (eds) (1999) *Public Sector Pay Determination in the European Union.* London: Macmillan

Elliott, R. (2003) Labour markets in the NHS: An agenda for research. *Health Economics*, 12, 797–801. https://doi.org/10.1002/hec.842

Elliott, R. (2010) The utilization of migrant labour in healthcare, a commentary. In Ruhs, M. and Anderson, B. (eds) *Who Needs Migrant Workers? Labour Shortages, Immigration, and Public Policy*, pp. 119–124. Oxford: Oxford University Press; online edn, Oxford Academic, 1 Jan. 2011). https://doi.org/10.1093/acprof:oso/9780199580590.001.0001

Elliott, B., Scott, A., Skåtun, D., Farrar, S., and Napper, M. (2003) The Impact of Local Labour Market Factors on the Organisation and Delivery of Health Services. Report to the National Co-ordinating Centre for NHS Service Delivery and Organisation R & D (NCCSDO), November. http://www.netscc.ac.uk/netscc/hsdr/files/project/SDO_FR_08-1319-052_V01.pdf

Elliott, R., Bell, D., Scott, A., Ma, A., and Roberts, E. (2007) Geographically differentiated pay in the labour market for nurses. *Journal of Health Economics*, 26, 190–212. https://doi.org/10.1016/j.jhealeco.2006.05.002

Elliott, R., Sutton, M., Ma, A., Skåtun D., McConnachie, A., Morris, S., and Rice, N. (2010) The Role of the Staff MFF in Distributing NHS Funding: Taking account of differences in local labour market conditions. *Health Economics*, 19 (May), 532–548. https://doi.org/10.1002/hec.1489

Elliott, R. and Scott, A. (2004) Programmes and Policies to Redistribute Physicians to High Need Areas: The case of the UK. Paper presented to the 8th International Medical Workforce Conference, Washington, DC, USA.

Ellis, R.P. and McGuire, T.G. (1990) Optimal payment systems for health services. *Journal of Health Economics*, 9(4), 375–396. https://doi.org/10.1016/0167-6296(90)90001-J

Fallick, J.L. and Elliott, R.F. (eds) (1981). George Allen and Unwin. Republished 2016. London: Routledge Library Editions

Ferns, T., Stacey, C., and Cork, A. (2006) Violence and aggression in the emergency department: Factors impinging on nursing research. *Accident and Emergency Nursing*, 14(1) (January), 49–55. https://doi.org/10.1016/j.aaen.2005.08.004

Forder, J. and Allan, S. (2011) *Competition in the Care Homes Market. Report for the OHE Commission on Competition in the NHS.* London: Office of Health Economics. https://www.ohe.org/wp-content/uploads/2012/01/Competition-in-care-home-market-2011.pdf

Foundation Trust Network (2013) Briefing Operating Theatres—maximising a valuable resource. https://nhsproviders.org/media/1128/operating-theatres-final.pdf

Frehywot, S., Mullan, F., Payne, P.W., and Ross, H. (2010) Compulsory service programmes for recruiting health workers in remote and rural areas: Do they work? *Bulletin of the World Health Organization*, 88(5), 364–370. https://doi.org/10.2471/BLT.09.071605.

Frakt, A. (2018) The Astonishing High Administrative Cost of U.S. Health Care, *The New York Times*, 16 July. https://www.nytimes.com/2018/07/16/upshot/costs-health-care-us.html?smid=em-share

Frijters, P., Shields, M.A., and Price, S.W. (2007) Investigating the quitting decision of nurses: Panel data evidence from the British National Health Service. *Health Economics*, 16, 57–73. https://doi.org/10.1002/hec.1144

Gagné, R., and Léger, P.T. (2005) Determinants of physicians' decisions to specialize. *Health Economics*, 14, 721–735. https://doi.org/10.1002/hec.970

General Medical Council (2017) Our data on medical students and doctors in training in the UK. https://www.gmc-uk.org/static/documents/content/SoMEP_2017_chapter_2.pdf

General Medical Council (2019) The state of medical education and practice in the UK: The workforce report 2019. https://www.gmc-uk.org/-/media/documents/somep-2019—full-report_pdf-81131156.pdf

Gershlick, B., Kraindler, J., Idriss, O., and Charlesworth A. (2019) Health and Social Care Funding: Priorities for the new government. The Health Foundation, 23 November. https://www.health.org.uk/publications/long-reads/health-and-social-care-funding

Gordon, D. and Vaughan, R. (2011) The Historical Role of the Production Function in Economics and Business. *American Journal of Business Education*, 4(4) (April). https://doi.org/10.19030/ajbe.v4i4.4191

Godager, G. and Wiesen, D. (2013) Profit or patients' health benefit? Exploring the heterogeneity in physician altruism. *Journal of Health Economics*, 32(6) (December), 1105–1116. https://doi.org/10.1016/j.jhealeco.2013.08.008

Gosden, T., Pedersen, L., and Torgerson, D. (1999) How should we pay doctors? A systematic review of salary payments and their effect on doctor behaviour. *Quarterly Journal of Medicine: An International Journal of Medicine*, 92(1) (January), 47–55. https://doi.org/10.1093/qjmed/92.1.47

Gosden, T., Forland, F., Kristiansen, K., Sutton, M., Leese, B., Giuffrida, A., Sergison, M., and Pedersen, L. (2000) Capitation, salary, fee-for-service and mixed systems of payment: Effects on the behaviour of primary care physicians. *Cochrane Database Systematic Review*. https://doi.org/10.1002/14651858.CD002215.

Grant, A.M. and Berg, J.M. (2012) Prosocial motivation at work. In Cameron, K.S. and Spreitzer, G.M. (eds) *The Oxford Handbook of Positive Organizational Scholarship*, pp. 28–44. Oxford: Oxford University Press

Gravelle, G., Sutton, M., and Ma, A. (2010) Doctor behaviour under a pay for performance contract: treating, cheating and case finding? *The Economic Journal*, 120(542) (1 February), F129–F156. https://doi.org/10.1111/j.1468-0297.2009.02340.x

Grobler, L., Marais, B.J., and Mabunda, S. (2015) Interventions for increasing the proportion of health professionals practising in rural and other underserved areas. *Cochrane Database of Systematic Rezviews*, 6. Art. No.: CD005314. https://doi.org/10.1002/14651858.CD005314.pub3

Hanel, B., Kalb, G., and Scott, A. (2014). Nurses' labour supply elasticities: the importance of accounting for extensive margins. *Journal of Health Economics*, 33, 94–112. https://doi.org/10.1016/j.jhealeco.2013.11.001

Harkness, S. (1996) The gender earnings gap: evidence from the UK. *Fiscal Studies*, 17(2), 1–36. Institute for Fiscal Studies. https://www.jstor.org/stable/24437860

Hawe, E. (2008) Sixty Years of the NHS: Changes in Demographics, Expenditure, Workforce and Family Services. London. Office of Health Economics. https://www.ohe.org/publications/sixty-years-nhs-changes-demographics-expenditure-workforce-and-family-services/

Health Education England (2015) Return to practice: Healthcare professionals https://www.hee.nhs.uk/our-work/return-practice

Health Foundation (2018) One in four student nurses drop out of their degrees before graduation, press, 3 September 2018.

Health Foundation (2019) Stemming the tide: Retaining the social care workforce, Newsletter, 30 April. https://www.health.org.uk/news-and-comment/newsletter-features/stemming-the-tide-retaining-the-social-care-workforce

Hennig-Schmidt, H., Selten, R., and Wiesen, D. (2011) How payment systems affect physicians' provision behavior—an experimental investigation. *Journal of Health Economics*, 30, 637–646. https://doi.org/10.1016/j.jhealeco.2011.05.001

Hicks, John (1932). *The Theory of Wages*. 2nd ed., London: Macmillan.

HM Treasury (2018) *The Green Book: Appraisal and evaluation in central government*. Annex 2. London: HM Treasury. https://www.gov.uk/government/publications/the-green-book-appraisal-and-evaluation-in-central-governent

Hoeve, Y.T., Jansen, G., and Roodbol, P. (2014) The nursing profession: Public image, self-concept and professional identity. A discussion paper. *Journal of Advanced Nursing*, 70, 295–309. https://doi.org/10.1111/jan.12177.

Home Office (2020) The UK's points-based immigration system: Policy statement, February. London. https://www.gov.uk/government/publications/the-uks-points-based-immigration-system-policy-statement/the-uks-points-based-immigration-system-policy-statement

Hospital and Community Health Services (2019) Workforce statistics: Equality and Diversity in NHS Trusts and CCGs in England, March. https://digital.nhs.uk/about-nhs-digital/corporate-information-and-documents/annual-inclusion-reports/our-workforce-demographics-2019#chapter-index

House of Commons Health Committee (2006) Public Expenditure on Health and Personal Social Services, HC1692-i. https://publications.parliament.uk/pa/cm200506/cmselect/cmhealth/1692-i/1692-i.pdf

Hughes, D., and Yule, B. (1992) The effect of per-item fees on the behaviour of general practitioners. *Journal of Health Economics*, 11(4), 413–437. https://doi.org/10.1016/0167-6296(92)90014-r

Humphreys, P., Spratt, B., Tariverdi, M., Burdett, R.L., Cook, D., Yarlagadda, P.K.D.V., and Corry, P. (2022) An overview of hospital capacity planning and optimisation. *Healthcare (Basel)* (April) 10(5): 826. https://doi.org/10.3390/healthcare10050826. PMID: 35627963; PMCID: PMC9140785.

International Labour Organisation (2011) Global Employment Trends 2011. https://www.ilo.org/wcmsp5/groups/public/@dgreports/@dcomm/@publ/documents/publication/wcms_150440.pdf

Kerry, V.B., Ndung'u, T., Walensky, R.P., Lee, P.T., Kayanja, V.F.I.B., and Bangsberg, D.R. (2011) Managing the demand for Global Health Education. *PloS Med*, 8(11), e1001118. https://doi.org/10.1371/journal.pmed.1001118

Keynes, J.M. (1972) *Essays in Biography. The Collected Writings of John Maynard Keynes*. London: Palgrave MacMillan/Royal Economic Society.

King's Fund, The (2018) Spending on and availability of healthcare resources: How does the UK compare to other countries? May. https://www.kingsfund.org.uk/publications/spending-and-availability-health-care-resources

King's Fund The (2021) Social Care 360: expenditure, 26 April 2021.

Lachish, S., Goldacre, M.J., and Lambert, T.W. (2018) Views of UK doctors in training on the timing of choosing a clinical specialty: Quantitative and qualitative analysis of surveys 3 years after graduation. *Postgraduate Medical Journal*, 94, 621–626. https://doi.org/10.1136/postgradmedj-2017-135460

Lazear, E.P. and Rosen, S. (1981) Rank-Order tournaments as optimum labour contracts. *Journal of Political Economy*, 89, 841–864. https://doi.org/10.1086/261010

Jefferson, L., Bloor, K., and Maynard, A. (2015) Women in medicine: Historical perspectives and recent trends. *British Medical Bulletin*, 114(1) (June), 5–15. https://doi.org/10.1093/bmb/ldv007

Lavetti, K. (2020) The estimation of compensating wage differentials: Lessons from the Deadliest Catch. *Journal of Business & Economic Statistics*, 38(1), 165–182, https://doi.org/10.1080/07350015.2018.1470000

Lee, T., Propper, C., and Stoye, G. (2019) Medical Labour Supply and the Production of Healthcare. *Fiscal Studies*, 40(4), 621–661. https://doi.org/10.1111/1475-5890.12198

Low Pay Commission Report 2019 (2020) National Minimum Wage, January. https://www.gov.uk/government/publications/low-pay-commission-report-2019

McCartney, G., Collins, C., Walsh, D., and Batty, D. (2011) Accounting for Scotland's Excess Mortality: towards a synthesis, Glasgow Centre for Population Health, April. https://www.gcph.co.uk/assets/0000/1080/GLA147851_Hypothesis_Report__2_.pdf

Maestas, N., Mullen, K.J., Powell, D., von Wachter, T., and Wenger, J.B. (2018) The Value of Working Conditions in the United States and Implications for the Structure of Wages, NBER Working Paper 25204. https://doi.org/10.3386/w25204

Marshall, A. (1920) *Principles of Economic*, 8th edition, London: MacMillan

Mclaughlin, K., Moutray, M., and Moore, C. (2010) Career motivation in nursing students and the perceived influence of significant others. *Journal of Advanced Nursing*, 66(2), 404–412, https://doi.org/10.1111/j.1365-2648.2009.05147.x

Mason, A., Rodriguez Santana, I., Aragón, M.J., Rice, N., Chalkley, M., Wittenberg, R., and Fernandez, J-L. (2019) Drivers of healthcare expenditure: Final report. Centre for Health Economics, Research Paper 169, University of York, UK. https://www.york.ac.uk/che/news/news-2019/che-research-paper-169/

Makepeace, G. and Marcenaro-Gutierrez, O. (2006) The earnings of workers covered by pay review bodies: Evidence from the labour force survey report for the office of Manpower Economics. http://www.ome.uk.com/research.cfm (accessed 12 April 2010).

Maier, C.B., Koppen, J., Busse, R., and the MUNROS Team (2018) Task shifting between physicians and nurses in acute care hospitals: Cross-sectional study in nine countries. *Human Resources for Health*, 16, 24, https://doi.org/10.1186/s12960-018-0285-9

Marshall, M. and Roland, M. (2017) The future of the Quality and Outcomes Framework in England. *British Medical Journal*; 359:j4681, https://doi.org/10.1136/bmj.j4681

McHarg, J., Mattick, K., and Knight, L.V. (2007) Why people apply to medical school: Implications for widening participation activities. *Medical Education*, 41(8) (August), 815–821. https://doi.org/10.1111/j.1365-2923.2007.02798.x.

McPake, B., Squires, A., Mahat, A., and Araujo, E. (2015) The Economics of Health Professional Education and Careers: Insights from a literature review. World Bank Group. https://doi.org/10.1596/978-1-4648-0616-2

McIsaac, M., Scott, A., and Kalb, G. (2019) The role of financial factors in the mobility and location choices of General Practitioners in Australia. *Human Resources for Health* 17, 34. https://doi.org/10.1186/s12960-019-0374-4

Mbemba, G., Gagnon, M.P., Paré, G., and Côté, J. (2013) Interventions for supporting nurse retention in rural and remote areas: An umbrella review. *Human Resources for Health*, 11(44) (11 September). https://doi.org/10.1186/1478-4491-11-44. PMID: 24025429; PMCID: PMC3847170

Medical Schools Council (2018) Selection Alliance 2018 Report. An update on the Medical Schools Council's work in selection and widening participation.

Milton, C.W., Torrance, G., and McGuire, A. (2009) QALYs: The Basics. *Value in Health*, 12 (Supplement 1), S5–S9. ISSN 1098–3015. https://doi.org/10.1111/j.1524-4733.2009.00515.x.

Mitton, C.R. and Donaldson, C. (2003) Setting priorities and allocating resources in health regions: Lessons from a project evaluating program budgeting and marginal analysis (PBMA). *Health Policy*, 64(3) (June), 335–348. https://doi.org/10.1016/S0168-8510(02)00198-7

Mincer, J. (1974) *Schooling, Experience and Earnings*. New York: National Bureau of Economic Research.

Moggeridge, D. (ed.) (1973) *The Collected Writings of John Maynard Keynes*, Vol 14 London: Macmillan

Mossialos, E., Wenzl M., Osborn R., and Sarnak, D. (2016) International Profiles of Healthcare Systems, 2015. The Commonwealth Fund, January. https://www.commonwealthfund.org/publications/fund-reports/2016/jan/international-profiles-health-care-systems-2015

Morris, S., Elliott, B., Ma, A., McConnachie, A., Rice, N., Skåtun D., and Sutton, M. (2008) Analysis of consultants' NHS and private incomes in England in 2003/4. *Journal of the Royal Society of Medicine*, 101, 372–380. https://doi.org/10.1258/jrsm.2008.080004

Mullan, F. (2005) The metrics of the physician brain drain. *New England Journal of Medicine*, 353, 1810–1818. https://doi.org/10.1056/NEJMsa050004

Murphy, G.T., Birch, S., Mackenzie, A., Rigby, J., and Langley, J. (2017) An integrated needs-based approach to health service and health workforce planning: applications for Pandemic Influenza. *Health Policy*, 13(1) (August), 28–42. https://doi.org/10.12927/hcpol.2017.25193. PMID: 28906234; PMCID: PMC5595212.

National Audit Office (2007) Pay Modernisation: A new contract for NHS consultants in England. 19 April 2007 https://www.nao.org.uk/reports/pay-modernisation-a-new-contract-for-nhs-consultants-in-england/

National Audit Office (2016) Managing the supply of NHS clinical staff in England, HC 736 Session 2015–16, 5 February 2016. https://www.nao.org.uk/wp-content/uploads/2016/02/Managing-the-supply-of-NHS-clinical-staff-in-England.pdf

National Institute for Health and Care Excellence (2022a) NICE health technology evaluations: The manual. https://www.nice.org.uk/process/pmg36/resources/nice-health-technology-evaluations-the-manual-pdf-72286779244741

National Institute for Health and Care Excellence (2022b) Charter. https://www.nice.org.uk/about/who-we-are/our-charter

Nesje, K. (2015) Nursing students' prosocial motivation: does it predict professional commitment and involvement in the job? *Journal of Advanced Nursing*, 71(1), 115–125. https://doi.org/10.1111/jan.12456

NHS Digital (2018) Factsheet—NHS staff numbers from 1949. https://digital.nhs.uk/news-and-events/news/workforce-factsheet

NHS Education for Scotland (2018) TURAS Data Intelligence, The Dental Workforce in Scotland. November. https://turasdata.nes.nhs.scot/data-and-reports/other-workforce-statistics/dental-workforce/the-dental-workforce-in-scotland-2018/?pageid=6202

NHS England (2018) Report of the Review of the Quality and Outcomes Framework in England. NHS England, 4 July 2018. https://www.england.nhs.uk/wp-content/uploads/2018/07/05-a-i-pb-04-07-2018-qof-report.pdf

NHS Pay Review Body (2018) Thirty-First Report, June, Cm 9641. https://assets.publishing.service.gov.uk/government/uploads/system/uploads/attachment_data/file/720320/NHSPRB_2018_report_Web_Accessible.pdf

NHS Digital, NHS Workforce Statistics (2019) https://digital.nhs.uk/data-andinformation/publications/statistical/nhs-workforce-statistics/

NHS England Shared Business Services (2019) Newsletter, May. https://www.sbs.nhs.uk/newsletter-may-2019-workforce-efficiencies

NHS Improvement England (2019) NHS Workforce Race Equality Standard: An overview of workforce data for nurses, midwives and health visitors in the NHS. March. https://www.england.nhs.uk/wp-content/uploads/2019/03/wres-nursing-strategy.pdf

NHS Improvement England (2019a) The national retention programme: Two years on. July. https://www.england.nhs.uk/2019/07/nhs-rolls-out-staff-retention-scheme-as-part-of-the-long-term-plan/

NHS Pay Review Body (2019) Thirty-Second Report July, Cm 147. https://assets.publishing.service.gov.uk/government/uploads/system/uploads/attachment_data/file/819464/NHSPRB_2019_Report_Web_Accessible__1_.pdf

NHS Scotland (2019) Scottish Diabetes Survey 2019. Scottish Diabetes Data Group https://www.diabetesinscotland.org.uk/wp-content/uploads/2020/10/Diabetes-Scottish-Diabetes-Survey-2019.pdf

NHS Scotland, COSLA, Scottish Government (2019) An Integrated Health and Social Care Workforce Plan for Scotland. December. https://www.gov.scot/publications/national-health-social-care-integrated-workforce-plan/

NHS Digital (2020) https://digital.nhs.uk/data-andinformation/publications/statistical/personal-social-services-staff-of-social-services-departments/england-2019/individual-worker-characteristics#ethnicity

NHS Health Careers (2020) https://www.healthcareers.nhs.uk/explore-roles/wider-healthcare-team/roles-wider-healthcare-team/clinical-support-

NHS Outcomes Framework (2020) https://digital.nhs.uk/data-and-information/publications/statistical/nhs-outcomes-framework/may-2020#related-links

NHS Scotland Workforce (2020) https://turasdata.nes.nhs.scot/data-and-reports/official-workforce-statistics/all-official-statistics-publications/?pageid=1302

NHS Workforce (2020) https://www.ethnicity-facts-figures.service.gov.uk/workforce-and-business/workforce-diversity/nhs-workforce/latest#main-facts-and-figures.

NHS Choices (2021) https://www.nhs.uk/using-the-nhs/about-the-nhs/your-choices-in-the-nhs/

Nuffield Trust (2019) The NHS workforce in numbers: Facts on staffing and staff shortages in England. May 2019. https://www.nuffieldtrust.org.uk/resource/the-nhs-workforce-in-numbers

Nuffield Trust (2020) What does the social care workforce look like across the four countries? https://www.nuffieldtrust.org.uk/news-item/what-does-the-social-care-workforce-look-like-across-the-four-countries

Nursing Standard (2019) What employers need to learn from nurse suicides. *Nursing Standard*, 34(1), 36–38. https://doi.org/10.7748/ns.34.1.36.s16.

OECD (2011) *Divided We Stand: Why Inequality Keeps Rising.* Paris: OECD Publishing https://www.oecd.org/els/soc/dividedwestandwhyinequalitykeepsrising.htm

OECD (2015) *International Migration Outlook 2015.* Paris: OECD Publishing. https://doi.org/10.1787/migr_outlook-2015-en

OECD (2015a) *Library, Health Statistics.* Paris: OECD Publishing.

OECD (2017) *Health at a Glance 2017. OECD Indicators* Paris: OECD Publishing. https://www.oecd.org/social/health-at-a-glance-19991312.htm

OECD (2019a) *Health at a Glance 2019: OECD Indicators.* Paris: OECD Publishing. https://doi.org/10.1787/4dd50c09-en

OECD (2019b) *Recent Trends in International Migration of Doctors, Nurses and Medical Students.* Paris: OECD Publishing. https://doi.org/10.1787/5571ef48-en

OECD (2021) *Health at a Glance 2021: OECD Indicators.* Paris: OECD Publishing. https://doi.org/10.1787/ae3016b9-en

Office for National Statistics (2012) A comparison of the 2011 Census and the Labour Force Survey (LFS) labour market indicators. December https://www.ons.gov.uk/people populationandcommunity/populationandmigration/populationestimates/articles/ acomparisonofthe2011censusandthelabourforcesurveylfslabourmarketindicators/2012-12-11

Office for National Statistics (2017) Healthcare expenditure. UK Health Accounts: 2017. https://www.ons.gov.uk/peoplepopulationandcommunity/healthandsocialcare/health caresystem/bulletins/ukhealthaccounts/2017#:~:text=In%202017%2C%20spending %20on%20healthcare,equal%20to%209.7%25%20of%20GDP

Office for National Statistics (2018a) Healthcare expenditure. UK Health Accounts: 2018. https://www.ons.gov.uk/peoplepopulationandcommunity/healthandsocialcare/health caresystem/bulletins/ukhealthaccounts/2018#:~:text=1.-,Main%20points,2017%20and %206.9%25%20in%201997

Office for National Statistics (2018) Public service productivity estimates, healthcare: 2015. January. https://www.ons.gov.uk/economy/economicoutputandproductivity/ publicservicesproductivity/articles/publicservicesproductivityestimateshealthcare/ healthcare2015

Office for National Statistics (2019) International migration and the healthcare workforce, 15 August 2019. https://www.ons.gov.uk/peoplepopulationandcommunity/population andmigration/internationalmigration/articles/internationalmigrationandthehealthcare workforce/2019-08-15

Office for National Statistics (2019a) What are the vacancy trends in the public sector? 6 August 2019. https://www.ons.gov.uk/economy/governmentpublicsectorandtaxes/ publicspending/articles/whatarethevacancytrendsinthepublicsector/2019-08-06

Office for National Statistics (2020) UK and non-UK people in the labour market: February. https://www.ons.gov.uk/employmentandlabourmarket/peopleinwork/ employmentandemployeetypes/articles/ukandnonukpeopleinthelabourmarket/ february2020

Office for National Statistics (2022) Vacancies by Industry: March. https://www.ons. gov.uk/employmentandlabourmarket/peopleinwork/employmentandemployeetypes/ bulletins/jobsandvacanciesintheuk/march2022

Ozegowski, S. (2013) Effective policy mechanisms for an equitable geographical distribution of general practitioners: A qualitative comparative analysis of the accessibility of primary care in Europe. *Journal of Health Services & Research Policy*, 18(3), 151–159. https://doi.org/10.1177/1355819613482885

Pandya, A., Doran, T., Zhu, J. et al. (2018) Modelling the cost-effectiveness of pay-for-performance in primary care in the UK. *BMC Medicine*, 16(35). https://doi.org/10.1186/ s12916-018-1126-3

Personal Social Services Research Unit (2014) Unit Costs of Health and Social Care 2014. https://www.pssru.ac.uk/project-pages/unit-costs/unit-costs-2014/

Pond, B. and McPake, B. (2006) The health migration crisis: The role of four Organisation for Economic Cooperation and Development countries. *The Lancet*, 367(9520) (29 April–5 May 2006), 1448–1455. https://doi.org/10.1016/ S0140-6736(06)68346-3

Prefect, D. (2011) Gender pay gaps. Equality and Human Rights Commission, Briefing Paper 2. https://www.equalityhumanrights.com/sites/default/files/briefing-paper-2-gender-pay-gap_0.pdf

Price, S.L. (2009) Becoming a nurse: A meta-study of early professional socialisation and career choice in nursing. *Journal of Advance Nursing*, 65(1), 11–19. https://doi.org/10.1111/j.1365-2648.2008.04839.x

Propper, C. and Van Reenen, J. (2010) Can Pay Regulation Kill? Panel Data Evidence on the Effect of Labor Markets on Hospital Performance. *Journal of Political Economy*, 118(2), 222–273. https://doi.org/10.1086/653137

Propper, C., Stockton, I., and Stoye, G. (2021) Cost of living and the impact on nursing labour outcomes in NHS acute trusts. The Institute for Fiscal Studies, February. https://ifs.org.uk/publications/cost-living-and-impact-nursing-labour-outcomes-nhs-acute-trusts

Public Health England (2016) Diabetes Prevalence Model. https://assets.publishing.service.gov.uk/government/uploads/system/uploads/attachment_data/file/612306/Diabetesprevalencemodelbriefing.pdf

Punshon, G., Maclaine, K., Trevatt, P., Radford, M., Shanley, O., and Leary, A. (2019) Nursing pay by gender distribution in the UK—Does the Glass Escalator still exist? *International Journal of Nursing Studies*, 93 (May), 21–29. https://doi.org/10.1016/j.ijnurstu.2019.02.008

Rice, N. (2005). *The labour supply of nurses in the UK: evidence from the British Household Panel Survey*. University of York, Health Economics Resource Centre.

Rios-Diaz, A.J., Lam, J., Ramos, M. S., Moscoso, A.V., Vaughn, P., Zogg, C.K., and Caterson, E.J. (2016) Global Patterns of QALY and DALY Use in Surgical Cost-Utility Analyses: A Systematic Review. *PLOS One* (10 February). https://doi.org/10.1371/journal.pone.0148304

Roland, M. and Guthrie, B. (2016) Quality and Outcomes Framework: What have we learnt? *British Medical Journal*, 354(i4060). https://doi.org/10.1136/bmj.i4060

Rosen, S. (1986) The theory of equalizing differences. In Ashenfelter, O.C. and Layard, R. (eds) *Handbook of Labor Economics*, Volume 1, pp.641–692. Amsterdam: Elsevier.

Royal College of Nursing, Wales (2019) The Nursing Workforce in Wales 2019 https://www.rcn.org.uk.media.2019.october

Ruhs, M. and Anderson, B. (eds) (2010) *Who Needs Migrant Workers? Labour Shortages, Immigration, and Public Policy*. Oxford: Oxford University Press

Runge, J., Hudson-Shap, N., and Rolfe, H. (2017) Use of agency Workers in the Public Sector, Report to OME. NIESR, February. https://www.niesr.ac.uk/wp-content/uploads/2021/10/NIESR_agency_working_report_final.pdf

Siciliani, L. (2009) Paying for performance and motivation crowding out. *Economics Letters*, 103(2) (May), 68–71. https://ideas.repec.org/a/eee/ecolet/v103y2009i2p68-71.html

Scheil, X. and Nove, A. (2017) Global estimates of the size of the health workforce contributing to the health economy. In Buchan, J., Dhillon, I.S., and Campbell, J. (eds) *Health Employment and Economic Growth: An Evidence Base*, pp. 139–170. Geneva. WHO. https://apps.who.int/iris/handle/10665/326411

Shields, M. (2004) Addressing nurse shortages: what can policy makers learn from the econometric evidence on nurse labour supply. *The Economic Journal*, 114, F464–F498. https://www.jstor.org/stable/3590168

Scott, A. (2001) "Eliciting GPs' Preferences for Pecuniary and Non-pecuniary Job Characteristics." *Journal of Health Economics* 20: 329–47.

Scott, A., Witt, J., Humphreys, J., Joyce, C., Kalb, G., Jeon, S.H., and Mcgrail, M. (2013) Getting doctors into the bush: General practitioners' preferences for rural location. *Social Science & Medicine*, 96, 33–44. https://doi.org/10.1016/j.socscimed.2013.07.002

Scott, A., Witt, J., Duffield, C., and Kalb, G. (2015) What do nurses and midwives value about their jobs? Results from a discrete choice experiment. *Journal of Health Services Research & Policy*, 20 (1), S. 31–38. https://doi.org/10.1177/1355819614554924

Sheiner, L. and Malinovskaya, A. (2016) Measuring productivity in healthcare: An analysis of the literature. Hutchins Centre on Fiscal and Monetary Policy at Brookings, May https://www.brookings.edu/wp-content/uploads/2016/08/hp-lit-review_final.pdf

Sivey, P., Scott, A., Witt, J., Joyce, C., and Humphreys, J. (2012) Junior doctors' preferences for specialty choice. *Journal of Health Economics*, 31(6), 813–823. https://doi.org/10.1016/j.jhealeco.2012.07.001

Sizmur, S. and Raleigh, V. (2018) The risks to care quality and staff wellbeing of an NHS system under pressure. The King's Fund: 31 January. Oxford, 24. https://www.researchgate.net/profile/Steve-Sizmur/publication/322853647_The_risks_to_care_quality_and_staff_wellbeing_of_an_NHS_system_under_pressure/links/5a72d661a6fdcc53fe1323c0/The-risks-to-care-quality-and-staff-wellbeing-of-an-NHS-system-under-pressure.pdf

Skills for Care (2015) Practical approaches to workforce planning: A guide to support workforce planning processes and plans for adult social care support services. November. https://www.bl.uk/collection-items/practical-approaches-to-workforce-planning-a-guide-to-support-workforce-planning-processes-and-plans-for-adult-social-care-support-services

Skills for Care (2020) The state of the adult social care sector and workforce in England. October. https://www.pslhub.org/learn/patient-safety-in-health-and-care/social-care/skills-for-care-the-state-of-the-adult-social-care-sector-and-workforce-in-england-october-2020-r3376/

Smith, A. (1776) *An Inquiry into the Nature and Causes of The Wealth of Nations*, Book 1, Chapter X, The Glasgow edition. 1976. Edited by Todd, W. B. General editors: Campbell, R. H., Raphael, D. D. and Skinner. A. S. Oxford: Oxford: University Press.

Stilwell, B., Diallo, K., Zurn, P., Vujicic, M., Adams, O., and Dal Poz, M. (2004) Migration of health-care workers from developing countries: Strategic approaches to its management. *Bull World Health Organization*, 82(8) (August), 595–600. Epub 2004 Sep 13. PMID: 15375449; PMCID: PMC2622931.

Sutton, M., Elder, R., Guthrie, B., and Watt, G. (2010) Record rewards: The effects of targeted quality incentives on the recording of risk factors by primary care providers. *Health Economics*, 19(1), 1–13. https://doi.org/10.1002/hec.1440

The Conversation (2020) New points-based immigration system will lead to care crisis. July. https://theconversation.com/new-points-based-immigration-system-will-lead-to-care-crisis–143299

The Lancet Editorial (2017) Suicide among health-care workers: Time to act. *The Lancet*, 389(10064), 2, (7 January). https://doi.org/10.1016/S0140-6736(17)30005-3

University and Colleges Admission System. https://www.ucas.com/about-us/news-and-key-documents

Vadean, F. and Allan, S. (2021) The Effects of Minimum Wage Policy on the Long-Term Care Sector in England. *British Journal of Industrial Relations*, 59: 307–334. https://doi.org/10.1111/bjir.12572

Vess, D.M. (1967) The Collapse and Revival of Medical Education in France: A Consequence of Revolution and War, 1789–1795. *History of Education Quarterly*, 7(1) (Spring), 71–92. https://www.jstor.org/stable/367234

Viscusi, W.K., and Aldy, J.E. (2003) The value of a statistical life: A critical review of market estimates throughout the world. *Journal of Risk and Uncertainty*, 27(1) (August), 5–76. http://camra.msu.edu/documents/ViscusiandAldy2003.pdf

Walker, S., Mason, A.R., Claxton, K., Cookson, R., Fenwick, E., Fleetcroft, R., and Sculpher, M. (2010) Value for money and the Quality and Outcomes Framework in primary care in the UK NHS. *The British Journal of General Practice: The journal of the Royal College of General Practitioners*, 60(574), e213–e220. https://doi.org/10.3399/bjgp10X501859

West, P.D., Dyrbye, L.N., Erwin, P.J., and Shanafelt, T.D. (2016) Interventions to prevent and reduce physician burnout: a systematic review and meta-analysis. *The Lancet*, 388(10057) (5 November), 2272–2281. https://doi.org/10.1016/S0140-6736(16)31279-X

World Economic Forum (2021) What we can learn from Japan's adoption of robots in the service sector. https://www.weforum.org/agenda/2021/02/study-robots-service-sector-japan

Wootton, B. (1955) *The Social Foundations of Wage Policy*. London: Allen and Unwin

World Bank (2020) Data, Current health expenditure (% of GDP)—United States | Data. https://data.worldbank.org/indicator/SH.XPD.CHEX.GD.ZS

WHO (2008) World Health Report. https://apps.who.int/iris/handle/10665/43949

WHO (2017) Global Health Workforce Statistics, Global Health Observatory data repository. Geneva: World Health Organization. http://www.who.int/hrh/statistics/hwfstats/

WHO (2018) Decade for health workforce strengthening in the South-East Asia Region 2015–2024: Second review of progress. https://apps.who.int/iris/handle/10665/274310

WHO (2019) African Health Observatory. Geneva: World Health Organization. https://www.afro.who.int/health-topics/health-financing

WHO (2019a) International Health Worker Mobility. IOM Migration Health Division Global Training, 16 May. https://emm.iom.int/handbooks/health-and-migration

Winkelmann-Gleed, A. (2006) *Migrant Nurses. Motivation, Integration and Contribution*. Oxford: Radcliffe

Wu, L.T., Low, M.M.J., Tan, K.K., Lopez, K.K., and Liaw, V.S.Y. (2015) Why not nursing? A systematic review of factors influencing career choice among healthcare students. *International Nursing Review*, 62(4), 547–562. https://doi.org/10.1111/inr.12220

Wrzesniewski, A. (2012) Callings. In Cameron, K.S. and Spreitzer, G.M. (eds) *The Oxford Handbook of Positive Organizational Scholarship*, pp. 45–55. Oxford: Oxford University Press

Index

For the benefit of digital users, indexed terms that span two pages (e.g., 52–53) may, on occasion, appear on only one of those pages.

Tables, figures and boxes are indicated by an italic *t*, *f* and *b*, following the page number.